Fearing Burr

Garden Vegetables, and How to Cultivate Them

Fearing Burr

Garden Vegetables, and How to Cultivate Them

ISBN/EAN: 9783337069032

Printed in Europe, USA, Canada, Australia, Japan

Cover: Foto ©Lupo / pixelio.de

More available books at **www.hansebooks.com**

GARDEN VEGETABLES,

AND

HOW TO CULTIVATE THEM.

BY

FEARING BURR, Jr.

BOSTON:
J. E. TILTON & COMPANY.
1866.

Entered, according to Act of Congress, in the year 1866,

BY FEARING BURR, JR.,

In the Clerk's Office of the District Court of the District of Massachusetts.

STEREOTYPED BY C. J. PETERS AND SON,

PRESS OF GEO. C. RAND AND AVERY.

TO

THE MEMORY OF MY FATHER,

FEARING BURR,

IN GRATEFUL ACKNOWLEDGMENT OF MY INDEBTEDNESS TO HIS
EXAMPLE AND KIND PARENTAL INSTRUCTION FOR ANY
MERIT THAT MAY BE FOUND IN ITS PAGES,

THIS VOLUME IS DEDICATED,

WITH THE WARMEST FILIAL AFFECTION,

BY THE AUTHOR.

PREFACE.

THE object of this volume is to give full descriptions of the vegetables common to the gardens of this country, together with the most approved methods by which they are raised, preserved, and used.

That it may be acceptable to the agriculturist, seedsman, and to all who may possess, cultivate, or find pleasure in, a garden, is the sincere wish of the author.

HINGHAM, May 1, 1866.

ACKNOWLEDGMENTS.

To the numerous friends who have rendered me valuable aid in the preparation of this work, I would here express my grateful obligations.

The illustrations, so finely delineated, are from the pencil of Mr. ISAAC SPRAGUE, of Grantville, Mass.

My acknowledgments are also due to J. F. C. HYDE, Esq., of Newton, Mass.; to Rev. E. PORTER DYER, of Somerville, Mass.; to Hon. JOSEPH BRECK, author of "Book of Flowers," and late President of the Massachusetts Horticultural Society; to CHARLES M. HOVEY, Esq., editor of "The Magazine of Horticulture," and President of the Massachusetts Horticultural Society; to PHINEAS B. HOVEY, Esq., nurseryman and seedsman, of Cambridge, Mass.; and to DANIEL T. CURTIS, Esq., seedsman and florist, and for many years Chairman of the Committee on Vegetables of the Massachusetts Horticultural Society.

For information or other very acceptable assistance, I am also indebted to Rev. CALVIN LINCOLN, of Hingham, Mass.; Rev. JOHN L. RUSSELL, of Salem, Mass.; JOHN A. BUTLER, Esq., of Chelsea, Mass.; EDWARD S. RAND, Jun., Esq., of Boston; Mr. AUSTIN BRONSON, of Enfield, N.H.; GEORGE W. PRATT, Esq., of Boston; Mr. E. HENRY GREENWOOD, of Needham, Mass.; Mr. CALVIN A. LINCOLN, of Hingham, Mass.; Dr. THOMAS M. BREWER, of

Boston, Mass.; JOHN M. IVES, Esq., of Salem, Mass.; Mr. JAMES SCOTT, of Hatfield, Mass.; Mr. ALONZO CRAFTS, of Whately, Mass.; Mr. JOHN C. HOVEY, of Cambridge, Mass.; Mr. ISAAC P. RAND, of Dorchester, Mass.; Mr. GEORGE EVERETT, of Concord, Mass.; and Mr. CALEB BATES, of Kingston, Mass.

From a work entitled "Descriptions des Plantes Potagères, par VILMORIN, ANDRIEUX, et CIE., Paris;" from CHARLES MCINTOSH's excellent "Book of the Garden;" the "Gardener's Assistant," by ROBERT THOMPSON; Rogers's "Vegetable Cultivator;" and Lawson's "Agriculturist's Manual," — I have made liberal extracts; and if, in the course of the volume, any omission of authority may occur where it should have been accredited, my indebtedness to the valuable publications above mentioned is here candidly confessed.

ABBREVIATIONS AND AUTHORITIES.

Am. Agr. — The American Agriculturist. By ORANGE JUDD, A.M. New York. Monthly. 1842 to the present time.

Big. — Plants of Boston and Vicinity. By JACOB BIGELOW, M.D. Boston, 1840.

Bon Jard. — Le Bon Jardinier pour l'Année 1859. Par A. POITEAU et M. VILMORIN.

Corb. — The American Gardener. By WILLIAM CORBETT. Concord, Boston, and New York, 1842.

Cot. Gard. — The Cottage Gardener. By GEORGE W. JOHNSON and ROBERT HOGG. Weekly. London.

Count. Gent. — The Country Gentleman. By LUTHER TUCKER and SON. Weekly. Albany, N.Y.

De Cand. — De Candolle's Systema Naturale. By Prof. DE CANDOLLE. 2 vols. 8vo. Paris, 1818, 1821.

Down. — The Fruit and Fruit-trees of America. By A. J. DOWNING. Revised and corrected by CHARLES DOWNING, 1858.

Gard. Chron. — The Gardener's Chronicle. Weekly. By Prof. LINDLEY. 1844 to the present time.

Gray. — Manual of the Botany of the Northern United States. By Prof. ASA GRAY. New York, 1857.

Hort. — The Horticulturist, and Journal of Art and Rural Taste. Monthly. By P. BARRY and J. JAY SMITH. Philadelphia.

Hov. Mag. — The Magazine of Horticulture, Botany, and Rural Affairs. By C. M. HOVEY. Boston. Monthly. 1834 to the present time.

Law. — The Agriculturist's Manual. By PETER LAWSON and SON. Edinburgh, 1836.

Lind. — A Guide to the Orchard and Kitchen Garden. By GEORGE LINDLEY. London, 1831.

Loud. — Encyclopædia of Gardening. By J. C. LOUDON. London, 1850.

Loud. — Encyclopædia of Agriculture. By J. C. LOUDON. London, 1844.

Low. — The Elements of Practical Agriculture. By DAVID LOW. London. 1843.

McInt.—The Book of the Garden. By CHARLES MCINTOSH. 2 vols. Edinburgh and London, 1855.

Mill.—The Gardener's and Botanist's Dictionary. By PHILIP MILLER. Revised by Prof. MARTYN. London, 1819.

Neill.—Neill's Journal of a Horticultural Tour, &c. 8vo. Edinburgh, 1823.

New Am. Cyclopædia.—New American Cyclopædia. D. APPLETON & Co., New York. 16 vols. royal 8vo. 1857 to 1863.

Rog.—The Vegetable Cultivator. By JOHN ROGERS. London, 1851.

Thomp.—The Gardener's Assistant. By ROBERT THOMPSON.

Trans.—The Transactions of the London Horticultural Society. Commenced 1815, and continued at intervals to the present time.

Vil.—Description des Plantes Potagères. Par VILMORIN, ANDRIEUX, et CIE. Paris, 1856.

CONTENTS.

CHAPTER I.
ESCULENT ROOTS.
The Beet. — Carrot. — Parsnip. — Potato. — Radish. — Swede or Ruta-baga Turnip. — Salsify, or Oyster-plant. — Sweet Potato. — Turnip 1

CHAPTER II.
ALLIACEOUS PLANTS.
The Garlic. — Leek. — Onion 65

CHAPTER III.
ASPARAGINOUS PLANTS.
Asparagus 77

CHAPTER IV.
CUCURBITACEOUS PLANTS.
The Cucumber. — The Melon. — Muskmelon. — Persian Melons. — Watermelon. — Prickly-fruited Gherkin. — Pumpkin. — Squash 83

CHAPTER V.
BRASSICACEOUS PLANTS.
Borecole, or Kale. — Broccoli. — Brussels Sprouts. — Cabbage. — Cauliflower. — Kohl Rabi. — Savoy. — Sea-kale 127

CHAPTER VI.
SPINACEOUS PLANTS.
Leaf-beet, or Swiss Chard. — New-Zealand Spinach. — Spinach. — Orach . 153

CHAPTER VII.

CORN.

Garden, Table, and Field Varieties 161

CHAPTER VIII.

SALAD PLANTS.

Celery. — Celeriac, or Turnip-rooted Celery. — Chiccory, or Succory. — Cress, or Peppergrass. — Endive. — Horse-radish. — Lettuce. — Mustard . . . 177

CHAPTER IX.

OLERACEOUS PLANTS.

Balm. — Basil. — Caraway. — Coriander. — Lavender. — Marjoram. — Parsley. — Rosemary. — Sage. — Savory. — Spearmint. — Thyme 211

CHAPTER X.

EGG-PLANT, PEPPER, AND TOMATO.

Egg-plant. — Pepper. — Tomato 229

CHAPTER XI.

LEGUMINOUS PLANTS.

American Garden-bean. — Asparagus-bean. — Lima Bean. — Scarlet-runner. — Sieva Bean. — English Bean. — Pea 253

CHAPTER XII.

MISCELLANEOUS VEGETABLES.

Alkekengi, or Ground Cherry. — Martynia. — Okra, or Gumbo. — Rhubarb, or Pie-plant. — Tobacco 327

INDEX 343

GARDEN VEGETABLES.

FIELD AND GARDEN VEGETABLES.

CHAPTER I.

ESCULENT ROOTS.

The Beet. — Carrot. — Parsnip. — Potato. — Radish. — Swede or Ruta-baga Turnip. — Salsify, or Oyster-plant. — Sweet Potato. — Turnip.

THE BEET.

Beta vulgaris.

THE Common Beet, sometimes termed the Red Beet, is a half-hardy biennial plant; and is cultivated for its large, succulent, sweet, and tender roots. These attain their full size during the first year, but will not survive the winter in the open ground. The seed is produced the second year; after the ripening of which, the plant perishes.

When fully developed, the beet-plant rises about four feet in height, with an angular, channelled stem; long, slender branches; and large, oblong, smooth, thick, and fleshy leaves. The flowers are small, green, and are either sessile, or produced on very short peduncles. The calyxes, before maturity, are soft and fleshy; when ripe, hard and wood-like in texture. These calyxes, which are formed in small, united, rounded groups, or clusters, are of a brownish color, and about one-fourth of an inch in diameter; the size, however, as well as depth of color, varying, to some extent, in the different varieties. Each of these clusters of dried calyxes contains from two to four of the true seeds, which are quite small, smooth, kidney-shaped, and of a deep reddish-brown color.

These dried clusters, or groups, are usually recognized as the seeds, about fifteen hundred of which will weigh one ounce. They retain their vitality from seven to ten years.

Soil and Fertilizers. — The soil best adapted to the beet is a deep, light, well-enriched, sandy loam. When grown on thin, gravelly soil, the roots are generally tough and fibrous; and when cultivated in cold, wet, clayey localities, they are often coarse, watery, and insipid, worthless for the table, and comparatively of little value for agricultural purposes.

A well-digested compost, formed of barn-yard manure, loam, and salt, makes the best fertilizer. The application of coarse, undigested, strawy manure tends to the production of forked and misshapen roots, and should be avoided.

Propagation and Culture. — Beets are always raised from seed. For early use, sowings are sometimes made in November; but the general practice is to sow the seed in April, as soon as the frost is out of the ground, or as soon as the soil can be worked. For use in autumn, the seed should be sown about the middle or 20th of May; and, for the winter supply, from the first to the middle of June. Lay out the ground in beds five or six feet in width, and of a length proportionate to the supply required; spade or fork the soil deeply and thoroughly over; rake the surface smooth and even; and draw the drills across the bed, fourteen inches apart, and an inch and a half in depth. Sow the seeds thickly enough to secure a plant for every two or three inches, and cover to the depth of the drills. Should the weather be warm and wet, the young plants will appear in seven or eight days. When they are two inches in height, they should be thinned to five or six inches apart, extracting the weaker, and filling vacant spaces by transplanting. The after-culture consists simply in keeping the plants free from weeds, and the earth in the spaces between the rows loose and open by frequent hoeings.

Taking the Crop. — Roots from the first sowings will be ready for use early in July; from which time, until October, the table may be supplied directly from the garden. They should be drawn as fast as they attain a size fit for use, which will allow more time and space for the development of those remaining.

For winter use, the roots must be taken up before the occurrence of heavy frosts, as severe cold not only greatly impairs their quality, but causes them to decay at the crown.

In harvesting, avoid cutting or bruising the skin; and, in removing the leaves, be careful not to cut or wound the crown. After being spread a few hours in the sun to dry, they should be packed in earth or sand, slightly moist, and stored out of reach of frost for the winter.

If harvested before receiving injury from cold, and properly packed, they will retain, in a good degree, their freshness and sweetness until the new crop is suitable for use.

Seed. — To raise seed, select smooth and well-developed roots, having the form, size, and color by which the pure variety is distinguished; and, in April, transplant them eighteen inches or two feet apart, sinking the crowns to a level with the surface of the ground. As the stalks increase in height, tie them to stakes for support. The plants will blossom in June and July, and the seeds will ripen in August.

In harvesting, cut off the plants near the ground, and spread them in a light and airy situation till they are sufficiently dried for threshing, or stripping off the seeds; after which the seeds should be exposed, to evaporate any remaining moisture.

An ounce of seed will sow from one hundred to one hundred and fifty feet of drill, according to the size of the variety; and about four pounds will be required for an acre.

Use. — Roots of medium size are generally to be preferred for table use. When their growth has been rapid and unchecked, they will be found succulent, free from fibre, and of good quality. The deepest or brightest colors are most esteemed.

The young plants make an excellent substitute for spinach; and the leaves of some of the kinds, boiled when nearly full grown, and served as greens, are tender and well-flavored.

Some of the larger varieties are remarkably productive, and are extensively cultivated for agricultural purposes. From a single acre of land in good condition, thirty or forty tons are frequently harvested; and exceptional crops are recorded of fifty and even sixty tons. In France, the White Sugar-beet is largely employed for the manufacture of sugar, the amount produced during one year being estimated to exceed that annually made from the sugar-cane in the State of Louisiana.

For sheep, dairy-stock, and the fattening of cattle, experience has proved the beet to be at once healthful, nutritious, and economical.

Varieties. — The varieties are quite numerous, and vary to a considerable extent in size, form, color, and quality.

The kinds now in cultivation are as follow; viz.: —

Bark-skinned Beet.

Bark-skinned. Root broadest near the crown, and thence tapering regularly to a point; average specimens measuring four inches in their greatest diameter, and one foot in depth. Skin dark-brown, thick, hard, and wrinkled, much resembling the bark of some descriptions of trees; whence the name. Flesh deep purplish-red, fine-grained, sugary, and tender.

It is an early French variety, of fine flavor, excellent for summer use, and, if sown as late as the second week in June, equally valuable for the table during winter. Not recommended for field culture.

Bulb flattened; six or seven inches in diameter by three or four inches in depth; not very regular or symmetrical, but often somewhat ribbed, and terminating in a small, slender tap-root. The skin is of fine texture; brown above ground; below the surface, clear rose-red. Flesh white, circled or zoned with bright pink; not close-grained, but sugary and well-flavored. The leaves are numerous, erect, of a lively green color, forming many separate groups or tufts, covering the entire top, or crown of the root.

Bassano. Early Bassano. Extra Early.

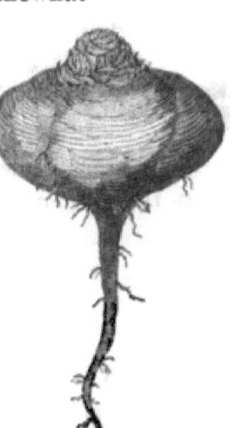

Bassano Beet.

It is an Italian variety, and generally considered the earliest of garden-beets, being from seven to ten days earlier than the Early Blood Turnip-rooted. The flesh, although much coarser than that of many other sorts, is tender, sweet, and of good quality. Roots from early sowings are, however, not suited for winter use; as, when overgrown, they become too tough, coarse, and fibrous for table use. To have them in perfection during winter, the seed should not be sown till near the close of June.

In dry, poor soil, it succeeds much better than the Early Blood Turnip-rooted.

A sub-variety of the Long Red Mangel-wurzel, growing mostly above ground. Root two feet and a half in length, and nearly three inches in diameter at its broadest part; often grooved or furrowed

Cow-horn Mangel-wurzel. Serpent-like Beet.

lengthwise, and frequently bent and distorted, — the effect either of the wind, or of the weight of its foliage. Flesh greenish-white, circled with red at the centre.

It derives its different names from its various contorted forms, sometimes resembling a horn, and often assuming a shape not unlike that of a serpent.

The variety is much esteemed and extensively cultivated in some parts of Europe, although less productive than the White Sugar or Long Red Mangel-wurzel.

Early Mangel-wurzel. Aside from its smaller size, this variety much resembles the Common Red Mangel-wurzel.

It is remarkable for the symmetry of its roots, which grow rapidly, and, if pulled while young, are tender, sweet, and well-flavored. Planted the last of June, it makes a table-beet of more than average quality for winter use.

When sown early, it attains a large size, and should have a space of twenty inches between the rows; but, when sown late, fifteen inches between the rows, and six inches between the plants in the rows, will afford ample space for their development.

Early Blood Turnip-rooted.
EARLY TURNIP BEET.

Early Blood Turnip-rooted.

The roots of this familiar variety are produced almost entirely within the earth, and measure, when of average size, from four to four and a half inches in depth, and four inches in diameter. Form turbinate, flattened, smooth, and symmetrical. Neck small. Tap-root very slender, and regularly tapering. Skin deep purplish-red. Flesh deep blood-red, sometimes circled and rayed with paler red; remarkably sweet and tender. Leaves erect, not numerous, and of a deep-red color, sometimes inclining to green, but the stems and nerves always of a deep brilliant red.

The Early Blood Turnip Beet succeeds well from Canada to the Gulf of Mexico; and in almost every section of the United States is more esteemed, and more generally cultivated for early use, than any other variety. Among market-gardeners, it is the most popular of the summer beets. It makes a rapid growth, comes early to the table, and, when sown late, keeps well, and is nearly as valuable for use in winter as in summer and autumn.

In common with most of the table sorts, the turnip-rooted beets are much sweeter and more tender if pulled before they are fully grown; and consequently, to have a continued supply in their greatest perfection, sowings should be made from the beginning of April to the last of June, at intervals of two or three weeks.

The roots, especially those intended for seed, should be harvested before severe frosts, as they are liable to decay when frozen at the crown, or even chilled.

Sow in drills fourteen inches apart; and, when two inches in height, thin out the plants to six inches apart in the drills. An acre of land in good cultivation will yield from seven to eight hundred bushels.

An improved variety of the Long Red Mangel-wurzel, almost regularly cylindrical, and terminating at the lower extremity in an obtuse cone. *German Red Mangel-wurzel.* It grows much out of ground: the neck or crown is quite small; it is rarely forked or deformed by small side-roots, and is generally much neater and more regular than the Long Red. Well-developed specimens measure from eighteen to twenty inches in length, and seven or eight inches in diameter.

For agricultural purposes, this variety is superior to the Long Red, as it is larger, more productive, and more easily harvested.

German Yellow Mangel-wurzel. Root produced half above ground, nearly cylindrical for two-thirds its length, terminating rather bluntly, and often branched or deformed by small side-roots. Well-grown specimens measure sixteen or eighteen inches deep, six or seven inches in diameter, and weigh from twelve to fifteen pounds. Skin above ground, greenish-brown; below, yellow. Flesh white, occasionally zoned or marked with yellow.

While young and small, the roots are tender and well-flavored; but this is a field rather than a table beet. In point of productiveness, it differs little from the Common Long Red, and should be cultivated as directed for that variety.

Half Long Blood.
Dwarf Blood.
Fine Dwarf Red.
Root produced within the earth, usually measuring about three inches in thickness near the crown, and tapering regularly to a point; the length being ten or twelve inches. Skin smooth, deep purplish-red. Flesh deep blood-red, circled and rayed with paler red, remarkably fine-grained, and of firm texture.

It is an excellent half-early garden variety, sweet and well-flavored, a good keeper, and by many considered superior to the Common Long Blood. When full grown, it is still tender and fine-grained, and much less stringy and fibrous than the last named at an equally advanced stage of growth. It may be classed as one of the best table-beets, and is well worthy of cultivation.

Improved Long Blood.
Long Smooth Blood.
This is an improved variety of the Common Long Blood, attaining a much larger size, and differing in its form, and manner of growth. When matured in good soil, its length is from eighteen inches to two feet; and its diameter, which is retained for more than half its length, is from four to five inches. It

is seldom symmetrical in its form; for, though it has but few straggling side-roots, it is generally more or less bent and distorted. Skin smooth, very deep or blackish purple. Flesh dark blood-red, sweet, tender, and fine-grained, while the root is young and small, but liable to be tough and fibrous when full grown. Leaves small, erect.

This beet, like the Common Long Blood, is a popular winter sort, retaining its color well when boiled. It is of larger size than the last named, grows more above the surface of the ground, and has fewer fibrous and accidental small side-roots. While young, it compares favorably with the old variety; but, when full grown, can hardly be said to be much superior. To have the variety in its greatest perfection for winter use, the seed should not be sown before the 10th of June, as the roots of this, as well as those of nearly all the table varieties, are much more tender and succulent when rapidly grown, and of about two-thirds their full size.

Improved Long Blood Beet.

Long Blood.
COMMON LONG BLOOD.

The roots of this familiar variety are produced within the earth. They are long, tapering, and slender, and vary in size according to the depth and richness of the soil. Skin dark-purple, sometimes purplish-black. Flesh deep blood-red, fine-grained, and sugary, retaining its color well after being boiled.

It is one of the most popular of winter beets; but, for late keeping, the seed should not be sown before the middle of June, as the roots, when large, are frequently tough and fibrous.

The Improved Long Blood is a variety of this, and has, to

a considerable extent, superseded it in the vegetable garden; rather, it would seem, on account of its greater size than from any real superiority as respects its quality, or keeping properties.

Long Red Mangel-wurzel.
Red Mangel-Wurzel.

Root fusiform, contracted at the crown, which, in the genuine variety, rises six or eight inches above the surface of the ground. When grown in good soil, it attains a large size, often measuring eighteen inches in length, and six or seven inches in diameter. Skin below ground purplish-rose, brownish-red where exposed to the air and light. Leaves green; the stems and nerves washed or stained with rose-red. Flesh white, zoned and clouded with different shades of red.

The Long Red Mangel-wurzel is hardy, keeps well, grows rapidly, is very productive, and, in this country, is more generally cultivated for agricultural purposes than any other variety. According to Lawson, the marbled or mixed color of its flesh seems particularly liable to vary: in some specimens, it is almost of a uniform red; while in others the red is scarcely, and often not at all, perceptible. These variations in color are, however, of no importance as respects the quality of the roots.

The seed may be sown from the middle of April till the last of May. If sown in drills, they should be at least eighteen inches apart, and the plants should be thinned to ten inches in the drills. If sown on ridges, the sowing should be made in double rows; the ridges being three and a half or four feet apart, and the rows fifteen inches apart. The yield varies with the quality of the soil and the state of cultivation; thirty and thirty-five tons being frequently harvested from an acre.

While young, the roots are tender and well-flavored, and are sometimes employed for table use.

THE BEET.

Long Yellow Mangel-wurzel.

Root somewhat fusiform, contracted towards the crown, which rises six or eight inches above the surface of the ground. Size remarkably large; when grown in deep rich soil, often measuring twenty inches in length, and five or six inches in thickness. Skin yellow, bordering on orange-color. Flesh pale-yellow, zoned or circled with white, not close-grained, but sugary.

The variety is one of the most productive of the field beets; but the roots are neither smooth nor symmetrical, a majority being forked or much branched.

In the vicinity of Paris, it is extensively cultivated, and is much esteemed by dairy farmers on account of the rich color which it imparts to milk when fed to dairy-stock. Compared with the German Yellow, the roots of this variety are longer, not so thick, but more tapering; and the flesh is of a much deeper color. It has also larger foliage.

Long Yellow Mangel-wurzel Beet.

Olive-shaped Mangel-wurzel (Red).

Red Oval Mangel-Wurzel.

Recently introduced. Bulb ovoid; intermediate in form between the Red Globe and common Red Mangel-wurzel; smooth and symmetrical. Flesh solid; somewhat variable in color, usually white, shaded or zoned with red, but sometimes with very little coloring. It is hardy, grows vigorously, and is said to yield quite as much to the acre as either of the last-named varieties.

Olive-shaped Mangel-wurzel, (Yellow.)

Yellow Oval Mangel-Wurzel.

A recently introduced sort, like the foregoing, which it resembles in form, hardiness, and productiveness. Flesh solid, white, zoned or clouded with different shades of yellow.

Pine-apple Short Top.
Hov. Mag.

Root of medium size, fusiform. Skin deep purplish-red. Flesh very deep blood-red, fine-grained, as sweet as the Bassano, tender, and of excellent quality for table use. Leaves short, and few in number, reddish-green; leaf-stems and nerves blood-red.

In its foliage, as well as in the color of the root, it strongly resembles some of the Long-Blood varieties; but it is not so large, is much finer in texture, and superior in flavor. It is strictly a garden or table beet, and, whether for fall or winter use, is well deserving of cultivation.

Red Castelnaudary.
Trans.

This beet derives its name from a town in the province of Languedoc in France, where the soil is particularly adapted to the growth of these vegetables, and where this variety, which is so much esteemed in France for its nut-like flavor, was originally produced.

The root is little more than two inches in diameter at the top, tapering gradually to the length of nine inches. The flesh, which is of a deep-purple, and exhibits dark rings, preserves its fine color when boiled, is very tender and sweet, and presents a delicate appearance when sliced.

Being small in its whole habit, it occupies but little space in the ground, and may be sown closer than other varieties usually are.

Not generally known or much cultivated in this country. There is a variety with yellow flesh.

Red Globe Mangel-wurzel.
Vil.

Root nearly spherical, seven or eight inches in diameter, and nine or ten inches in depth. Skin smooth, and of a rich purplish rose-color below ground, but brown above the surface where exposed to the sun. Flesh white, rarely circled with rose-red.

This variety is productive, keeps well, and, like the Yellow Globe, is well adapted to hard and shallow soils. It is usually cultivated for agricultural purposes, although the yield is less than that of the last named.

THE BEET. 13

In moist soils, the Yellow Globe succeeds best; and, as its quality is considered superior, it is now more generally cultivated than the Red.

Sutton's Large Yellow Globe Mangel-wurzel. An improved variety of the Yellow Globe Mangel-wurzel, recommended for size, symmetry of form, and solidity. It is also hardy, yields abundantly, and appears to be adapted to all descriptions of soil.

White Globe Mangel-wurzel. A sub-variety of the Yellow and Red Globe, which in form, and manner of growth, it much resembles. Skin, above ground, green; below, white. Flesh white and sugary; but, like the foregoing sorts, not fine-grained, or suited for table use.

Productive, easily harvested, excellent and profitable for farm-purposes, and remarkably well adapted for cultivation in hard, shallow soil.

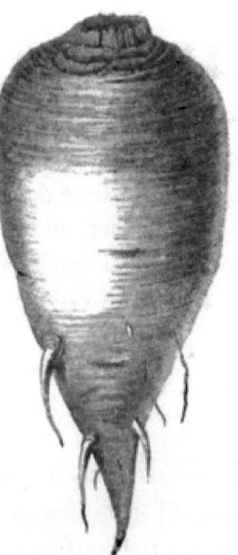

White Sugar Beet.

White Sugar. WHITE SILESIAN. Root fusiform, sixteen inches in length, six or seven inches in its greatest diameter, contracted towards the crown, thickest just below the surface of the soil, but nearly retaining its size for half the depth, and thence tapering regularly to a point. Skin white, washed with green, or rose-red at the crown. Flesh white, crisp, and sugary. Leaves green; the leaf-stems clear green, or green stained with light red, according to the variety.

The White Sugar Beet is quite extensively grown in this country, and is employed almost exclusively as feed for stock; although the young roots are sweet, tender, and well-flavored, and in all respects superior for the table to many garden varieties. In France, it is largely cultivated for the manufacture of sugar, and for distillation.

Of the two sub-varieties, some cultivators prefer the Green-top; others the Rose-colored, or Red-top. The latter is the larger, more productive, and the better keeper; but the former is the more sugary. It is, however, very difficult to preserve the varieties in a pure state; much of the seed usually sown containing, in some degree, a mixture of both.

It is cultivated in all respects as the Long Red Mangel-wurzel, and the yield per acre varies from twenty to thirty tons.

White Turnip-rooted. A variety of the Early Blood Turnip-rooted, with green leaves and white flesh. It is sweet and tender, but, on account of its color, not so marketable as the last named.

Wyatt's Dark Crimson. Root sixteen inches long, and five inches in diameter. Crown conical, brownish. Skin smooth, slate-black. Flesh deep purplish-red, circled and rayed with yet deeper shades of red; fine-grained, and remarkably sugary.

The variety is not early, but of fine quality; keeps well, and is recommended for cultivation for winter and spring use. Much esteemed in England.

Yellow Globe Mangel-wurzel.
Orange Globe Mangel-wurzel. This is a globular-formed beet, measuring eight or ten inches in diameter, and weighing ten or twelve pounds; nearly one-half of the root growing above ground. Skin yellow, where it is covered by the soil, and yellowish-brown above the surface where exposed to light and air. Flesh white, zoned or marked with yellow; close-grained, and

sugary. Leaves not large or numerous, erect, green; the stems and ribs paler, and sometimes yellowish.

The Yellow Globe is one of the most productive of all the varieties; and, though not adapted to table use, is particularly excellent for stock of all descriptions, as the roots are not only remarkably sugary, but contain a considerable portion of albumen. It retains its soundness and freshness till the season has far advanced, does not sprout so early in spring as many others, and is especially adapted for cultivation in hard, shallow soil.

Yellow Globe Mangle-wurzel Beet.

The yield varies from thirty to forty tons per acre, according to soil, season, and culture; although crops are recorded of fifty tons and upwards.

Sow from the last of April to the last of May; but early sowings succeed best. If sown in drills, they should be made twenty inches apart, and the plants should be thinned to ten inches apart in the drills: if sown on ridges, sow in double rows, making the ridges three feet and a half, and the rows sixteen inches apart. On account of its globular form, the crop can be harvested with great facility by the use of a common plough.

Yellow Turnip-rooted. A sub-variety of the Early Blood Turnip-rooted, with yellowish-green foliage and yellow flesh.

Not much cultivated, on account of its color; the Red varieties being preferred for table use.

Additional varieties, and more complete descriptions of many of the foregoing kinds, may be found in the "FIELD AND GARDEN VEGETABLES OF AMERICA."

THE CARROT.

Daucus carota.

Soil, Sowing, and Culture. — The Carrot flourishes best in a good, light, well-enriched loam. Where there is a choice of situations, heavy and wet soils should be avoided; and, where extremes are alternatives, preference should be given to the light and dry. If possible, the ground should be stirred to the depth of twelve or fifteen inches, incorporating a liberal application of well-digested compost, and well pulverizing the soil in the operation. The surface should next be levelled, cleared as much as possible of stones and hard lumps of earth, and made mellow and friable; in which state, if the ground contains sufficient moisture to color the surface when it is stirred, it will be ready for the seed. This may be sown from the 1st of April to the 20th of May; but early sowings succeed best. The drills should be made an inch in depth; and, for the smaller garden varieties, ten inches apart. The larger sorts are grown in drills fourteen inches apart, the plants in the rows being thinned to five or six inches asunder.

Harvesting. — The roots attain their full size by the autumn of the first year, and, as they are not perfectly hardy, should be dug and housed before the ground is frozen. When large quantities are raised for stock, they are generally placed in bulk in the cellar, without packing; but the finer sorts, when intended for the table, are usually packed in earth or sand in order to retain their freshness and flavor. With ordinary precaution, they will remain sound and fresh until May or June.

Seeds. — The seeds of the several varieties differ little in size, form, or color, and are not generally distinguishable from each other. They will keep well two years; and if preserved from dampness, and placed in a cool situation, a large percentage will vegetate when three years old.

In the vegetable garden, an ounce of seed is allowed for one hundred and fifty feet of drill; and for field culture, about two pounds for an acre.

An ounce contains twenty-four thousand seeds.

Use. — Though not relished by all palates, carrots are extensively employed for culinary purposes. They form an important ingredient in soups, stews, and French dishes of various descriptions; and by many are much esteemed when simply boiled, and served with meats or fish. They are also considered valuable for almost all descriptions of farm stock, and are more or less extensively cultivated throughout the country for this purpose. For horses, they are palatable and healthful; and for dairy cows, few kinds of food are better suited, as they are not only highly nutritious, but impart color and flavor to butter.

The varieties are as follow: —

The Altrincham Carrot measures about fourteen inches in length by two inches in diameter. It retains its thickness for nearly two-thirds its length; but the surface is seldom regular or smooth, the genuine variety being generally characterized by numerous crosswise elevations and corresponding depressions. Neck small and conical, rising one or two inches above the surface of the soil. Skin nearly bright red; the root having a semi-transparent appearance. Flesh bright and lively, crisp and breaking in its texture; and the heart, in proportion to the size of the root, is smaller than that of the Long Orange. Leaves long, but not large or numerous.

Altrincham.
Law.
ALTRINGHAM.

It is a good field carrot, but less productive than the Long Orange and some others; mild, and well-flavored for table, and one of the best sorts for cultivation for market.

In seedmen's lists, it is frequently but erroneously called the Altringham.

ESCULENT ROOTS.

Early Frame.
EARLY FORCING HORN.
EARLY SHORT SCARLET.

Early Frame.

Root grooved, or furrowed, at the crown; roundish, or somewhat globular; rather more than two inches in diameter, nearly the same in depth, and tapering suddenly to a slender tap-root. Skin red, or reddish-orange; brown, or greenish, where it comes to the surface of the ground. Foliage small, and finely cut or divided; not so large or luxuriant as that of the Early Horn.

The Early Frame is the earliest of all varieties, and is especially adapted for cultivation under glass, both on account of its earliness, and the shortness and small size of its roots. It is also one of the best sorts for the table, as the flesh is peculiarly mild and delicate.

Where space is limited, it may be grown in rows six inches apart, thinned to three inches apart in the rows; or sown broadcast, and the young plants thinned to three inches apart in each direction.

Early Half-long Scarlet.
HALF-LONG RED.
VII.

Root slender and tapering, measuring seven or eight inches in length, and two inches in its greatest diameter. Crown hollow. Skin red below the surface of the ground, green or brown above. Flesh reddish-orange, fine-grained, mild, and pleasant. Foliage similar to that of the Early Frame, but not abundant.

The variety is remarkably productive; good soil and favorable seasons often yielding an amount per acre approaching that of the Long Orange. Season intermediate between the early garden and late field sorts.

Early Horn.
DUTCH HORN.

Root six inches in length, two inches and a half in diameter, nearly cylindrical, and tapering abruptly to a very slender tap-root. Skin orange-red, but green or brown where it comes to the surface of the ground. Flesh deep orange-yellow, fine-grained, and of superior flavor and delicacy. The crown of the root is hollow, and the foliage short and small.

The variety is early, and, as a table carrot, much esteemed, both on account of the smallness of its heart and the tenderness of its fibre. As the roots are quite short, it is well adapted for shallow soils, and, on poor, thin land, will often yield a greater product per acre than the Long Orange or the White Belgian, when sown under like circumstances.

Sow in rows one foot apart, and thin to four inches in the rows.

Early Horn Carrot.

Root long, thickest at or near the crown, and tapering regularly to a point. Size very variable, being much affected by soil, season, and cultivation. Well-grown specimens measure fifteen inches in length, and three inches in diameter at the crown. Skin smooth, of a reddish-orange color. Flesh comparatively close-grained, succulent, and tender, of a light-reddish vermilion or orange color; the heart lighter, and large in proportion to the size of the root. Foliage not abundant, but healthy and vigorous, and collected into a small neck. The roots are usually produced entirely within the earth.

Long Orange.

If pulled while young and small, they are mild, fine-grained, and good for table use; but, when full grown, the texture is coarser, and the flavor stronger and less agreeable.

The Long Orange is more cultivated in this country for agricultural purposes than all other varieties. With respect to its value for stock, its great productiveness, and its keeping properties, it is considered the best of all the sorts for field culture. A well-enriched soil will yield from six hundred to eight hundred bushels per acre. The seed is usually sown in drills about fourteen inches apart, but sometimes on ridges eighteen or twenty inches apart, formed by turning two furrows together; the ridges yielding the largest roots, and the drills the greatest quantity.

Two pounds of seed are usually allowed to an acre; but, if sown by a well-regulated machine, about one-half this quantity will be sufficient.

Long Red Belgian.
YELLOW BELGIAN.

Root very long, fusiform; when grown in deep soil, often measuring twenty inches in length, and nearly three inches in diameter. The crown rises four or five inches above the surface of the ground, and is of a green color; below the surface, the skin is reddish-yellow. Flesh orange-red.

This variety, like the White, originated in Belgium. In Europe, it is much esteemed by agriculturists, and is preferred to the White Belgian, as it is not only nearly as productive, but has none of its defects.

Long Yellow.
LONG LEMON.

Root fusiform, three inches in diameter at the crown, and from twelve to fourteen inches in depth. Skin pale yellow; flesh yellow; the heart paler, and, like that of the Long Orange, of large size.

Long Red Belgian Carrot.

The Long Yellow is easily harvested, and is very productive, yielding nearly the same quantity to the acre as the Long Orange, which variety it much resembles in its general character, and with which it is frequently, to a greater or less extent, intermixed.

Long Surrey.
LONG RED.
JAMES'S SCARLET.

This variety resembles the Long Orange: the roots, however, are more slender, the heart is smaller, and the color deeper.

It is popular in some parts of England, and is cultivated to a considerable extent on the Continent.

An English variety, of recent introduction. **New Intermediate.** Root broadest at the crown, and thence tapering regularly to a point. Well-grown specimens measure nearly three inches in diameter at the broadest part, and one foot in length. Skin bright orange-red. Flesh orange-yellow, fine-grained, sweet, well-flavored, and, while young, excellent for table use.

Very hardy and productive; yielding, according to the best English authority, a greater weight per acre than any other yellow-fleshed variety

Root fusiform; fourteen inches in length by **Purple or Blood Red.** *Vil.* two inches and a half in diameter at the top or broadest part. Skin deep-purple, varying to some extent in depth of shade, but generally quite dark. Flesh purple at the outer part of the root, and yellow at the centre, or heart; fine-grained and well-flavored.

Not much cultivated for the table, on account of the brown color it imparts to soups or other dishes of which it may be an ingredient. It is also inclined to run to seed the year it is sown. It has, however, the reputation of flourishing better in wet, heavy soil than any other variety.

Root very long, fusiform, frequently **White Belgian.** **Green-Top White.** measuring eighteen or twenty inches in length, and four or five inches in diameter. Skin green above, white below ground. Flesh white, tending to citron-yellow at the centre, or heart, of the root; somewhat coarse in texture. Foliage large and vigorous.

The White Belgian Carrot is remarkable for its productiveness, surpassing in this respect all other varieties, and exceeding that of the Long Orange by nearly one-fourth. It can be harvested with great facility, and gives a good return even on poor soils.

The variety is not considered of any value as a table esculent, and is grown almost exclusively for feeding stock; for which purpose it is, however, esteemed less valuable than the yellow-fleshed sorts, because less nutritious, and more liable to decay during winter.

The same amount of seed will be required as of the Long Orange; and the general method of culture should be the same, with the exception, that, in thinning out the plants, the White Belgian should have more space.

THE PARSNIP.

Pastinaca sativa.

The Parsnip is a hardy biennial, and is cultivated for its roots, which are fusiform, often much elongated, sometimes turbinate, and attain their full size during the first year. The flowers and seeds are produced the second year, the plant then measuring five or six feet in height, with a grooved, or furrowed, hollow, branching stem. The seeds ripen in July and August; are nearly circular; one-fourth of an inch in diameter; flat, thin, very light, membranous on the borders, and of a pale yellowish-brown or yellowish-green color. They vary but little in size, form, or color in the different varieties, and retain their vitality two years. Six thousand seeds are contained in an ounce.

Half an ounce of seed is usually allowed for one hundred feet of drill, and six pounds for an acre.

Soil, Sowing, and Cultivation. — The soil should be mellow, deep, of a rich vegetable texture, and not recently turned from the sward. As the roots of most of the varieties are long and slender, the deeper and more thoroughly the soil is stirred, the better. Where the soil is thin, and the subsoil clayey or hard and gravelly, the Parsnip rarely succeeds well; the roots being not only short and branched, but deficient in the mild, tender, and sugary properties which they possess when grown under more favorable conditions.

The Parsnip is always propagated from seeds sown annually. As early in April as the soil becomes dry and warm, prepare the land as for the Carrot and other esculent roots, raking the surface fine and smooth; and sow the seeds rather thickly, in drills fifteen inches asunder, and an inch and a half in depth. When the young plants are well up, thin them to five or six inches apart, and cultivate in the usual manner during the season.

The roots are sometimes drawn for use early in September; but they are at this season generally small, and comparatively flavorless. Their full size and excellence are not acquired till the decay of the leaves, when they are ready for harvesting.

Harvesting. — The Parsnip sustains no injury when left in the open ground during winter; and it is a common practice to take up in the fall a certain quantity of roots to meet a limited demand in the winter months, allowing the rest to remain in the ground until spring. The roots thus treated are considered to have a finer flavor; that is to say, are better when recently taken from the ground.

In taking up the crop, remove the soil, and be careful not to break or bruise the roots. The thrust of the spade that easily lifts a carrot without essential injury, will, if applied to the parsnip, break the roots of nine in ten at scarcely half their length from the surface of the ground. As the roots keep much fresher, and retain their flavor much better, when taken up entire, the best method is to throw out a trench beside the rows, to the depth of the roots, when they can be easily, as well as perfectly, removed. They should be dug in pleasant weather, and laid on the ground, exposed to the sun for a few hours to dry; after which remove the foliage, and pack in sand, dried leaves, or common loam not too moist. Thus treated, they will remain fresh, kept in almost any location, either in the cellar or storehouse.

If the roots which have remained in the ground during winter be taken up in spring, and the tops removed as before directed, they may be packed in sand or earth, and will remain fresh, and in good condition for use, until May or June.

Use. — The use of the Parsnip as an esculent is well known. The roots are considered healthful, and are esteemed for their delicate, pleasant flavor. They contain a considerable portion of sugar, and are considered more nutritive than carrots or turnips.

Aside from the value of the Parsnip as a table vegetable, it is one of the most economical roots for cultivation for farm-purposes, as it not only produces an abundant and almost certain crop, but furnishes very nourishing food particularly adapted to and relished by dairy-stock.

Varieties. — The varieties are as follow: —

Common, or Dutch. *Trans.*
Long Smooth Dutch.

The leaves of the Common, or Dutch Parsnip, are strong and numerous; generally two feet long or high. The roots are from twenty to thirty inches in length, and from three to four inches in diameter at the shoulder, regularly tapering to the end, occasionally producing a few strong fangs. The crown is short and narrow, elevated, and contracts gradually from the shoulder, which is generally below the surface of the ground.

Seeds from America, Holland, and Germany, sown in the garden of the London Horticultural Society, all proved alike; though some were superior to others in the size of their roots, owing, it was thought, both to a careful selection of seed-roots, and to the age of the seeds. It was found that new seeds uniformly produced the largest roots.

Early Short-horn. *McInt.*

A recently introduced variety, similar to the Turnip-rooted, but shorter. Very delicate and fine-flavored.

The leaves of this variety grow much **Guernsey.** stronger and somewhat taller than those of *Trans.* the Common Parsnip. The only distinguish- **Long Smooth.** able difference in the roots is, that those of the Guernsey Parsnip are the larger and more perfect, being sometimes three feet long. Roots produced from seed obtained from Guernsey were evidently much superior to those which were grown from seed raised in other localities; from which it would appear that the Guernsey Parsnip is only an improved variety of the common, arising from soil and cultivation in that island. Dr. McCulloch states, that, in Guernsey, its roots grow to the length of four feet. In its flavor, it differs little from the Common Dutch Parsnip.

In this variety, the leaves are shorter and not **Hollow-** so numerous as those of the Common Parsnip. **Crowned.** *Trans.* The roots are oblong, eighteen inches in length, and four inches in diameter at the shoulder, more swollen at the top, and not tapering gradually, but ending somewhat abruptly with a small tap-root. The crown is short, and quite sunk into the shoulder, so as to form a hollow ring around the insertion of the stalks of the leaves, and grows mostly below the surface of the ground.

It is a good sort for general cultivation, especially as it does not require so deep a soil as either the Common or Guernsey. There is little difference in the flavor or general qualities of the three varieties.

Root fusiform, varying in length from fifteen **The Student.** to twenty inches, according to soil and culture. **Sutton's Student.** The crown is broad and rounded, hollowed at the insertion of the leaves, and, in well-grown specimens, measures nearly three inches in diameter. Compared with the Common Dutch or Hollow-crowned, the root is more free from fibres, and tapers more suddenly, and with greater regularity, from the crown of the point. The flavor is peculiarly sweet, mild, and pleasant, and is described as excelling that of any other sort now in cultivation.

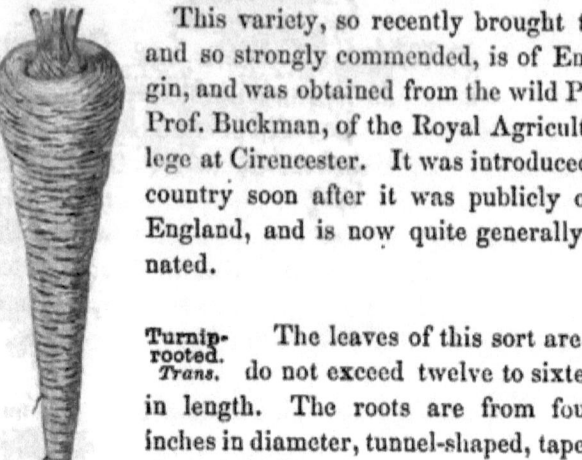

This variety, so recently brought to notice, and so strongly commended, is of English origin, and was obtained from the wild Parsnip by Prof. Buckman, of the Royal Agricultural College at Cirencester. It was introduced into this country soon after it was publicly offered in England, and is now quite generally disseminated.

Turnip-rooted.
Trans. The leaves of this sort are few, and do not exceed twelve to sixteen inches in length. The roots are from four to six inches in diameter, tunnel-shaped, tapering very abruptly, with a strong tap-root; the whole being from twelve to fifteen inches in length. The rind is rougher than either of the other sorts; the shoulder very broad, growing above the surface of the soil; convex, with a small, short crown. It is much the earliest of the Parsnips, and, if left in the ground, is liable to rot in the crown. The leaves also decay much sooner than those of most other sorts.

Student Parsnip.

It is particularly adapted to hard and shallow soils, and, from its coming into use much earlier than any other kind, very desirable. In flavor it is mild and pleasant, though less sugary than the long-rooted kinds. The flesh, when dressed, is more yellow than that of any other variety.

Turnip-rooted Parsnip,

THE POTATO.

Solanum tuberosum.

The Potato is a native of Central or Tropical America. In its wild or natural state, as found growing on the mountains of Mexico or South America, the tubers rarely exceed an inch in diameter, and are comparatively unpalatable. During the last half-century, its cultivation within the United States has greatly increased; and it is now considered the most important of all esculent roots, and next to the cereals in value as an article of human subsistence.

Soil. — The soils best suited to the Potato are of the dryer and lighter descriptions; pasture-lands, or new land, with the turf freshly turned, producing the most abundant as well as the most certain crops. On land of a stiff, clayey texture, or in wet soils, they are not only extremely liable to disease, but the quality is usually very inferior.

Where the land has been long under cultivation, they seldom produce well, and the quality, even when quite free from disease, is usually much below that of tubers raised on new soil.

Fertilizers. — If the soil is good, but little manure will be required. In highly enriched soil, the plants appear to be more liable to disease than when grown in soil that is naturally good.

The best fertilizers are those of a dry or absorbent nature, as plaster, lime, superphosphate of lime, and bone-dust. For wet soils, these are particularly beneficial, as they not only promote growth, but prevent disease. On dry, warm land, muck-compost or barn-yard manure may be applied advantageously. Decaying leaves make an excellent fertilizer; but all applications of very rich manure, particularly in the hill about the sets, at the time of planting, should be avoided. Ashes are a safe manure, and crops in

England treated with these alone suffered very little from disease; while others, under the application of manure in the ordinary forms, were more than half destroyed.

Propagation. — The Potato is propagated from the tubers, which are either divided into sets, or planted entire. Whichever of these practices may be adopted, experience has proved that plants from well-ripened tubers are not only more healthy and more productive, but actually come to perfection earlier, than those produced from immature sets.

Experiments for the purpose of testing the comparative value of the tubers entire, or divided into sets for planting, do not seem to be satisfactory. At the Chiswick Gardens, England, the divided tubers gave nearly one ton per acre more than those planted entire; this excess being the mean of two plantations, — one made early in the season, and another four weeks later: while another experiment, continued through a series of years, gave a mean result in favor of medium-sized tubers, planted entire.

The part of the Potato used for planting has been regarded as important; the point, or top, being thought to produce the most healthy and productive plants. Though there appears to be a physiological difference between the extremities, and though the results of the experiment made by the London Horticultural Society gave a large amount in favor of the eye, or top, of the tuber, still, practically considered, the part of the tuber to be used for planting is unimportant; a paramount consideration being its complete development, or full maturity.

With regard to the quantity of seed per acre, great diversity of opinion exists among cultivators. Much, of course, depends on the variety, as some sorts not only have more numerous eyes, but more luxuriant and stronger plants, than others. Of such varieties, a much less quantity will be required than of those of an opposite character. From a series of experiments carefully made for the purpose of ascertaining the amount of seed most profitable for an acre, it was found that from six to eight bushels, if planted in hills, answered better than more: for, when too much seed was used, there were many small tubers; and where the tubers had been divided into very small parts, or single eyes, the plants were more feeble, and the yield less in number and weight, though usually of larger size.

Methods of Planting and Cultivation. — Potatoes are usually planted either in hills or ridges, the former method being the more common in this country. If planted in hills, they should be made from three feet to three and a half apart, the distance to be regulated by the habit of the variety under cultivation. If in ridges or drills, they may be made from two and a half to three feet apart; although some of the earlier and smaller kinds may be successfully grown at eighteen or twenty inches.

Of sets formed by dividing a tuber of medium size into four parts, three may be allowed to a hill: if planted in drills, sets of this size should be placed ten inches apart. On light, warm soil, they require to be covered nearly four inches deep; but in cold, wet situations, two and a half or three inches will be sufficient.

Cultivation. — This should be commenced as soon as the young shoots are fairly above the surface. As the season advances, gather the earth gradually about the hills or along the drills, adding a little at each successive hoeing for the support of the growing plants, and to encourage the development of the side-roots; for it is at the extremities of these that the tubers are formed. After the appearance of the blossoms, cultivation should be discontinued; and no further attention will be required till the time for harvesting.

Forcing. — This should be commenced from three to four weeks before the season for planting in the open ground. The earliest varieties should be chosen for the purpose, selecting whole tubers of medium size, and placing them close together, in a single layer, among half-decayed leaves or very light loam, on the surface of a moderate hot-bed.

In a few weeks, the eyes will have started sufficiently for planting out. Divide the tubers into sets, as before directed, being careful not to break or injure the young shoots; set them in hills or drills, and cover three inches deep. A light application of horse-manure at the bottom of the hills or drills will afford the warmth which may be needed early in the season, and afterwards give support and vigor to the growing crop.

Taking the Crop, and Method of Preservation. — The season of maturity of the earlier sorts will be indicated by the decay of the plants. The later sorts will continue their growth until checked by frost; previous to which time, they will not be ready for harvesting.

In summer weather, when it is practicable, the table should be supplied from day to day directly from the field or garden, as the tubers rapidly deteriorate after being taken from the ground, particularly if exposed to a warm, light atmosphere, or kept in a warm and dry cellar.

In the preservation of potatoes, it is of the first importance that they be excluded from light. If this is neglected, they become not only injurious, but actually poisonous; and this is especially the fact when they are allowed to become of a green color, which they readily will do on exposure to the light. In a state of complete darkness, they should, therefore, be placed the day they are taken out of the ground; and it were even better that they were stored in rather a damp state, than that they should be exposed for a day to the light with a view to dry them.

Varieties. — Messrs. Peter Lawson & Sons describe one hundred and seventy-five, and other foreign authors enumerate upwards of five hundred varieties, describing the habit of the plant; size, form, and color of the tubers; quality and general excellence; and comparative value for cultivation.

Few of these foreign sorts have ever been cultivated to any extent in this country, and a large proportion are nearly worthless. Most varieties, from some yet unexplained cause, gradually deteriorate; and many kinds now generally free from disease, and universally classed as good, will probably soon be ranked with those unworthy of cultivation.

Sebec. Tubers yellowish-white, above medium size, somewhat irregular in form, but generally roundish, or oblong, and a little flattened; flesh perfectly white when cooked, with the delicate flavor, and dry, floury character, once peculiar to the Carter.

The variety is healthy, very productive, of good quality, and, whether for family use or the market, must be classed as one of the best, and is recommended for cultivation.

Some samples in bulk resemble the Jackson White; but the growing plants of the last named differ in a marked degree from those of the Sebec.

Buckeye. A Western variety; grown also to a considerable extent in some parts of the Middle States.

"It is a handsome, round potato; white throughout, except a little bright pink at the bottom of the eye; very early,— ripening as early as the Chenango; attains a good marketable size as soon as the Dykeman; cooks dry and light; and is fine-flavored, particularly when first matured. It throws up a thick, vigorous, and luxuriant vine; grows compactly in the hill, and to a large size, yielding abundantly."

For planting for early use, it is a promising variety; but for a late or medium crop, upon strong, rich ground, is said to grow so rapidly, and to so great a size, that many of the tubers are liable to be hollow-hearted, which considerably impairs their value for table use

Carter. A medium-sized, roundish, flattened, white potato, once esteemed the finest of all varieties, but at present nearly or quite superseded by the Jackson White, of which it is supposed to be the parent. Eyes rather numerous, and deeply sunk; flesh very white, remarkably dry, farinaceous, and well-flavored. Originated about thirty years ago, in Berkshire County, Mass., by Mr. John Carter.

Cuzco. A recent variety; originated by the late Rev. Chauncey E. Goodrich, of Utica, N.Y. The tubers are of medium size; and the flesh is white, light, and dry, when cooked.

In common with many of the kinds known as the "Goodrich Seedlings," the Cuzco appears to be very productive, free from disease, a good keeper, and in all respects desirable both for the field and garden.

Danvers Seedling.
DANVERS RED. Plant healthy and vigorous. The large, full-grown tubers are long; and the smaller, undeveloped ones, nearly round. Color, light red, with faint streaks of white; eyes moderately sunk; quality fair.

This variety originated in Danvers, Essex County, Mass., and, when first introduced, was not only of good size and quality, but remarkably productive. It has, however, much deteriorated; and is now, both as respects quality and yield, scarcely above an average. At one period, it had the reputation of being one of the best varieties for keeping, and of entirely withstanding the attacks of the potato disease.

Davis's Seedling.

Davis's Seedling. Tubers of good size, red, nearly round, though sometimes more or less flattened. Eyes deeply sunk, and not very numerous; flesh nearly white, slightly tinged with pink beneath the skin when cooked; quality good. It requires the full season for its complete perfection, and resists disease better than most varieties.

Dykeman.
EARLY DYKEMAN.

Plant of medium strength and vigor, rarely producing seed or blossoms; tubers large, roundish, often oblong; color white, clouded at the stem-end and about the eyes (which are moderately sunk and rather numerous) with purple; flesh white, or yellowish-white; its quality greatly affected by season and the soil in which the variety may be cultivated.

In certain descriptions of rather strong, clayey land, the yield is often remarkably great, and the quality much above medium. In such land, if warm and sheltered, the tubers attain a very large size quite early in the season, and find a ready sale in the market at greatly remunerative prices. Under other conditions, it frequently proves small, waxy, and inferior in quality, and profitless to the cultivator. Notwithstanding these defects, its size, earliness, and productiveness render it worthy of trial.

Early Blue.

Tubers of medium size, roundish, of a bright purple or bluish color; eyes moderately deep; flesh, when cooked, white, or yellowish white, mealy, and well-flavored.

This old and familiar variety is one of the earliest of the garden potatoes, of fine quality, and one of the best for forcing for early crops. It retains its freshness and flavor till late in the spring; is of healthy habit; and, though but moderately productive, is worthy more general cultivation.

Early Handsworth.

A recently introduced, foreign potato, described as being not only healthy and prolific, but the earliest of all varieties. The tubers are of medium size, round, and cook white and flowery. It is one of the best for forcing; and, as an early garden-sort, is recommended for cultivation. Of more than seventy varieties experimentally grown by the London Horticultural Society, the Early Handsworth proved ten days the earliest.

3

ESCULENT ROOTS.

Early Goodrich. *Am. Agr.* Plant of hardy, healthy habit; tubers of full medium size, oblong, white, with rather large, prominent eyes; flesh white, light and dry, mild and delicate.

The variety was originated by the late Rev. C. E. Goodrich, of Utica, N.Y., after whom it was named; and is described as being a seedling of the Cuzco.

It was introduced in 1864; and has proved not only of fine quality, but early and productive. Of sixteen thousand seedlings raised by Mr. Goodrich, this promises to be one of the best.

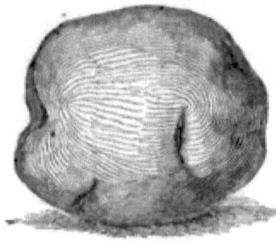

Garnet Chili.

Garnet Chili. Plant of medium height, rather erect, sturdy, and branching; flowers abundant, white or pale purple, showy, and generally abortive; tubers large, roundish or oblong, purplish-red or garnet-colored; eyes not abundant, and of moderate depth; flesh nearly white, dry and mealy when cooked, and, the size of the tubers considered, remarkably well flavored. Not early, but hardy, healthy, productive, and recommended for cultivation.

The Garnet Chili, now very generally disseminated, was originated in 1853 by Rev. Chauncey E.. Goodrich, of Utica, N.Y., from the seeds of a variety received from Chili, South America.

Gillyflower. Tubers large, oval or oblong, flattened, white, and comparatively smooth; flesh white, dry, and of fair quality. The plants are healthy, and the variety is very productive: but it is inferior to many others for table use; though its uniform good size, and its fair form and whiteness, make it attractive and salable in the market.

It is frequently sold for the State of Maine, which it much resembles.

Tubers white, of full medium size, oblong, with quite small, slightly sunken eyes; flesh white, floury, and of excellent quality.

<small>Harrison.
Am. Agr.</small>

This is one of the varieties recently introduced by the late Rev. C. E. Goodrich, and is said to have been obtained from the same seed-ball as the Early Goodrich.

Mr. A. W. Harrison of Philadelphia, who has experimentally grown many of the more recent sorts, and after whom the present variety was named, places the Early Goodrich and the Harrison "at the head of all varieties for every good quality."

Jackson White.

This comparatively new but very excellent variety originated in Maine, and is supposed to be a seedling from the celebrated Carter, which it much resembles. Tubers yellowish-white, varying in size from medium to large; form somewhat irregular, but generally roundish, though sometimes oblong and a little flattened; eyes rather numerous, and deeply sunk; flesh perfectly white when cooked, remarkably dry, mealy, farinaceous, and well-flavored.

The variety unquestionably attains its greatest perfection when grown in Maine, or the northern sections of Vermont and New Hampshire; but is nevertheless of good quality when raised in the warmer localities of New England and the Middle States. It is earlier than the Davis Seedling; comparatively free from disease; a good keeper; commands the highest market-price; and, every thing considered, must be classed as one of the best, and recommended for general cultivation.

The plants are very erect, the flowers nearly white, and the balls, or berries, are produced in remarkable abundance.

Like many other varieties, the plants seem to be more productive, and the tubers of better quality, when raised from seed obtained every year or two from Maine, Canada, or the Provinces. When grown for successive years from seed raised in the same locality, the variety becomes less productive, the plants less healthy and vigorous, and the tubers gradually lose the dry, floury character which they possess when in their full perfection, and for which they are so much esteemed.

Jenny Lind.
RHODE-ISLAND SEEDLING.

This is one of the largest of all the varieties. It is remarkably productive, keeps well, and, as an agricultural potato, rivals the Rohan. Requires the full season. It sports more than any potato; being exceedingly variable in size, form, and color. Not suited for table use.

Lady's Finger.
RUFFORT KIDNEY.
Law.

An old variety, of pretty appearance, long cultivated, and much esteemed as a baking potato; its peculiar form being remarkably well adapted for the purpose. It is, however, very liable to disease; and as many of the recently introduced seedlings are quite as good for baking, as well as far more hardy and productive, it cannot now be considered as a variety to be recommended for general culture.

Lapstone Kidney.
McInt.
NICHOLS EARLY.

A variety of English origin. McIntosh describes it as being decidedly the best kidney potato grown, and an excellent cropper. Tubers sometimes seven inches in length, and three inches in breadth. It is a good potato in August and September; and will keep in excellent condition till May following, without losing either its mealiness or flavor,

Long Red.

A few years since, this variety was exceedingly abundant in the market, and was esteemed one of the best sorts for use late in spring and early in summer. It was also remarkably healthy and productive, and was considered one of the most valuable kinds for general cultivation. The Jenny Lind and other varieties are now rapidly superseding it in most localities.

Mercer.

CHENANGO. WHITE CHENANGO.
MESHANNOCK.

An old and familiar variety; at one period almost everywhere known, and generally acknowledged as the best of all varieties. As a potato for early planting, whether for family use or for the market, it was a general favorite; but, within a few years past, it has not only greatly deteriorated in quality and productiveness, but has been peculiarly liable to disease and premature decay of the plants.

When well grown, the tubers are of good size, rather long, a little flattened, and comparatively smooth; eyes slightly sunk; color white, with blotches of purple, — before cooking, somewhat purple under the skin; flesh, when cooked, often stained with pale purple; in its crude state, zoned with bright purple. Quality good; dry, mealy, and well-flavored.

It originated in Mercer County, Penn.: whence the name. Mr. Paschal Morris, of Philadelphia, states that it went West, taking the name of Meshannock, from the name of the stream, in Mercer County, along which it originated. In Canada, the Provinces, and throughout most of New England, it is known as the Chenango, or White Chenango.

Monitor.
Am. Agr.

Originated with Mr. D. A. Bulkley, Massachusetts. Tubers very large, oblong, of a dull, rusty, pinkish-red color, and strongly depressed eyes; flesh light and dry, and described as of good quality for the table.

Is very productive, rarely hollow-hearted, and is recommended as being worthy cultivation. Fifty specimens weighed sixty pounds, and measured one bushel.

Peach-blow. Tubers similar in form to the Davis Seedling, but more smooth and regular; color red, the eyes not deeply sunk; flesh yellow when cooked, dry and mealy, but only of medium quality, on account of its strong flavor.

It is hardy, and quite productive; keeps well; and, at one period, was extensively cultivated for market in the northern parts of New England and the State of New York, as well as in the Canadas.

Pink-eyed. Tubers nearly round; eyes rather large and deep; color mostly white, with spots and splashes of pink, particularly about the eyes; flesh yellow.

The Pink-eyed is an old but inferior variety, hardly superior in quality to the Vermont White. Though quite productive, it is generally esteemed unworthy of cultivation.

Rohan. Tubers very large, in form much resembling the Jenny Lind; color yellowish-white, with clouds or patches of pink or rose; flesh greenish-white when cooked, yellowish, watery, and strong-flavored.

State of Maine.

The State of Maine Potato is quite early, but more liable to disease than the Davis Seedling and some other varieties. In Maine it is grown in great perfection, nearly equalling the Jackson White and Carter as a table potato. On light soil, it is only moderately productive; but on strong land, in high cultivation, yields abundantly.

Western Red. — Plant erect, stout, and branching; stem and foliage deep green; flowers lilac-purple; tubers large, roundish or oblong, like those of the Garnet Chili, purplish-red; eyes not numerous, set in shallow basins; flesh yellowish-white, and, if well grown, dry, and of fair quality.

The variety is hardy, yields abundantly, and is extensively grown in many sections of the country, but can hardly be considered superior in quality or productiveness to the Garnet Chili, besides being quite as liable to disease.

White Peach-blow. — The tubers resemble the Buckeye. They are somewhat above medium size, white, stained with pink about the eye; flesh white, dry, and floury. The plant is a good grower, and of healthy habit.

Besides being quite as productive as the old Peach-blow, it is greatly superior to it for the table. It is also a fine market potato, and is recommended for general cultivation. Requires nearly the entire season for its full maturity. Originated in Monmouth County, N. J.

THE RADISH

Raphanus sativus.

The Radish is a hardy annual plant, originally from China. The roots vary greatly in form; some being round or ovoid, some turbinate, and others long, slender, and tapering. When in flower, the plant rises from three to four feet in height, with an erect, smooth, and branching stem. The flowers are quite large, and, in the different kinds, vary in color from clear white to various shades of purple. The seeds are round, often irregularly flattened or compressed: those of the smaller, or spring and summer varieties, being of a grayish-red color; and those of the winter, or larger-rooted sorts, of a yellowish-red. An ounce contains from three thousand three hundred to three thousand six hundred seeds, and they retain their vitality five years.

Soil, Propagation, and Cultivation. — All the varieties thrive best in a light, rich, sandy loam; dry for early spring sowings, moister for the summer.

Like all annuals, the Radish is propagated by seeds, which may be sown either broadcast or in drills; but the latter method is preferable, as allowing the roots to be drawn regularly, with less waste. For the spindle-rooted kinds, mark out the drills half an inch deep, and five or six inches apart; for the small, turnip-rooted kinds, three-quarters of an inch deep, and six inches asunder. As the plants advance in growth, thin them so as to leave the spindle-rooted an inch apart, and the larger-growing sorts proportionally farther.

Open Culture. — Sow in spring, as soon as the ground can be worked. If space is limited, radishes may be sown with onions or lettuce. When grown with the former, they are said to be less affected by the maggot. For a succession, a small sowing should be made each fortnight until midsummer, as the early-sown plants are liable to become rank, and unfit for use, as they increase in size.

Radishes usually suffer from the drought and heat incident to the summer, and, when grown at this season, are generally fibrous and very pungent. To secure the requisite shade and moisture, they are sometimes sown in beds of asparagus, that the branching stems may afford shade for the young radishes, and render them more crisp and tender. A good criterion by which to judge of the quality of a radish is to break it asunder by bending it at right angles. If the parts divide squarely and freely, it is fit for use.

Seed. — An ounce and a half of seed will sow a bed five feet in width and twelve feet in length. Ten pounds are required for seeding an acre.

The excellence of a radish consists in its being succulent, mild, crisp, and tender; but, as these qualities are secured only by rapid growth, the plants should be frequently and copiously watered in dry weather. The varieties are divided into two classes; viz., spring or summer, and autumn or winter, radishes.

SPRING OR SUMMER RADISHES.

These varieties are all hardy, and may be sown in the open ground as early in spring as the soil is in good working condition.

Early radishes are easily grown in a common hot-bed; and, as the plants will withstand cold and moisture, the seeds may be sown in February; or they may be successfully grown in frames with early lettuce, sowing the seeds in any of the winter months, or early in March.

Early Scarlet Turnip-rooted.

Bulb spherical, or a little flattened, — often bursting or cracking longitudinally before attaining its full dimensions; skin deep scarlet; flesh rose-colored, crisp, mild, and pleasant; neck small; leaves few in number, and of smaller size than those of the common Scarlet Turnip-rooted. Season quite early, — two or three days in advance of the last named.

As a variety for forcing, it is considered one of the best; but the small size of the leaves renders it inconvenient for bunching, and it is consequently less cultivated for the market than many other sorts.

Extensively grown in the vicinity of Paris.

Early White Turnip-rooted. Skin and flesh white; form similar to that of the Scarlet Turnip-rooted. It is, however, of smaller size, and somewhat earlier. An excellent sort, and much cultivated.

Gray Olive-shaped. Form similar to the Scarlet Olive-shaped. Skin gray; flesh white, crisp, and well-flavored. A desirable variety.

Gray Turnip-rooted. The form of this variety may be called round, though it is somewhat irregular in shape. The outside coat is mottled with greenish-brown, wrinkled, and often marked with transverse white lines. The flesh is mild, not so solid as that of many varieties, and of a greenish-white color. Half early, and a good variety for summer use.

Long Purple. *Thomp.* Root long, a large portion growing above ground; skin deep purple; flesh white, and of good flavor.

The seed-leaves, which are quite large, are used as a small salad. The variety is early, and good for forcing. When the green tops are required for salading, the seeds should be sown in drills, as mustard or cress.

Long Scarlet. *Thomp.* **Early Scarlet Short-Top.** Root long, a considerable portion growing above the surface of the ground; outside, of a beautiful, deep-pink color, becoming paler towards the lower extremity; flesh white, transparent, crisp, and of good flavor, having less pungency than that of the Scarlet Turnip; leaves small, but larger than those of the last-named variety.

When of suitable size for use, the root measures seven or eight inches in length, and five-eighths or three-fourths of an inch in diameter at its largest part.

The Long Scarlet Radish, with its sub-varieties, is more

generally cultivated for market in the Eastern, Middle, and Western States, than any other, or perhaps even more than all other sorts. It is extensively grown about London, and is everywhere prized, not only for its fine qualities, but for its rich, bright color. It is also one of the hardiest of the radishes, and is raised readily in any common frame if planted as early as February.

Long White. Root long and slender, nearly of the size and form of the Long Scarlet; skin white, — when exposed to the light, tinged with green; flesh white, crisp, and mild.

It is deserving of cultivation, not only on account of its excellent qualities, but as forming an agreeable contrast at table when served with the red varieties.

Long Scarlet Radish.

Olive-shaped Scarlet. Bulb an inch and a half deep, three-fourths of an inch in diameter, oblong, somewhat in the form of an olive, terminating in a very slim tap-root; skin fine scarlet; neck small; leaves not numerous, and of small size; flesh rose-colored, tender, and excellent. Early, and well adapted for forcing and for the general crop.

Olive Scarlet Radish.

Scarlet Turnip-rooted. Bulb spherical, — measuring in its greatest perfection an inch in diameter; skin fine, deep scarlet; flesh white, sometimes stained with red; leaves large and numerous.

The variety is early, and deserves more general cultivation, not only on account of its rich color, but for the crisp and tender properties of its flesh. It is much esteemed in England, and is grown extensively for the London market.

Scarlet Turnip-rooted Radish.

White Turnip-rooted. Bulb of the form and size of the Scarlet Turnip-rooted; skin white; flesh white and semi-transparent. It possesses less piquancy than the Scarlet, but is some days later.

Autumn and Winter Radishes.

These varieties may be sown from the 20th of July to the 10th of August; the soil being previously made rich, light, and friable. Thin out the young plants from four to six inches apart; and, in the absence of rain, water freely. During September and October, the table may be supplied directly from the garden. For winter use, the roots should be harvested before freezing weather, and packed in earth or sand, out of danger from frost. Before being used, they should be immersed for a short time in cold water.

Use. — All of the kinds are used as salad, and are served in all the forms of the spring and summer radishes.

Varieties: —

Black Spanish. *Trans.* Bulb ovoid, or rather regularly pear-shaped, with a long tap-root. At first the root is slender, and somewhat cylindrical in form; but it swells as it advances in age, and finally attains a large size, measuring eight or ten inches in length, and three or four inches in diameter. The outside is rough, and nearly black; the flesh is pungent, firm, solid, and white; the leaves are long, and inclined to grow horizontally; the leaf-stems are purple. It is one of the latest as well as one of the hardiest of the radishes, and is considered an excellent sort for winter use.

Large Purple Winter. *Trans.* **Purple Spanish.** The large Purple Winter Radish is a beautiful variety, derived, without doubt, from the Black Spanish, which, in shape and character, it much resembles. The outside, however, when cleaned, is of a beautiful purple, though it appears black when first drawn from the earth; and the coat, when cut through, shows the purple very finely.

Rose-colored Chinese.
SCARLET CHINESE WINTER.

Bulb rather elongated, somewhat cylindrical, contracted abruptly to a long, slender tap-root; size full medium, — average specimens measuring five inches in length, and two inches in diameter at the broadest part; skin bright rose; flesh firm, and rather piquant; leaves large, — the leaf-stems washed with rose-red. Season between that of the Gray Turnip-rooted and the Black Spanish.

Winter White Spanish.

Root somewhat fusiform, retaining its diameter for two-thirds the length, sharply conical at the base, and, when well grown, measuring seven or eight inches in length by nearly three inches in its fullest diameter; skin white, slightly wrinkled, sometimes tinged with purple where exposed to the sun; flesh white, solid, and pungent, though milder than that of the Black Spanish.

It succeeds best, and is of the best quality, when grown in light, sandy soil. Season intermediate.

RUTA-BAGA, OR SWEDE TURNIP.

Russian Turnip. — French Turnip. — Brassica campestris Ruta-baga. — De Cand.

The Ruta-baga, or Swede Turnip, is supposed by De Candolle to be analogous to the Kohl Rabi; the root being developed into a large, fleshy bulb, instead of the stem. In its natural state, the root is small and slender, and the stem smooth and branching, — not much exceeding two feet in height.

The bulbs or roots are fully developed during the first year. The plant flowers, and produces its seed, the second year, and then perishes. Although considered hardy, — not being affected by even severe frosts, — none of the varieties will withstand the winters of the Northern or Middle States in the open ground. The crop should therefore be harvested in October or November, and stored for the winter out of danger from freezing. Most of the sorts now cultivated retain their freshness and solidity till spring, and some even into the summer; requiring no particular care in their preservation, other than that usually given to the Carrot or the Potato.

Soil and Cultivation. — All the varieties succeed best in a deep, well-enriched, mellow soil, which, previous to planting, should be very deeply ploughed, and thoroughly pulverized by harrowing or otherwise. Some practise ridging, and others sow in simple drills. The ridges are usually formed by turning two furrows against each other, and, being thus made, are about two feet apart. If sown in simple drills, the surface should be raked smooth, and the drills made from sixteen to eighteen inches apart; the distance to be regulated by the strength of the soil.

Seed and Sowing. — About one pound of seed is usually allowed to an acre. Where the rows are close, rather more than this quantity will be required; while three-fourths of a pound will be amply sufficient if sown on ridges, or where the drills are eighteen inches apart. The sowing may be made from the middle of May to the 1st of July; the latter time being considered sufficiently early for growing for the table, and by some even for stock. Early sowings will, unquestionably, give the greatest product; while the later-grown bulbs, though of smaller dimensions, will prove of quite as good quality for the table.

The seeds are similar to those of the common garden and field turnip, and will keep from five to eight years.

Varieties. — The varieties are as follow : —

Ashcroft.

Bulb of medium size, ovoid, smooth, and symmetrical; neck very short, or wanting. Above ground, the skin is purple; below the surface, yellow. Flesh yellow; solid, fine-grained, and of excellent flavor. It forms its bulb quickly and regularly; keeps in fresh and sound condition until May or June; and well deserves cultivation, either for agricultural purposes or for the table.

Common Purple-top Yellow.

An old and long-cultivated sort, from which, in connection with the Green-top, have originated most of the more recent and improved yellow-fleshed varieties. Form regularly egg-shaped, smooth, but usually sending out a few small, straggling roots at its base, near the tap-root; neck short; size rather large, — usually measuring six or seven inches in depth, and four or five inches in its largest diameter; skin purple above ground, — below the surface, yellow; flesh yellow, of close, firm texture, and of good quality. It is very hardy; forms its bulb promptly and uniformly; and in rich, deep soils, yields abundantly. For thin and light soils, some of the other varieties should be selected.

Green-top Yellow.

In form and foliage, this variety resembles the Common Purple-top, but usually attains a larger size when grown in similar situations. Skin, above the surface of the soil, green; below ground, yellow. The flesh is solid, sweet, and well-flavored, but inferior to that of the Purple-top. It keeps well, is of fair quality for the table, and, on account of its great productiveness, one of the best of all varieties for growing for feeding stock.

Green-top White. The Green-top White differs from the Purple-top White, not only in color, but in size and quality; the bulbs being larger, and the flesh not quite so firm or well-flavored.

It is productive; continues its growth till the season has far advanced; is little affected by severe weather; and, when sown in good soil, will yield an agricultural crop of twenty-five or thirty tons to an acre.

Laing's Improved Purple-top.
Law. and Gen. Farmer.
This variety differs from most, if not all, of the varieties of Swedish turnips, in having entire cabbage-like leaves, which, by their horizontal growth, often nearly cover the surface of the ground. In form, hardiness, and quality, it is fully equal to any of the other sorts. It requires good land in high condition; and, under such circumstances, will yield abundantly, and is worthy of cultivation.

The bulb, when well grown, has an almost spherical form; a fine, smooth skin, purple above ground, yellow below, with yellow, solid, and well-flavored flesh

Purple-top White. Bulb oblong, tapering towards the lower extremity, five or six inches in diameter, seven or eight inches in depth, and less smooth and regular than many of the yellow-fleshed varieties. The skin is of a clear, rich purple, where it comes to air and light, but, below the ground, pure white; flesh white, very solid and fine-grained, sugary and well-flavored.

The variety is hardy, productive, keeps remarkably well, is good for table use, and may be profitably grown for agricultural purposes. Upwards of twenty-eight tons, or nine hundred and sixty bushels, have been raised from an acre.

THE RUTA-BAGA.

Root regularly turbinate, or fusiform, of full **River's.**
medium size, smooth, and with few small or
fibrous roots; neck two inches long; skin, above ground,
green, washed with purplish-red where most exposed to the
sun, — below ground, yellow; flesh yellow, firm, sweet, and
well-flavored.

Esteemed one of the best, either for stock or for the table.
Keeps fresh till May or June.

Bulb ovoid, or regularly turbinate, and **Skirving's**
rather deeper in proportion to its diameter **Purple-top.**
than the common Purple-top Yellow; surface **Skirving's Improved Purple-Top.**
smooth and even, with few fibrous roots, and
seldom deformed by larger accidental roots, although, in
unfavorable soils or seasons, a few coarse roots are put
forth in the vicinity of the tap-root; size full medium, —
five to seven inches in length, and four or five inches in
diameter. Neck short, but, when grown in poor soil, comparatively long; skin, above ground, fine, deep purple, — below ground, yellow, — the colors often richly blending together at the surface; flesh yellow, of solid texture, sweet, and well-flavored.

This variety was originated by Mr. William Skirving, of Liverpool, Eng. In this country it has been widely disseminated, and is now more generally cultivated for table use and for stock than any other of the Swede varieties. The plants seldom fail to form good-sized bulbs. It is a good keeper; is of more than average quality for the table; and long experience has proved it one of the best sorts for cultivation on land that is naturally shallow and in poor condition. On soils in a high state of cultivation, upwards of nine hundred bushels have been obtained from an acre.

In sowing, allow twenty inches between the rows, and thin to ten or twelve inches in the rows.

Sutton's Champion. An English prize sort, said to have received twelve silver cups in six years.

Skin bright purple above, yellow below ground; form smooth and regular; size large; flesh yellow, firm, and of good quality.

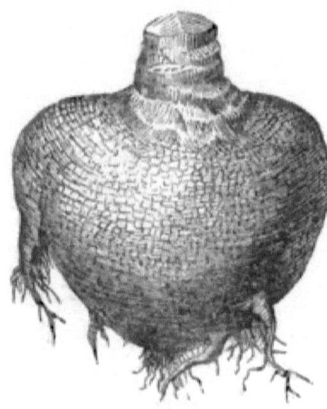

Sweet German Turnip.

It yields abundantly, keeps well, and deserves cultivation, either for farm stock or for the table.

Sweet German. Bulb four or five inches in diameter, six or seven inches in depth, turbinate, sometimes nearly fusiform. In good soil and favorable seasons, it is smooth and regular; but, under opposite conditions, often branched and uneven. Neck two or three inches in length; skin greenish-brown above ground, white beneath; flesh pure white, of firm texture, very sweet, mild, and well-flavored.

It retains its solidity and freshness till spring, and often at midsummer has no appearance of sponginess or decay. As a table variety, it must be classed as one of the best, and is recommended for general cultivation.

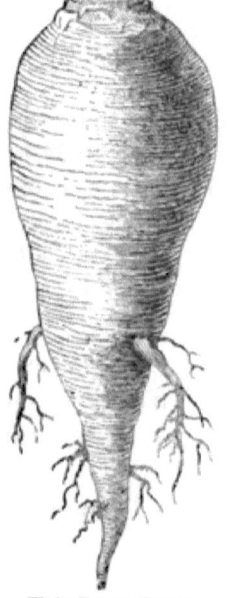

White French Turnip.

White French. LONG WHITE FRENCH. The roots of this variety are produced entirely within the earth. They are invariably fusiform; and, if well grown, measure four or five inches in diameter, and from eight to ten inches in length. Foliage not abundant, spreading; skin white; flesh white, solid, mild, sweet, and delicate. It is not so productive as some other varieties, and is therefore not so well adapted to field culture; but for table use it is surpassed by few, if any, of its class.

A rough-leaved, fusiform-rooted variety of the common garden turnip: is known by the name of "White French" in many localities; but, according to the most reliable authority, the term has not only long been used in connection with, but properly belongs to, the white turnip above described.

SALSIFY, OR OYSTER-PLANT.

Leek-leaved Salsify.—Vegetable Oyster.—Tragopogon porrifolius.

The Salsify is a hardy, biennial plant, and is principally cultivated for its roots, the flavor of which resembles that of the oyster; whence the popular name.

The leaves are long and grass-like, or leek-like; the roots are long and tapering, white within and without, and, when grown in good soil, measure twelve or fourteen inches in length, and rather more than an inch in diameter at the crown.

Soil and Cultivation. — The Oyster-plant succeeds best in a light, well-enriched, mellow soil, which, previous to sowing the seeds, should be stirred to the depth of twelve or fifteen inches. The seeds should be sown annually, in the same manner and at the same time as the seeds of the Carrot and Parsnip. Make the drills fourteen inches apart; cover the seeds an inch and a half in depth; and thin, while the plants are young, to four or five inches asunder. Cultivate in the usual manner during the summer; and by the last of September, or beginning of October, the roots will have attained their full growth, and be ready for use. The plants will sustain no injury during the winter, though left entirely unprotected in the open ground; and the table may be supplied directly from the garden, whenever the frost will admit of their removal. A portion of the crop should, however, be taken up in autumn, and stored in the cellar, like other roots, or, which is perhaps preferable, packed in earth or sand. Roots remaining in the ground may be drawn for use till April, or until the plants have begun to send up their stalks for flowering.

Seeds. — The seeds are brownish, long, and slender, and will keep four years.

An ounce contains three thousand two hundred seeds, and will sow a row eighty feet in length.

Use. — The roots are prepared in various forms; but, when simply boiled in the manner of beets and carrots, the flavor is sweet and delicate. The young flower-stalks, if cut in the spring of the second year, and dressed like asparagus, resemble it in taste, and make an excellent dish.

The roots are sometimes thinly sliced, and, with the addition of vinegar, salt, and pepper, served as a salad. They are also recommended as being remedial or alleviating in cases of consumptive tendency.

THE SWEET POTATO.

Spanish Potato.—Carolina Potato.—Convolvulus batatas.—Ipomœa batatas.

In tropical climates, where the growth of the Sweet Potato is natural, the plant is perennial.

Soil, Planting, and Cultivation. — In warm climates, the Sweet Potato is cultivated in much the same manner as the common Potato is treated at the North. It succeeds best in light, warm, mellow soil, which should be deeply stirred and well enriched. The slips, or sprouts, may be set on ridges, four feet apart, and fifteen inches from plant to plant; or in hills four or five feet apart in each direction, three plants being allowed to a hill. During the summer, give the vines ordinary culture; and late in September, or early in October, the tubers will have attained their growth, and be ready for harvesting.

The slips, or sprouts, are generally obtained by setting the tubers in a hot-bed in March or April, and breaking off, or separating, the sprouts from the tubers as they reach four or five inches in height, or attain a suitable size for transplanting. In favorable seasons, the plucking may be repeated three or four times. In setting out the slips, the lower part should be sunk from one-third to one-half the entire length; and, if very dry weather occurs, water should be moderately applied.

Keeping.—The essentials for the preservation of Sweet Potatoes are dryness, and a warm and even temperature. Where these conditions are not supplied, the tubers speedily decay. By packing in dry sand, and storing in a warm, dry room, they are sometimes preserved in the Northern States until the time of starting the plants in spring.

Varieties.—Though numerous other varieties, less marked and distinctive, are described by different authors, and catalogued by gardeners and seedsmen, the principal are as follow:—

Tubers red, or purplish-red, of medium size; flesh yellow, dry, sweet, and of good quality. A very prolific, hardy variety; recommended as the best red Sweet Potato for Northern culture.   Kentucky Early Red. *Murray.* Red Nansemond.

Tubers from six to ten inches in length; weight from six ounces to a pound, and upwards; skin dusky white; flesh nearly white, but with a shade of yellow. Not so fine-grained or so sweet as the Yellow or Purple, but quite farinaceous and well-flavored. It requires a long season in order to its full development;   Large White.

but, being remarkably hardy, it will succeed well in any of the Middle States, and attain a fair size in the warmer sections of New England.

Nansemond.
YELLOW NANSEMOND.
Tubers large, yellow, swollen at the middle, and tapering to the ends; flesh yellow, dry, unctuous, sweet, and well-flavored.

It is early fit for the table; matures in short seasons; is very productive; succeeds well in almost any tillable soil; and, having been long acclimated, is one of the best sorts for cultivation at the North, — very good crops having been obtained in Maine and the Canadas.

Red-skinned, or American Red.
Tubers long and slender, — the length often exceeding twelve inches, and the diameter rarely above two inches; weight from three to ten ounces; skin purplish-red, smooth, and shining; flesh yellow; very fine-grained, unctuous, sugary, and farinaceous.

This variety is early, quite hardy, productive, and excellent, but does not keep so well as the yellow or white sorts. It is well adapted for cultivation in the cooler sections of the United States, where, in favorable seasons, the crop has proved as certain, and the yield nearly as abundant, as that of the common Potato.

Yellow-skinned.
YELLOW CAROLINA.
Tubers from six to ten inches in length; weight from four to twelve ounces, and upwards; skin smooth, yellow; flesh yellow, fine-grained, unctuous, and remarkably sugary, — surpassing, in this last respect, nearly all other varieties.

When grown in the Southern States, it yields well; perfectly matures its crop; and, in color and flavor, the tubers will accord with the description above given. When grown in the Middle States, or in the warmer parts of New England, it decreases in size; the tubers become longer and more slender; the color, externally and internally, becomes much paler, or nearly white; and the flesh, to a great extent, loses the fine, dry, and sugary qualities which it possesses when grown in warm climates.

THE TURNIP.
English Turnip. — Brassica rapa.

The common Turnip is a hardy biennial, and the roots or bulbs of all the varieties attain their full size during the first year. The flowers are produced in May and June of the second year, and the seeds ripen in July. The latter are small, round, black, or reddish-brown, and are similar, in size, form, and color, in the different varieties: ten thousand are contained in an ounce, and they retain their vitality from five to seven years.

Propagation and Culture. — All the sorts are propagated by seeds, which should be sown where the plants are to remain. Sowings for early use may be made the last of April, or beginning of May; but as the bulbs are seldom produced in perfection in the early part of the season, or under the influence of extreme heat, the sowing should be confined to a limited space in the garden. The seeds may be sown broadcast or in drills: if sown in drills, they should be made fourteen inches apart, and half an inch in depth. The young plants should be thinned to five or six inches asunder. For a succession, a few seeds may be sown, at intervals of a fortnight, until the last week in July; from which time, until the 10th of August, the principal sowing is usually made for the winter's supply. In the Middle States and the warmer portion of New England, if the season is favorable, a good crop will be obtained from seed sown as late as the last week in August.

Harvesting. — Turnips for the table may be drawn directly from the garden or field until November, but must be harvested before severe freezing weather; for, though very hardy, few of the varieties will survive the winters of the Northern States in the open ground.

Seed. — An ounce of seed will sow eight rods of land, and a pound will be sufficient for an acre.

Varieties. — The varieties, which are numerous, are as follow : —

Altrincham.
Law.
ALTRINCHAM.

This is a yellow-fleshed, field variety, of less than average size. The bulb, however, is of a fine, globular shape, with a light green top, small neck and tap-root, and possessed of considerable solidity.

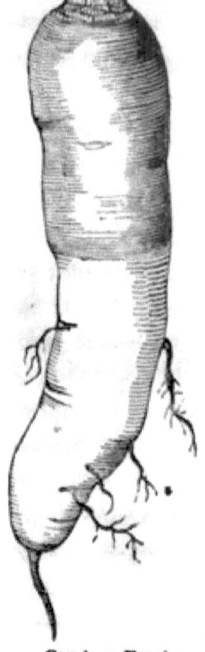

Cow-horn Turnip.

Chivas's Orange Jelly.
Thomp.

Bulb of a handsome, round form, with a small top; the skin is pale orange; and the flesh yellow, juicy, sweet, and tender. It has very little fibre; so that, when boiled, it almost acquires the consistence of a jelly.

Cow-horn. Root produced much above ground, nearly cylindrical, rounded at the end, ten or twelve inches in length, nearly three inches in diameter, and weighing from one and a half to two pounds. The skin is smooth and shining, — white below the surface of the ground, and green at the top; the flesh is white, tender, and sugary. Early, productive, and remarkable for its regular form and good quality. As a field-turnip, it is one of the best, and, when pulled young, good for table use. During winter, the roots often become dry and spongy.

An old and well-known early garden variety. Bulb round, much flattened, and produced mostly within the earth; the skin is white, somewhat washed with green at the insertion of the leaves. **Early Flat Dutch.** EARLY WHITE DUTCH. WHITE DUTCH.

Before the bulb has attained its full dimensions, the flesh is fine-grained, tender, and sweet; but when ripe, especially in dry seasons, it often becomes spongy and juiceless: in which condition it is of no value for the table, and, even for stock, is nearly worthless. Average specimens measure four inches in diameter, and two inches and a half in depth.

This variety, which somewhat resembles the Yellow Malta, has a small, globular root, of a pale-yellow color throughout. It **Early Yellow Dutch.** YELLOW DUTCH.

is early, tender, close-grained, and sugary, but better suited for use in summer and autumn than for winter. By some, the variety is esteemed the best of the yellow garden-turnips.

This is a beautiful medium-sized turnip, of a bright yellow throughout, even to the neck; somewhat similar to a firm Yellow Malta, but of finer color. The under part of the bulb is singularly depressed: from this depression issues a small, mouse-tail-like root. It is earlier, and also hardier, than the Yellow Malta. **Finland. — Law.**

The flesh is tender, close-grained, and of a sweet, sugary flavor. The bulbs measure two inches in thickness by four inches in diameter, and weigh eight or ten ounces. An excellent garden variety. Finland Turnip.

Bulb produced mostly within the earth, nearly globular, smooth, and symmetrical; skin bright yellow below ground, greenish **Golden Ball.** M'Int. Vil. YELLOW GLOBE.

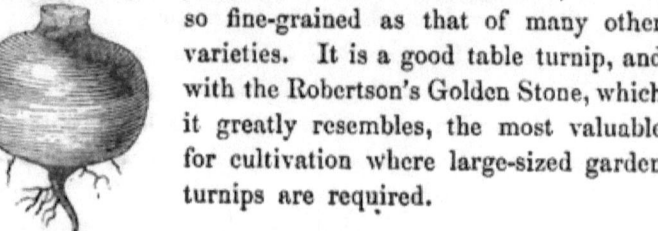
Golden-ball Turnip.

above; flesh pale yellow, sweet, and well-flavored, but not so fine-grained as that of many other varieties. It is a good table turnip, and with the Robertson's Golden Stone, which it greatly resembles, the most valuable for cultivation where large-sized garden turnips are required.

Green Globe. *Law.* Roots of a fine globular shape, with a small neck and tap-root; white below, and green above, the surface of the ground; of medium size, hardy, and firm in texture, but scarcely so much so as the Green Round. It is somewhat larger than the White Norfolk; grows strongly, and produces extraordinary crops: but it soon becomes spongy, and often decays in autumn, or early in winter.

Green Norfolk. *Law.* A sub-variety of the White Norfolk, of nearly the same form and size; the bulb differing principally in the color of the top, which is green.

The Norfolk turnips are all of a peculiar flattish form; rather hollowed towards their neck, as also on their under side. When grown to a large size, they become more or less irregular, or somewhat angular.

Green-top Flat. Similar, in size, form, and quality, to the common Purple-top Flat; skin, above ground, green.

Long grown in New England for feeding stock; and, in its young state, often used as a table turnip. Now very little cultivated.

Green-top Yellow Aberdeen. *Law.* An old and esteemed variety, similar in size and form to the Purple-top Yellow Aberdeen. The top of the bulb is bright green.

This variety has some resemblance to the Cow-horn, but is smaller, and the flesh is not so white.   <small>Long White Maltese.
Long White Clairfontaine.
Vil.</small>

Bulb of medium size, flattened, smooth, and regular; tap-root slender, issuing from a basin; skin blackish-purple above and below ground, sometimes changing to yellow about the tap-root of large or overgrown bulbs; flesh yellow, fine-grained, and tender if grown in cool weather, but liable to be fibrous and strong-flavored when grown during the summer months.   <small>Petrosowoodsks.</small>

The variety is early, and must be classed as a garden rather than as a field turnip.

Bulb round, flattened, nearly one-half growing above ground; neck and tap-root small; skin reddish-purple where exposed to light and air, white below the surface of the soil; flesh white, close-grained while young, and of a sugary but often bitter taste. During winter, it usually becomes dry and spongy. Average specimens measure two and a half inches in depth, four or five inches in diameter, and weigh from sixteen to twenty ounces.   <small>Purple-top Flat.
Red-Top Flat.</small>

This old and well-known variety at one period was the principal field as well as garden turnip of the Northern and Middle States. It is now, however, very little cultivated, being superseded by the Strap-leaved and other more desirable sorts.

Bulb flat, smooth, and regular in form, produced almost entirely above ground; tap-root slender; leaves few, upright, broad, rounded at the ends, and tapering to the neck, which is very small; skin above, clear, bright purple, — below, pure white, often finely clouded or shaded at the union of the colors; flesh   <small>Purple-top Strap-leaved.</small>

clear white, firm, solid, sugary, mild, and remarkably well-flavored; size medium,—measuring two inches and a half in depth by four or five inches in diameter, and weighing from ten to twelve ounces. Field-grown roots, with the benefit of a long season and rich soil, attain much greater dimensions; often, however, greatly deteriorating in quality as they increase over the average size.

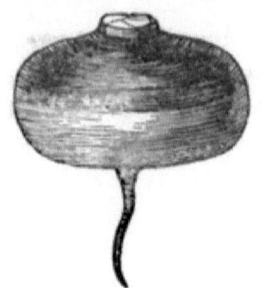

Purple-top Strap-leaved Turnip.

This variety is unquestionably one of the best of the flat turnips, either for the garden or field. It is early, hardy, thrives in almost any description of soil, is of excellent quality, and rarely fails to yield a good crop. It is the best of all the flat turnips for sowing among corn or potatoes, or upon small patches of the garden from which early pease or beans have been harvested.

Purple-top Yellow Aberdeen. Bulb globular, reddish-purple above, and deep yellow below; tap-root small; leaves short, and inclined to grow horizontally.

In rich soil and long seasons, the bulbs sometimes attain a weight of eight or ten pounds; but specimens of average size measure four inches in depth, nearly five inches in diameter, and weigh from sixteen to twenty ounces. The flesh is pale yellow, tender, sugary, and nearly equal to that of the Swedes in solidity.

The variety is hardy, and, although generally grown for farm-purposes, is really superior to many sorts cultivated exclusively for table use.

Red Globe. *Law.* An old, medium-sized, globular turnip, well suited for cultivation in light soil and on exposed or elevated situations. It is not suited for table use; and is generally field-grown, and fed to stock.

This is a sub-variety of the White Norfolk, **Red Norfolk.**
the size and form being nearly the same.
The bulb is red above, and white below.

Bulb produced partially above ground, **Red Tankard.**
pyriform, eight or nine inches in depth, four or five inches
in diameter, and weighing three pounds; below ground, the
skin is white,—above, purple or violet; flesh white.

It is recommended for its earliness and productiveness,
but must be considered a field rather than a table variety.

An excellent, half-early variety; form **Robertson's**
nearly globular; color deep orange through- **Golden Stone.**
out, sometimes tinged with green on the *McInt. Vil.*
top. Average specimens measure nearly four inches in
depth, four inches in diameter, and weigh from sixteen to
eighteen ounces; flesh firm and well-flavored.

The Robertson's Golden Stone is remarkably hardy, keeps
well, and is one of the best of the Yellows for autumn or
winter use.

Bulb produced much above ground, and of **Six Weeks.**
an irregular, globular form. It soon arrives *Law.*
at maturity; but, on account of its natural **Early Dwarf.**
softness of texture, should always be sown late, and used
before severe frosts. It is well suited for sowing after the
removal of early crops, or for making up blanks in turnip-
fields where the first sowing may have partially failed.

Though well-flavored when first harvested, it soon becomes dry and spongy, and is unsuitable for use during
winter. Skin white below the surface of the ground, greenish above. Field-grown specimens sometimes weigh three
pounds and upwards.

The bulbs of this variety are nearly spheri- **Snowball.**
cal, smooth, and regular: average specimens

measure four inches in diameter, four and a half in depth, and weigh from sixteen to twenty ounces. The neck is small, and the skin white. The flesh of the young bulbs is white, fine-grained, tender, and sugary; but if overgrown, or long kept, it is liable to become dry and spongy.

The variety is early, and, though classed by seedsmen as a garden turnip, is well adapted for field-culture, as it not only yields abundantly, but succeeds well when sown late in the season.

Stone Globe. Bulb globular, and regularly formed, growing mostly beneath the surface of the ground. It belongs to the White-Globe varieties, and is considered the hardiest and the best suited for winter use of any of its class.

Skin and flesh white; texture moderately close; flavor sweet, and its keeping properties good.

Waite's Hybrid Eclipse. A recent variety, of English origin, introduced by Mr. John G. Waite, a seed-merchant of London. As figured and described, it is of large size, richly colored, and remarkably smooth and regular.

It is recommended as a turnip of good quality, and as being very productive, but, when cultivated in this country, has generally fallen short of the excellence it is represented as attaining in England. It is apparently not adapted to the dry and warm summers of the United States.

White Globe. *Law.* Root globular; skin smooth, perfectly white; flesh also white; neck and tap-root small; diameter from four to six inches.

This variety is better adapted to field-culture than to the garden, as it is altogether too coarse in texture for table use. It is a poor keeper, and, in unfavorable seasons, sometimes decays before the time of harvesting. Specimens have been grown weighing fifteen and even eighteen pounds.

THE TURNIP.

White Norfolk.

The White Norfolk is but a sub-variety of the Common Flat Turnip, and oftentimes attains a most extraordinary size. For the garden, it possesses no value. It is grown exclusively as an agricultural or field turnip, but is very liable to rot, soon becomes spongy, and can only be classed as third-rate even for feeding stock.

White Stone. Early Stone.

This common and well-known garden turnip somewhat resembles the White Dutch, but has stronger foliage, is rounder in form, and finer in texture. A sub-variety is known by the name of Mouse-tail Turnip; and, in addition, some catalogues contain varieties under the name of Red-topped Mouse-tail, &c.

Skin and flesh white; size full medium, measuring three and a half to four inches in depth by four and a half or five inches in diameter.

White-top Flat.

Bulb similar in size and form to the Green-top Flat; skin uniformly white; flesh white, firm, sugary, and well-flavored. As a table variety, it is superior to the Purple-top Flat or the Green-top.

White-top Strap-leaved.

This is a sub-variety of the Purple-top Strap-leaved; differing little, except in color. The flesh is white, fine-grained, saccharine, mild, and excellent.

Early, productive, and recommended as one of the best varieties for field or garden culture.

The Strap-leaved turnips appear to be peculiarly adapted to the climate of the Northern States, and are greatly superior in all respects to the Common White and Purple-top Flat varieties. Though recently introduced, they have been widely disseminated; and, wherever grown, are highly esteemed.

Yellow Malta. *McInt.* A beautiful, small bulbed, early variety, slightly flattened above, somewhat concave about the tap-root, which, as well as the neck, is remarkably small; skin smooth, bright orange-yellow; foliage small, and not abundant, — on which account, the plants may be grown quite close to each other; flesh pale yellow, fine-grained, and well-flavored.

It is a good garden variety, and one of the best of the Yellows for summer use. Average bulbs measure two inches in depth, four inches in diameter, and weigh ten ounces.

Yellow Stone. Similar to the Golden Ball or Yellow Globe. Compared with these varieties, the bulb of the Yellow Stone is produced more above ground, and the upper surface is more colored with green. One of the best of garden turnips.

For other esculent roots, including the Earth Almond, Tuberous-rooted Chervil, Chinese Potato, German Rampion, Jerusalem Artichoke, Tuberous-rooted Oxalis, Rampion, Scolymus, Scorzonera, Skirret, Tuberous-rooted Vetch and Tropœolum, see "FIELD AND GARDEN VEGETABLES OF AMERICA."

CHAPTER II.

ALLIACEOUS PLANTS.

The Garlic. — Leek. — Onion.

COMMON GARLIC.

Allium sativum.

THIS is a perennial plant, from the south of Europe. The root is composed of from ten to fifteen small bulbs, called "cloves," which are enclosed in a thin, white, semi-transparent skin, or pellicle. The leaves are long and narrow. The flower-stem is cylindrical, eighteen inches in height, and terminates in an umbel, or group of pale-pink flowers, intermixed with small bulbs. The seeds are black, and, in form, irregular, but are seldom employed for propagation; the cloves, or small bulbs, succeeding better.

Garlic.

Planting and Cultivation. — Garlic thrives best in a light, well-enriched soil; and the bulbs should be planted in April or May, an inch deep, in rows or on ridges, fourteen inches apart, and five or six inches apart in the rows. Keep the soil loose, and the plants clear of weeds; and, when the tops wither, the bulbs will have attained their growth, and be ready for harvesting.

Use. — It is cultivated for its bulbs, or cloves, which possess more of the flavor of the Onion than any other alliaceous plant. These are sometimes employed in soups, stews, and other dishes; and, in some parts of Europe, are eaten in a crude state with bread.

The bulbs of the Common Garlic, as seen in the markets of this country, generally average about an inch in diameter; but McIntosh states, that, where they are skilfully treated, they sometimes attain a circumference of seven and a half inches. Twenty well-grown bulbs weigh one pound.

Early Rose Garlic. This is a sub-variety of the Common Garlic. The pellicle, in which the small bulbs are enclosed, is rose-colored; and this is its principal distinguishing characteristic. It is, however, nearly a fortnight earlier.

Great-headed Garlic.
Vil.
ALLIUM AMPELO-
PRASUM.
This species is a hardy perennial, and is remarkable for the size of its bulbs; which, as in the foregoing species and variety, separate into smaller bulbs, or cloves. It is used and cultivated as the Common Garlic.

THE LEEK.

Allium porum.

The Leek is a hardy biennial, and produces an oblong, tunicated bulb; from the base of which, rootlets are put forth in great numbers. The plant, when full grown, much resembles what are commonly known as "Scallions;" the lower, blanched portion, being the part eaten. This varies in length from four to eight inches, and in diameter from less than an inch to more than three inches. The seeds are black, somewhat triangular in form, and, with the exception of their smaller size, are similar to those of the Onion. Twelve thousand seeds are contained in an ounce, and they retain their vitality two years.

THE LEEK.

Soil, Sowing, and Cultivation. — The Leek is very hardy, and easily cultivated. It succeeds best in a light but well-enriched soil. The seed should be sown in April, at the bottom of drills made six or eight inches deep, and eighteen inches asunder. Sow the seeds thinly, cover half an inch deep, and thin the young plants to nine inches distant in the drills. As the plants increase in size, draw the earth gradually into the drills, and around the stems of the leeks, until the drills are filled. By this process the bulbs are blanched, and rendered tender and mild-flavored. In October the leeks will be suitable for use, and, until the closing-up of the ground, may be drawn from time to time as required for the table. For winter use, they should be preserved in earth or sand.

Early leeks may be obtained by sowing the seeds in a hot-bed in February or March, and transplanting to the open ground in June or July.

Use. — The whole plant has the flavor and general properties of the Onion: but the lower or blanched portion is the part generally eaten; and this is used in soups, or boiled and served as asparagus.

Varieties : —

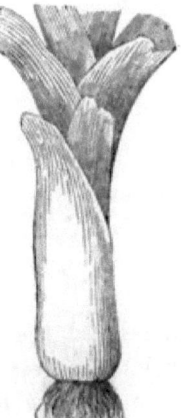

Large Rouen Leek.

Common Flag.
Vil.
LONG FLAG.

The stem, or blanched portion, of this variety is about six inches in depth, and an inch in diameter.

It is remarkably hardy, and well suited for open culture.

Large Rouen.
Thomp.

Stem short, but very thick, sometimes measuring nearly four inches in diameter.

It is now the variety most cultivated near Paris, and, since its general dissemination, has been much approved by all who have grown it. It is found to be the best kind for forcing, as it acquires a sufficient thickness of stem sooner than any other. In England, it is pronounced one of the best, if not the best, of all varieties.

London Flag.
LARGE FLAG.
BROAD FLAG.
Stem four inches in length, and nearly an inch and a half in diameter.

The London Flag Leek is hardy and of good quality, and is more generally cultivated in this country than any other variety.

Musselburg.
Thomp.
SCOTCH FLAG.
Stem somewhat shorter than that of the London Flag, but of equal thickness. The swelling at the base has the same form. Hardy, and of excellent quality.

Yellow Poitou.
Thomp.
A remarkably large variety; the leaves having sometimes measured five feet in length, and six inches in breadth. The underground or blanched portion of the stem is yellowish-white, and is more tender than that of any other variety. On this account, and also for its large size, it deserves cultivation.

THE ONION.

Allium cepa.

The Onion is a half-hardy biennial plant: the roots and leaves, however, are annual, as they usually perish during the first year. The bulbs, for which the plant is generally cultivated, are biennial, and differ, to a considerable extent, in their size, form, and color. The flower-stalk, which is developed the second year, is from three to four feet in height, leafless, hollow, swollen just below the middle, and tapers to the top. The flowers are either white or rose-colored, and are produced at the extremity of the stalk, in a regular, globular group, or umbel. The seeds ripen in August. They are deep blue-black, somewhat triangular, and similar in size and form in all the varieties. An ounce contains about seventy-five hundred seeds, which retain their vitality two years.

Soil and Cultivation. — The Onion requires a light, loamy, mellow soil; and, unlike most kinds of garden or field vegetables, succeeds well when cultivated on the same land for successive years. With the exception of the Top and the Potato Onion, all the varieties are raised from seed. Previous to sowing, the ground should be thoroughly spaded over or deeply ploughed, and the surface made smooth and even. The seed should be sown as early in spring as the soil may be in good working condition. Sow in drills fourteen inches apart, and half an inch in depth. When the plants are three or four inches high, thin them to two inches asunder; and, in the process of culture, be careful not to stir the soil too deeply, or to collect it about the growing bulbs. The onions will ripen in August, or early in September; and their full maturity will be indicated by the perfect decay of the leaves, or tops. The bulbs may be drawn from the drills by the hand, or by the use of a common garden-rake. After being exposed for a few days to the sun for drying, they will be ready for storing or the market.

Preservation. — The essentials for the preservation of the bulbs are a low temperature, freedom from frost, dryness, and thorough ventilation.

Seed. — For the production of seed, select the ripest, firmest, and best-formed bulbs; and, in April, transplant them to lines two feet and a half or three feet distant, and from nine to twelve inches apart in the lines, sinking the crowns just below the surface of the ground.

An ounce of seed will sow two hundred feet of drill, and three pounds are usually allowed to an acre.

Varieties. — Few of the numerous varieties are cultivated

to any extent in this country. Many of the kinds succeed only in warm latitudes, and others are quite unimportant. The Danvers, Large Red, Silver-skin, and the Yellow, seem peculiarly adapted to our soil and climate. The annual product of these varieties greatly exceeds that of all the other sorts combined.

Danvers Red. A recently introduced variety, with the color and general quality of the Large Red Wethersfield, and the form of the Danvers Yellow. It is recommended as being hardy, keeping well, and as rivalling the first named in productiveness.

Danvers Yellow.
DANVERS.

Danvers Onion.

This somewhat recent variety was obtained by selection from the Common Yellow. It is above medium size, and inclined to globular in its form. Average bulbs measure three inches in diameter, and two inches and three-fourths in depth. The skin is yellowish-brown, but becomes darker by age, and greenish-brown if long exposed to the sun; the flesh is similar to that of the Yellow, — white, sugary, comparatively mild, and well-flavored.

The superiority of the Danvers Onion over the last named consists principally, if not solely, in its greater productiveness. When grown under like conditions, it yields, on the average, nearly one-fourth more; and on this account the variety is generally employed for field-culture. It is, however, not so good a keeper; and for shipping-purposes is decidedly inferior to the Yellow, its globular form rendering it more liable to decay from the heat and dampness incident to sea-voyages.

Deptford.
Thomp.
BROWN DEPT-FORD.

Similar to, if not identical with, the English Strasburg. "It sometimes exactly agrees with the description of that variety: but it occasionally has a pale-brown skin, without any tinge of red; and, when this is the case, its flavor is milder than that of the last named."

With the exception of its more globular form, the bulb much resembles the Yellow Onion of this country.

A sub-variety of the Large Red Wethersfield, and the earliest of the red onions. **Early Red Wethersfield.** Form and color nearly the same as the Large Red; bulb small, measuring two inches and a half in diameter, and an inch and a half in depth. It is close-grained, mild, a good keeper; forms its bulbs, with few exceptions, and ripens, the last of July, being three or four weeks earlier than the Large Red. Cultivated to a limited extent in various places on the coast of New England, for early consumption at home, and for shipment to the South and West.

This variety and the Intermediate are liable to degenerate: they tend to grow larger and later, approaching the original variety; and can be preserved in a pure state only by a careful selection of the bulbs set for seed.

This is a small, early variety of the Silver-skin, measuring two inches and three-fourths **Early Silver-skin.** in diameter, and an inch and three-fourths in depth. The neck is small, and the skin silvery-white. It is much esteemed for its earliness and mild flavor, and is one of the best of all varieties for pickling. When cultivated for the latter purpose, it should be sown and treated as directed for the Silver-skin.

An early variety of the common Large Red. Bulb of medium size, flattened; neck **Intermediate Red Wethersfield.** small; color deep purple.

It is rather pungent, yet milder than the Large Red; keeps well, and is grown to a considerable extent, in certain localities in New England, for shipping.

Large Red.
WETHERSFIELD LARGE RED.

Bulb sometimes roundish, but, when pure, more or less flattened. It is of very large size, and, when grown in favorable soil, often measures five inches or more in diameter, and three inches in depth. Skin deep purplish-red; neck of medium size; flesh purplish-white, moderately fine-grained, and stronger flavored than that of the Yellow and earlier Red varieties. It is quite productive; one of the best to keep; and is grown to a large extent, in many places on the sea-coast of New England, for shipping to the South and West. It is almost everywhere seen in vegetable markets, and, with perhaps the exception of the Yellow or Danvers, is the most prominent of the sorts employed for commercial purposes. It derives its name from Wethersfield, Conn., where it is extensively cultivated, and where it has the reputation of having originated.

Wethersfield Large Red Onion.

New Deep Blood Red.

Bulb small, flattened, — two inches and a quarter in diameter, and an inch and a half in depth; neck small; skin deep violet-red, approaching black. A half early variety, remarkable for its intense purplish-red color.

Blood-red Onion.

Potato Onion.
UNDERGROUND ONION.

Bulb flattened, from two and a half to three inches in diameter, and two inches in depth; skin copper-yellow; flavor sugary, mild, and excellent. It does not keep so well as many other varieties, but remains sound longer if the leaves are cut two or three inches above the top of the bulb at the time of harvesting.

The Potato Onion produces no seeds, neither small bulbs

upon its stalks, in the manner of many of the species of the Onion family; but, if a full-grown bulb be set in spring, a number of bulbs of various sizes will be formed beneath the surface of the ground, about the parent bulb.

Like other varieties of onions, it requires a rich, deep soil. In April, select the large bulbs, and set them ten inches apart, in rows fifteen inches asunder, with the crown of the bulbs just below the surface of the ground. As soon as the tops are entirely dead, they will be ready for harvesting. It is very prolific, yielding from four to six fold.

Silver-skin.
WHITE PORTUGAL OF NEW ENGLAND.

Bulb of medium size, flattened, — average specimens measuring three inches in diameter, and an inch and a half or two inches in thickness; neck small; skin silvery-white. After the removal of the outer envelope, the upper part of the bulb is often veined and clouded with green, while the portion produced below ground is generally clear white. Flesh white, fine-grained, sugary, and remarkably mild-flavored.

It forms its bulb early and regularly, ripens off well, and is quite productive; an average yield being about four hundred bushels per acre. It is a poor keeper, and this is its most serious objection. The best method for its preservation is to spread the roots in a dry, light, and airy situation.

Silver-skin Onion.

The Silver-skin Onion is much esteemed in the middle and southern sections of the United States, and is cultivated to a considerable extent in New England. It is well adapted for sowing in August or the beginning of September, for early use, and for marketing during the ensuing spring. Where the winters are mild, the crop, with slight protection, will sustain no injury in the open ground. In Europe, it is much esteemed, and extensively grown for pickling, as its "white color, in contrast with the fine green veins, or lines, gives it a very agreeable appearance. For pickling, the seed should be sown thickly, then slightly covered with fine soil, and afterwards rolled. If the seed is covered more deeply, the bulb, from not being quite on the surface, has a larger and thicker neck; so that it loses its finely rounded form, and is, moreover, less compact."

This variety, erroneously known in New England as the White Portugal, is unquestionably the true Silver-skin, as described both by English and French authors. The application of the term "Silver-skin" to the Common Yellow Onion, as extensively practised by seedsmen and marketmen in the Eastern States, is neither pertinent nor authorized.

Strasburg.
McInt.
YELLOW STRASBURG.

This is the variety most generally cultivated in Great Britain. Its form varies from flat to globular or oval; bulb large, three inches wide, and full two inches in depth; outside coating brown, of firm texture. Divested of this, the color is reddish-brown, tinged with green. Flavor mild and pleasant. It is a very hardy sort, succeeds in cold localities, and keeps well.

Strasburg Onion.

The Strasburg and Deptford Onions much resemble the common Yellow Onion of New England; and the difference between the sorts is not great, when English-grown bulbs of the first-named varieties are compared with the bulbs of the Yellow Onion, American-grown: but seeds of the Strasburg or Deptford, raised in England, and sown in this country, rarely produce plants that form bulbs so generally or so perfectly as American-grown seeds of the Yellow Onion.

The Dutch, Essex, and Flanders, found on seedsmen's catalogues, are not distinguishable from the Common Strasburg.

THE ONION.

Bulb large, a little flattened; producing, instead of seeds, a number of small bulbs, or onions, about the size of a filbert, which serve as a substitute for seeds in propagation. The flesh is coarse; and the bulbs are liable to decay during winter, unless kept in a cool and dry situation. The variety has been considered rather curious than useful.

Top or Tree Onion.
EGYPTIAN.

Propagation and Culture. — It is propagated from the bulbs, which are set in April or May, in rows fifteen inches apart, and ten inches asunder in the rows. The small bulbs produced upon the stalk are sometimes used for propagation, and are set at the same season with the underground bulbs in rows one foot apart, and four inches apart in the rows. These small bulbs are obtained by setting mature or fully developed bulbs in April or May, and treating as directed for raising the seeds of the Common Onion.

Form nearly ovoid, very regular and symmetrical; skin greenish-yellow, marked with rose-colored lines, — the pellicle changing to white on drying. The bulb measures four inches in depth, and two inches and three-fourths in its largest diameter. It keeps well, and is an excellent variety.

White Globe.
Thomp.

White Globe Onion.

A recent sort, known as the New White Globe, is similar to the foregoing, though somewhat flatter in form.

Nearly allied to the preceding variety; the size and form being the same. Skin reddish-yellow. In color, quality, and in its keeping properties, it resembles the Yellow Onion, though much less productive.

Yellow Globe.

Yellow Onion.
Silver-Skin of New England.

One of the oldest varieties, and, as a market-onion, probably better known and more generally cultivated in this country than any other sort. The true Yellow Onion has a flattened form and a small neck. Its size is rather above medium, measuring, when well grown, from three inches to three inches and a half in diameter, and from two inches to two inches and a half in depth. Skin yellowish-brown or copper-yellow,—becoming somewhat deeper by age, or if exposed long to the sun; flesh white, fine-grained, mild, sugary, and well flavored. It keeps well, and is very prolific: few of the plants, in good soils and seasons, fail to produce good-sized and well-ripened bulbs. For the vegetable-garden, as well as for field-culture, it may be considered a standard sort.

Yellow Onion.

The Danvers Onion, which is but a sub-variety of the Common Yellow, may prove somewhat more profitable for extensive cultivation, on account of its globular form; but neither in its flavor nor in its keeping properties can it be said to possess any superiority over the last named.

The term "Silver-skin," by which this onion is very generally though erroneously known throughout New England, has created great confusion between seedsmen and dealers. Much perplexity might be avoided if its application to the Yellow Onion were entirely abandoned. The genuine Silver-skin, as its name implies, has a skin of pure, silvery whiteness, and is in other respects very dissimilar to the present variety.

The yield per acre varies from four to six hundred bushels.

For the "*Cive*," for varieties of the "*Shallot*" and "*Welsh Onion*," and also for numerous additional varieties of the "*Common Onion*," see "FIELD AND GARDEN VEGETABLES OF AMERICA."

CHAPTER III.

ASPARAGINOUS PLANTS.

ASPARAGUS.

Asparagus officinalis.

ASPARAGUS is a hardy, perennial, maritime plant. It rises to the height of five feet and upwards, with an erect, branching stem; short, slender, nearly cylindrical leaves; and greenish, drooping flowers. The seeds, which are produced in globular, scarlet berries, are black, somewhat triangular, and retain their germinative powers four years. Twelve hundred and fifty weigh an ounce.

Propagation. — It is propagated from seed, sown either in autumn, just before the closing-up of the ground, or in spring, as soon as the soil is in good working condition. It should not be sown thickly; and the drills should be twelve or fourteen inches apart, and an inch in depth. An ounce of seed is sufficient for fifty or sixty feet of drill.

When the plants are well up, thin them to three inches asunder, and cultivate in the usual manner during the summer.

Good plants of one year's growth are preferred by experienced growers for setting; but some choose those of two years, and they may be used when three years old.

Soil and Planting. — A deep, rich, mellow soil is best adapted to the growth of Asparagus.

Before planting out the roots, the ground should be thoroughly trenched two feet or more in depth. As the soil can hardly be made too rich, incorporate in the process of trenching a very liberal quantity of well-decomposed manure with a free mixture of common salt.

Lay out the land in beds five feet apart, and running north and south, or east and west, as may be most convenient. Along these beds set three rows of roots, the outer rows being one foot from the borders of the bed, and the roots one foot from each other in the rows.

The roots may be set in April, or early in May. Throw out a trench along the length of the bed, ten inches or a foot in width, and deep enough to allow the crowns to be covered three or four inches beneath the surface. There are various methods of placing the roots in the trench. Some spread them out like a fan against the side; some form little hillocks of fine soil, over which the roots are spread, extending like the sticks of an umbrella; others make a ridge along the centre of the trench, and spread the roots on either side; while others remove the soil from the bed, rake the surface smooth, and spread out the roots at right angles on the level, afterwards replacing the soil, covering to the depth of about three inches.

During the summer, nothing will be necessary but to keep the plants clear of weeds. In the autumn, the beds should be lightly dug over, and two or three inches of rich loam, intermixed with well-digested compost, and salt at the rate of two quarts to the square rod, should be applied; which will leave the crowns of the roots five inches below the surface.

Second Year. — Early in spring, dig over the beds, taking care not to disturb the roots; rake the surface smooth; and, during the summer, cultivate as before directed: but none of the shoots should be cut for use. In the autumn, stir the surface of the bed, and add an inch of soil and manure, which will bring the crowns six or seven inches below ground, — a depth preferred, by a majority of cultivators, for established plantations.

Third Year. — Early in spring, stir the ground as directed for the two previous years. Some cultivators make a slight cutting during this season; but the future strength of the plants will be increased by allowing the crop to grow naturally, as during the first and second years. In autumn, dig over the surface; add a dressing of manure; and, in the ensuing spring, the beds may be cut freely for use.

"Asparagus-beds should be enriched every autumn with a liberal application of good compost, containing some mixture of salt.

"In general, transplanted Asparagus comes up quite slender the first year; is larger the second; and, the third year, a few shoots may be fit for cutting. It is nearly in perfection the fourth year."

Cutting. — "The shoots should be cut angularly, from two to three inches below the surface of the ground; taking care not to wound the younger buds. It is in the best condition for cutting when the shoots are four or five inches above ground, and while the head, or bud, remains close and firm."

In the Middle States, the cutting should be discontinued from the 10th to the 15th of June; and from the 15th to the 25th of the same month in the Eastern States and the Canadas.

Asparagus-beds will continue from twenty to thirty years; and there are instances of beds being regularly cut, and remaining in good condition for more than fifty years.

Use. — The young shoots are boiled twenty minutes or half an hour, until they become soft; and are principally served on toasted bread, with melted butter. It is the practice of some to boil the shoots entire; others cut or break the sprout just above the more tough or fibrous part, and cook only the part which is tender and eatable. This is snapped or cut into small sections, which are boiled, buttered, seasoned, and served on toast in the usual form.

"The smaller sprouts are sometimes cut into pieces three-eighths of an inch long, and cooked and served as green pease." The sprouts are also excellent when made into soup.

It is one of the most productive, economical, and healthful of all garden vegetables.

Varieties. — "The names of numerous varieties occur in the catalogues of seedsmen; but there seems to be little permanency of character in the plants. What are called the Red-topped and Green-topped may perhaps be somewhat distinct, and considered as varieties." — *Glenny.*

Soil and location have, unquestionably, much influence, both as respects the quality and size of the sprouts. A bed of Asparagus in one locality produced shoots seldom reaching a diameter of half an inch, and of a very tough and fibrous character; while a bed in another situation, formed of plants taken from the same nursery-bed, actually produced sprouts so large and fine as to obtain the prize of the Massachusetts Horticultural Society.

If any variety really exists peculiar in size, form, color, or quality, it cannot be propagated by seed. Large sprouts may afford seeds, which, as a general rule, will produce finer Asparagus than seeds from smaller plants; but a variety, when it occurs, can be propagated only by a division of the roots.

Mr. Thompson states, that on one part of Mr. Grayson's extensive plantation, on the south side of the Thames, near London, the so-called Grayson's Giant was produced; and in another section, the common sort: but, when both were made to change places, the common acquired the dimensions of the Giant, whilst the latter diminished to the ordinary size.

Seeds of the following named and described sorts may be obtained of seedsmen, and will undoubtedly, in nearly all cases, afford fine Asparagus; but they will not produce plants which will uniformly possess the character of the parent variety: —

ASPARAGUS.

Battersea is famed for producing fine Aspara- **Battersea.**
gus, and the name is applied to the particular   *Rog.*
variety there grown. The heads are large, full, and close,
and the tops tinted with a reddish-green color. It is probably intermediate between the Green and Purple Topped.

Originated and named under like circum- **Gravesend.**
stances with the Battersea. The top is greener,   *Rog.*
and not generally so plump and close; but it is considered
finer flavored. Both varieties are, however, held in great
estimation.

This variety, as also the Deptford, Mortlake, **Grayson's**
and Reading, all originated and were named un- **Giant.**
der the same conditions as the varieties before described.
All are fine sorts; but the difference between them, and,
indeed, between all of the kinds, if important, is certainly
not permanent, so long as they are offered in the form of
seeds for propagation.

Mr. Grayson, the originator of this variety, produced a
hundred sprouts, the aggregate weight of which was forty-
two pounds, — the largest ever raised in Britain.

Sprout white; the top, as it breaks ground,   **Giant**
purple; size very large, sometimes measuring **Purple-top.**
an inch and three-fourths in diameter, but   Dutch. Red-Top.
greatly affected by soil and cultivation.

A hundred sprouts of this variety have been produced,
which weighed twenty-five pounds.

This variety, when grown under the same con- **Green-top.**
ditions as the Giant Purple-top, is generally smaller or more
slender. The top of the sprout, and the scales on the sides,
are often slightly tinged with purple. The plant, when full
grown, is perceptibly more green than that of the Giant
Purple-top. From most nursery-beds, plants of both varie-

ties will probably be obtained, with every intervening grade of size and color.

Additional asparaginous plants, including the Cardoon, Artichoke, Hop, Oosung, and Phytolacca, will be found in the "FIELD AND GARDEN VEGETABLES OF AMERICA."

CHAPTER IV.

CUCURBITACEOUS PLANTS.

The Cucumber. — The Melon. — Muskmelon. — Persian Melons. — Watermelon. — Prickly-fruited Gherkin. — Pumpkin. — Squash.

THE CUCUMBER.

Cucumis sativus.

Soil and Culture. — Cucumbers succeed decidedly best in warm, moist, rich, loamy ground. The essentials to their growth are heat and a fair proportion of moisture. They should not be planted or set in the open air until there is a prospect of continued warm and pleasant weather; as, when planted early, not only are the seeds liable to decay in the ground, but the young plants are frequently cut off by frost.

The hills should be five or six feet apart in each direction. Make them fifteen or eighteen inches in diameter, and a foot in depth; fill them three-fourths full of thoroughly digested compost, and then draw four or five inches of earth over the whole, raising the hill a little above the level of the ground; plant fifteen or twenty seeds in each, cover half an inch deep, and press the earth smoothly over with the back of the hoe. When all danger from bugs and worms is past, thin out the plants, leaving but three or four of the strongest or healthiest to a hill.

Taking the Crop. — As fast as the cucumbers attain a

suitable size, they should be plucked, whether required for use or not. The imperfectly formed, as well as the symmetrical, should all be removed. Fruit, however inferior, left to ripen on the vines, soon destroys their productiveness.

Seed. — As cucumbers readily intermix or hybridize when grown together, it is necessary, in order to retain any variety in its purity, to grow it apart from all other sorts. When a few seeds are desired for the vegetable-garden, two or three of the finest-formed cucumbers should be selected early in the season, and allowed to ripen on the plants. In September, or when fully ripe, cut them open, take out the seeds, and allow them to stand a day or two, or until the pulp attached to them begins to separate, when they should be washed clean, thoroughly dried, and packed away for future use.

The seeds of the different varieties are similar in size, form, and color. Twelve hundred are contained in an ounce, and they retain their vitality ten years.

For Pickling. — The land for raising cucumbers for pickling may be either swarded or stubble; but it must be in good condition, and such as is not easily affected by drought. It should be deeply ploughed, and the surface afterwards made fine and friable by being thoroughly harrowed. The hills should be six feet apart, and are generally formed by furrowing the land at this distance in each direction. Manure the hills with well-digested compost, level off, draw over a little fine earth, and the land is ready for planting.

This may be done at any time from the middle of June to the first week in July. The quantity of seed allowed to an acre varies from three-fourths of a pound upwards. In most cases, growers seed very liberally, to provide against the depredation of worms and bugs; usually putting six or eight times as many seeds in a hill as will be really required for the crop. When the plants are well established and beyond danger, the field is examined, and the hills thinned to three or four plants, or, where there is a deficiency of plants, replanted.

As fast as the cucumbers attain the proper size, they should be plucked; the usual practice being to go over the plantation daily. In gathering, all the fruit should be removed, — the misshapen and unmarketable, as well as those which are well formed; for, when any portion of the crop is allowed to remain and ripen, the plants become much less productive.

In favorable seasons, and under a high state of cultivation, a hundred and twenty-five thousand are obtained from an acre; while, under opposite conditions, the crop may not exceed fifty thousand. The average price is about a dollar and twenty-five cents per thousand.

Varieties: —

Early Cluster.
EARLY GREEN CLUSTER.

A popular, early cucumber, producing its fruit in clusters near the root of the plant: whence the name. The plant is healthy, hardy, and vigorous; fruit short and thick. Its usual length is five inches, and its diameter about two inches; skin prickly, green, — often paler or nearly white at the blossom-end, — brownish-yellow when ripe; flesh white, seedy, tender, and well flavored, but less crispy or brittle than that of many other varieties.

It is a good early garden sort, and is quite productive; but is not well adapted for pickling, on account of the soft and seedy character of its flesh.

Early Cluster Cucumber.

Early Frame.
SHORT GREEN.

One of the oldest of the garden sorts, justly styled a standard variety. Plant healthy and vigorous, six to ten feet in length; fruit

CUCURBITACEOUS PLANTS.

straight and well formed, five inches and a half long, and two inches and a half in diameter; skin deep green, paler at the blossom-end, changing to clear yellow as it approaches maturity, and, when fully ripe, of a yellowish, russet-brown color; flesh greenish-white, rather seedy, but tender, and of an agreeable flavor. It is a few days later than the Early Cluster.

Early Frame Cucumber.

The variety is universally popular, and is found in almost every vegetable-garden. It is also very productive; succeeds well, whether grown in open culture or under glass; and, if plucked while young and small, makes an excellent pickle.

Early Russian. This somewhat recent variety resembles the Early Cluster. Fruit from three to four inches in length, and an inch and a half or two inches in diameter, and generally produced in pairs; flesh tender, crisp, and well flavored. When ripe, the fruit is deep yellow or yellowish-brown.

Its merits are its hardiness, extreme earliness, and great productiveness. It comes into use nearly ten days in advance of the Early Cluster, and is the earliest garden variety now cultivated. Its small size is, however, considered an objection; and some of the larger kinds are generally preferred for the main crop.

London Long Green. *McInt.* Fruit nearly a foot in length, tapering towards the extremities; skin very deep green while the fruit is young, yellow when it is ripe; flesh greenish-white, firm, and crisp; flavor good.

This variety is nearly related to the numerous prize sorts which in England are cultivated under glass, and forced during the winter. There is little permanency in the slight variations of character by which they are distinguished;

and old varieties are constantly being dropped from the catalogues, and others, with different names, substituted. Amongst the most prominent of these sub-varieties are the following : —

Carter's Champion — Recently introduced. Represented as one of the largest and finest of the forcing varieties.

Coleshill. — A recent sort, measuring on the average twenty inches in length. With the exception of the neck, which is short and handsome, the fruit is perfectly cylindrical. The skin is smooth, pale green, and thickly covered with bloom. Hardy, productive, and of excellent quality.

Conqueror of the West. — Eighteen to twenty inches in length. It is a fine prize sort, and succeeds well in open culture.

Cuthill's Black Spine. — Six to nine inches in length, hardy, early, and productive. An excellent sort for starting in a hot-bed. Fruit very firm and attractive.

The Doctor. — Sixteen to eighteen inches in length, and contracted towards the stem in the form of a neck. In favorable seasons, it will attain a good size if grown in the open ground. Crisp, tender, and well flavored.

Eggleston's Conqueror. — " Very prolific, good for forcing, of fine flavor, hardy, and a really useful sort. Specimens have been grown measuring twenty-eight inches in length, nine inches and a half in circumference, and weighing five pounds."

Flanigan's Prize. — An old, established variety; having been grown in England upwards of thirty years. Length fifteen inches.

The Doctor Cucumber.

Manchester Prize Cucumber.

Giant of Arnstadt.—Length twenty-four inches; fine rich color, and productive.

Henderson's Number One Black-spined.—Length seventeen inches, straight and even; color deep and fine. Of a hundred and eighteen varieties fruited at the Chiswick Gardens, England, this proved one of the best.

Hunter's Prolific.—Length eighteen inches. Very crisp and excellent, but requires more heat than most other varieties. Spines white; fruit covered with a good bloom, and not liable to turn yellow at the base.

Improved Sion House.—This variety has received many prizes in England. Not only is it well adapted for the summer crop, but it succeeds remarkably well when grown under glass.

Irishman.—Length twenty-two to twenty-five inches. Handsome, and excellent for exhibition.

Lord Kenyon's Favorite.—Length twelve to eighteen inches. A fine sort for winter forcing.

Manchester Prize.—This, like the Nepal, is one of the largest of the English greenhouse prize varieties. It sometimes measures two feet in length, and weighs twelve pounds. In favorable seasons, it will attain a large size in open culture, and sometimes perfect its seeds.

Napoleon III. — Hardy and very prolific. A fine new sort.

Nepal. — One of the largest of all varieties; length twenty-four inches; weight ten to twelve pounds.

Norman's Stitchworth-Park Hero. — A recently introduced variety, hardy, long, handsome, very prolific, and fine flavored.

Old Sion House. — Length nine inches. This is a well-tried, winter, forcing variety. Like the improved Sion House, it also succeeds well in open culture. Quality good, though the extremities are sometimes bitter.

Prize-fighter. — Length sixteen inches. Good for the summer crop, or for exhibition.

Rifleman. — This variety is described as one of the best prize cucumbers. It has a black spine; always grows very even from stem to point, with scarcely any handle; carries its bloom well; keeps a good fresh color; and is not liable to turn yellow as many other sorts. Length twenty-four to twenty-eight inches. An abundant bearer.

Ringleader. — A prominent prize sort, fifteen inches in length. It succeeds well, whether grown under glass or in the open ground.

Roman Emperor. — Length twelve to fifteen inches.

Star of the West. — Long, hardy, handsome; described as extra fine.

Stockwood. — One of the best sorts for forcing. It is remarkably hardy and prolific, and succeeds well grown in a common hot-bed. Length fifteen to twenty inches. It sometimes produces three or four fruit at a joint.

Southgate. — This variety has been pronounced the most productive, and the best for forcing, of all the prize sorts. It is not so late as many of the English varieties, and will frequently succeed well if grown in the open ground.

Sugden's Aldershott. — Remarkably large and handsome; one of the finest of the prize sorts. The fruit sometimes attains the length of three feet.

Victory of Bath. — Length seventeen inches. Well adapted for forcing, or for the general crop.

Long Green Prickly.
Long Prickly.
Early Long Green Prickly.

This is a large-sized variety, and somewhat later than the White-spined. The plant is a strong grower, and the foliage of a deep-green color; the fruit is seven inches in length, straight, and generally angular; skin dark green, changing to yellow as the fruit approaches maturity, — when fully ripe, it is reddish-brown, and is often reticulated about the insertion of the stem; prickles black; flesh white, somewhat seedy, but crisp, tender, and well flavored.

The Long Green Prickly is hardy and productive; makes a good pickle if plucked while young; and is well deserving of cultivation. It differs from the London Long Green and the Long Green Turkey in its form, which is much thicker in proportion to its length; and also in the character of its flesh, which is more pulpy and seedy.

Long Green Turkey.
Extra Long Green Turkey.

A distinct and well-defined variety; when full grown, sometimes measuring nearly eighteen inches in length. Form long and slender, contracted towards the stem in the form of a neck, and swollen towards the opposite extremity; seeds few, and usually produced nearest the blossom-end. The neck is generally solid. While the fruit is young, the skin is deep green; afterwards it changes to clear yellow, and finally assumes a rusty yellow or yellowish-brown. Flesh remarkably firm and crisp, exceeding, in these respects, that of any other cucumber. Very productive and excellent.

Its firm and crispy flesh, and the absence of seeds, render it serviceable for the table after it has reached a very considerable size. For the same reasons, it may be pickled at a stage of its growth when other more seedy and pulpy sorts would be almost worthless.

Short Prickly. SHORT GREEN PRICKLY. EARLY SHORT GREEN PRICKLY.

This variety somewhat resembles the Long Prickly; but it is shorter, and proportionally thicker. Its length, when suitable for use, is four inches. Skin prickly, green, changing to yellow at maturity; flesh transparent, greenish-white, rather seedy, but tender, crisp, and fine flavored.

The variety is hardy and productive, comes early into fruit, and is one of the best for pickling. It is a few days later than the Early Cluster.

White Spanish.

The form of this variety is similar to that of the White-spined. The fruit measures five inches in length, two inches in diameter, and is generally somewhat ribbed. When suitable for use, the skin is white; a characteristic by which the variety is readily distinguished from all others. The flesh is crisp, tender, and well flavored. At maturity, the fruit is yellow.

White-spined. EARLY WHITE-SPINED. NEW-YORK MARKET.

This very distinct variety is extensively grown for marketing, both at the North and South. The plants grow from six to ten feet in length; and, like those of the Early Frame, are of a healthy, luxurious habit. The fruit is of full medium size, straight, and well formed,—six inches in length, and two inches and a half in diameter; skin deep green; prickles white; flesh white, tender, crispy, and of remarkably fine flavor. As the fruit ripens, the skin gradually becomes paler, and, when fully ripe, is nearly white; by which peculiarity, in connection with its white spines, the variety is always readily distinguishable.

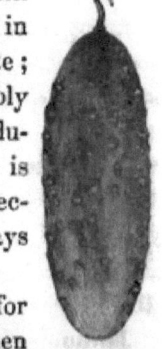

White-spined Cucumber.

The White-spined is one of the best sorts for the table; and is greatly prized by market-men on account of its color, which is never changed to yellow, though kept long after being plucked. It is generally thought to retain its freshness longer than any other variety, and consequently to be well fitted for transporting long distances; though, on account of its peculiar color, the freshness may be less real than apparent.

For the very general dissemination of this variety, the public are, in a great degree, indebted to the late Isaac Rand, Esq., of Boston, Mass., whose integrity as a merchant, and whose skill as a practical vegetable cultivator and horticulturist, will be long remembered.

THE MELON.

Of the Melon there are two species in general cultivation, — the Muskmelon (*Cucumis melo*) and the Watermelon (*Cucurbita citrullus*), — each, however, including many varieties. Like the Squash, they are tender, annual plants, of tropical origin, and only thrive well in a warm temperature. "The climate of the Middle and Southern States is remarkably favorable for them; indeed, far more so than that of England, France, or any of the temperate portions of Europe. Consequently, melons are raised as field-crops by market-gardeners; and, in the month of August, the finest citrons, or green-fleshed melons, may be seen in the markets of New York and Philadelphia in immense quantities; so abundant, in most seasons, as frequently to be sold at half a dollar per basket, containing nearly a bushel of fruit. The warm, dry soils of Long Island and New Jersey are peculiarly favorable to the growth of melons: and, even at low prices, the product is so large, that this crop is one of the most profitable." — *Downing.*

Through the extraordinary facilities now afforded by railroads and ocean steam-navigation, the markets of all the cities and large towns of the northern portions of the United States, and even of the Canadas, are abundantly supplied within two or three days from the time of gathering: and they are retailed at prices so low, as to allow of almost universal consumption; well ripened and delicious green-fleshed citron-melons being often sold from six to ten cents each.

Soil and Cultivation. — Both the Musk and the Watermelon thrive best in a warm, mellow, rich, sandy loam, and in a sheltered exposure. After thoroughly stirring the soil by ploughing or spading, make the hills six or seven feet apart in each direction. Previous to planting, these hills should be prepared as directed for the Squash; making them a foot and a half or two feet in diameter, and twelve or fifteen inches in depth. Thoroughly incorporate at the bottom of the hill a quantity of well-digested compost, equal to three-fourths of the earth removed; and then add sufficient fine loam to raise the hill two or three inches above the surrounding level. On the top of the hill thus formed, plant twelve or fifteen seeds; and, when the plants are well up, thin them out from time to time as they progress in size. Finally, when all danger from bugs and other insect depredators is past, leave but two or three of the most stocky and promising plants to a hill.

THE MUSKMELON.

Cucumis melo.

The seeds of the Muskmelon are oval, flattened, generally yellow, but sometimes nearly white, about four-tenths of an inch in length, and three-sixteenths of an inch in breadth, — the size, however, varying to a considerable extent in the different varieties. An ounce contains from nine hundred to eleven hundred seeds; and they retain their germinative properties from eight to ten years.

Varieties. — These are exceedingly numerous, in consequence of the great facility with which the various kinds intermix or hybridize. Varieties are, however, much more easily produced than retained; consequently, old names are almost annually discarded from the catalogues of seedsmen and gardeners, and new names, with superior recommendations, offered in their stead. The following list embraces most of the kinds of much prominence or value now cultivated: —

Beechwood. Fruit nearly spherical, but rather longer than broad, — usually five or six inches in diameter; skin greenish-yellow, thickly and regularly netted; flesh green, melting, sugary, and excellent. An early and fine variety.

Christiana. This variety was originated by the late Capt. Josiah Lovett, of Beverly, Mass. Form roundish; size rather small, — average specimens measuring nearly the same as the Green Citron; skin yellowish-green; flesh yellow, sweet, juicy, and of good quality. Its early maturity is its principal recommendation; the Green Citron, Nutmeg, and many other varieties, surpassing it in firmness of flesh, sweetness, and general excellence.

It would probably ripen at the North, or in short seasons when other sorts generally fail.

Citron.
GREEN-FLESHED CITRON. GREEN CITRON.
Fruit nearly round, but flattened slightly at the ends, — deeply and very regularly ribbed; size medium, or rather small, — average specimens measuring six inches in diameter, and five inches and a half in depth; skin green and thickly netted, — when fully mature, the green becomes more soft and mellow, or of a yellowish shade; flesh green, quite thick, very juicy, and of the richest and most sugary flavor. It is an abundant bearer, quite hardy, and remarkably uniform

in its quality. It is deservedly the most popular as a market sort; and for cultivation for family use, every thing considered, has few superiors.

In common with the Carolina Watermelon, the Green Citron is extensively grown at the South for shipping to the northern portions of the United States; appearing in the markets of New York and Boston three or four weeks in advance of the season of those raised in the same vicinity in the open ground.

Green Citron Melon.

This variety possesses little merit aside from its very early maturity. It is a roundish melon, flattened a little at the ends, ribbed, and of small size; usually measuring nearly five inches in diameter. Skin yellowish, often spotted with green, and sometimes a little warty; rind quite thick; flesh reddish-orange, sweet, and of good flavor.

Early Cantaloupe.

It is exceedingly variable in size, form, and color.

Fruit very oval, large, strongly ribbed; skin yellow, very thickly netted, sometimes so closely as to cover nearly the entire surface; flesh salmon-yellow, remarkably thick and sweet, but not fine-grained or melting when compared with the more recent and improved varieties.

Large-ribbed Netted.
COMMON MUSKMELON.

Hardy and productive. In good soil and favorable seasons, the fruit sometimes attains a length of fifteen inches, and weighs upwards of twenty pounds.

Monroe's Green Flesh. *Vil.* Fruit nearly spherical, but tapering slightly towards the stem, rather regularly as well as distinctly ribbed. Its diameter is about five inches. Cicatrix large; skin greenish-yellow, thickly and finely netted over the entire surface; rind thin; flesh green, remarkably transparent, thick, very melting, and highly perfumed.

Nutmeg. Fruit oval, regularly ribbed, eight or nine inches in length, and six inches in its broadest diameter; skin pale green, and thickly netted; rind thin; flesh light green, rich, sweet, melting, and highly perfumed.

The Nutmeg Melon has been long in cultivation, and is almost everywhere to be found in the vegetable-garden, though seldom in a perfectly unmixed state. When the variety is pure, and the fruit perfectly ripened, it is of most delicious excellence, and deservedly ranked as one of "the best."

Pine-apple. Form roundish, inclining to oval, either without ribs, or with rib-markings faintly defined; size small, — the average diameter being nearly five inches and a half; skin olive-green, with net-markings more or less abundant; rind thin; flesh green, melting, sweet, and perfumed. Season early.

It is an excellent sort, easily grown, and very productive.

Skillman's Fine-netted. This variety much resembles the Pine-apple. Form rounded, flattened slightly at the ends; flesh green, sugary, melting, and excellent. It has been pronounced "the earliest of the green-fleshed sorts."

Fruit of medium size, or small, round, **Ward's Nectar.** and regularly ribbed; skin green, sometimes softening into greenish-yellow at maturity, and so thickly netted, that the markings often nearly cover the entire surface; flesh green, moderately thick, very melting, and abounding in juice of remarkable sweetness and excellence.

The plants are prolific; the fruit ripens with the Green Citron, and the variety is recommended for cultivation.

A recently introduced, roundish, medium- **White Japan.** sized, or rather small variety; skin cream-white and very thin; flesh thick, remarkably sweet and fine flavored,—if the fruit is well matured, almost rivalling that of the Green Citron. It ripens early, and is quite productive.

Of the numerous new sorts that have been offered to the public within the past two or three years, this appears to be one of the most desirable.

White Japan Melon.

PERSIAN MELONS.—*Trans.*

These differ remarkably from the varieties commonly cultivated. They are destitute of the thick, hard rind which characterizes the common sorts, and which renders so large a portion of the fruit useless. On the contrary, the Persian Melons are protected by a skin so thin and delicate, that they are subject to injury from causes that would produce no perceptible effect on the sorts in general cultivation. As a class, they are not only prolific, but their flesh is extremely tender, rich, and sweet, and flows copiously with a cool juice, which renders them still more grateful. They are, however, not early, and, for their complete perfection, require a long and warm season.

7

The numerous varieties — few of which have been grown to any extent in this country — will be found described in the "FIELD AND GARDEN VEGETABLES OF AMERICA."

THE WATERMELON.

Cucurbita citrullus.

Plant running, — the length varying from eight to twelve feet; leaves bluish-green, five-lobed, the lobes rounded at the ends; flowers pale yellow, an inch in diameter; fruit large, roundish or oblong, green, or variegated with different shades of green; seeds oval, flattened, half an inch long, five-sixteenths of an inch broad, — the color varying according to the variety, being either red, white, black, yellowish, or grayish-brown. An ounce contains from a hundred and seventy-five to two hundred seeds, and they retain their vitality eight years.

The Watermelon is more vigorous in its habit than the Muskmelon, and requires more space in cultivation; the hills being usually made eight feet apart in each direction. It is less liable to injury from insects, and the crop is consequently much more certain. The seed should not be planted till May, or before established warm weather; and but two good plants allowed to a hill.

The varieties are as follow : —

Apple-seeded. A rather small, nearly round sort, deriving its name from its small, peculiar seeds, which, in form, size, and color, are somewhat similar to those of the apple. Skin deep, clear green; rind very thin; flesh bright red to the centre, sweet, tender, and well flavored. It is hardy, bears abundantly, seldom fails to ripen perfectly in the shortest seasons, and keeps a long time after being gathered.

THE WATERMELON.

Fruit of large size, roundish or oblong, **Black Spanish.** generally more or less distinctly ribbed; Spanish. skin very dark or blackish-green; rind half an inch thick; flesh deep red (contrasting finely with the deep-green color of the skin), fine-grained, sugary, and of excellent flavor. The variety is hardy, productive, matures its fruit in the Northern and Eastern States, and is decidedly one of the best for general cultivation. Seeds dark brown, or nearly black.

The Bradford is a highly prized South- **Bradford.** Carolina variety; size large; form oblong; *W. D. Brinckle.* skin dark green, with gray, longitudinal stripes, mottled and reticulated with green; rind not exceeding half an inch in thickness; seed yellowish-white, slightly mottled, and with a yellowish-brown stripe around the edge; flesh fine red to the centre; flavor fine and sugary; quality "best."

Fruit of large size, and of an oblong form, usually somewhat swollen towards the blossom- **Carolina.**

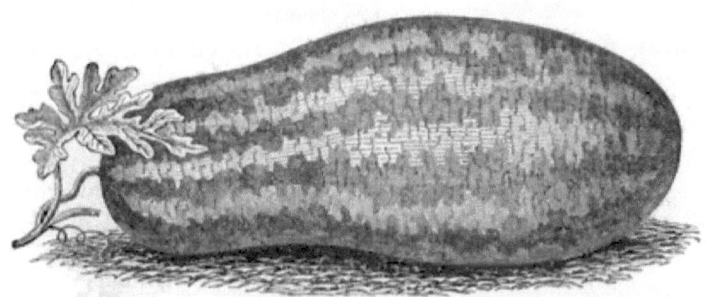

Carolina Watermelon.

end; skin deep green, variegated with pale green or white; flesh deep red, not fine-grained, but crisp, sweet, and of fair quality; fruit frequently hollow at the centre; seeds black.

This variety is extensively grown in the Southern States

for exportation to the North, where it appears in the markets about the beginning of August, and to some extent in July. Many of the specimens are much less marked with stripes and variegations than the true Carolina; and some shipments consist almost entirely of fruit of a uniform deep-green color, but of the form and quality of the Carolina.

Downing mentions a sub-variety with pale-yellow flesh and white seeds.

Citron Watermelon. Fruit nearly spherical, six or seven inches in diameter; color pale green, marbled with darker shades of green; flesh white, solid, tough, seedy, and very squashy and unpalatable in its crude state. It ripens late in the season, and will keep until December. "It is employed in the making of sweetmeats and preserves by removing the rind, or skin, and seeds, cutting the flesh into convenient bits, and boiling in sirup which has been flavored with ginger, lemon, or some agreeable article. Its cultivation is the same as that of other kinds of melons." — "*New American Cyclopædia.*"

Citron Watermelon.

Clarendon.
W. D. Brinckle.
DARK-SPECKLED.
Size large; form oblong; skin mottled-gray, with dark-green, interrupted, longitudinal stripes, irregular in their outline, and composed of a succession of peninsulas and isthmuses; rind thin, not exceeding half an inch; seed yellow, with a black stripe extending round the edge, and from one to three black spots on each side, — the form and number corresponding on the two sides; flesh scarlet to the centre; flavor sugary and exquisite, and quality "best."

This fine melon originated in Clarendon County, S.C.;

and, when pure, may at all times be readily recognized by the peculiarly characteristic markings of the seeds.

A large, pale-green sort; when unmixed, **Ice Cream.** readily distinguishable from all other varieties. Form nearly round, but sometimes a little depressed at the extremities; rind thicker than in most varieties; flesh white, sweet, and tender, and of fine flavor; seeds white.

It is prolific, early, and well adapted for cultivation in cold localities, or where the seasons are too short for the successful culture of the more tender and late kinds. Its pale-green skin, white flesh, and white seeds, are its prominent distinctive peculiarities.

This variety is said to have been introduced **Imperial.** from the Mediterranean. Fruit round or ob- *Down.* late, and of medium size; skin pale green, with stripes and variegations of white or paler green; rind thin; flesh pale red, crisp, sweet, and of excellent flavor; seeds reddish-brown. Very productive, but requires a warm situation and a long season for its complete perfection.

This variety is similar to the Mountain **Mountain** Sweet. It is of large size, long, and of an **Sprout.** oval form. Skin striped and marbled with paler and deeper shades of green; rind thin, measuring scarcely half an inch in thickness; flesh scarlet, a little hollow at the centre, crisp, sugary, and of excellent flavor.

Like the Mountain Sweet, it is a favorite market sort. It is not only of fine quality, but very productive. Seeds russet-brown.

A large, long, oval variety, often contract- **Mountain** ed towards the stem in the form of a neck; **Sweet.** skin striped and marbled with different shades of green;

rind rather thin, measuring scarcely half an inch in thickness; flesh scarlet, and solid quite to the centre; seeds pale

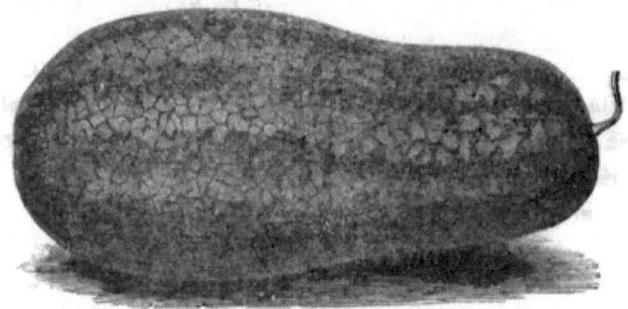

Mountain Sweet Watermelon.

russet-brown, but often of greater depth of color in perfectly matured specimens of fruit.

A popular and extensively cultivated variety, quite hardy, productive, and of good quality. "For many years it was universally conceded to be the best market sort cultivated in the Middle States, but of late has lost some of the properties that recommended it so highly to favor. This deterioration has probably been owing to the influence of pollen from inferior kinds grown in its vicinity." No variety will long remain pure, unless planted apart from all others.

Odell's Large White.
W. D. Brinckle.

A remarkably large variety; the fruit sometimes weighing sixty pounds; form round; skin gray, with fine green network spread over its uneven surface; rind nearly three-fourths of an inch in thickness; seeds large, grayish-black, and not numerous; flesh pale red; flavor fine; quality very good. Productiveness said to exceed that of most other kinds.

Its large size, and long-keeping quality after being separated from the vine, will recommend the variety, especially for the market.

Form oval, of medium size; skin pale **Orange.**
green, marbled with shades of deeper green;
rind half an inch in depth, or of medium thickness; flesh red, not fine-grained, but tender, sweet, and of good quality. When in its mature state, the rind separates readily from the flesh, in the manner of the peel from the flesh of an orange.

When first introduced, the variety was considered one of the best quality; but it appears to have in some degree deteriorated, and now compares unfavorably with many other sorts.

Fruit oblong, very large, often sixteen **Pie-melon.**
inches and upwards in length, and from eight CALIFORNIA
to ten inches in diameter; skin yellowish- PIE-MELON.
green, marbled with different shades of light-green or pea-green; flesh white, succulent, somewhat tender, but quite unpalatable, or with a squash-like flavor, in its crude state. As intimated by the name, it is used only for culinary purposes.

This melon should be cooked as follows: After removing the rind, cut the flesh into pieces of convenient size, and stew until soft and pulpy. Lemon-juice, sugar, and spices should then be added; after which, proceed in the usual manner of making pies from the apple or any other fruit. If kept from freezing, or from dampness and extreme cold, the Pie-melon may be preserved until March.

Size large; form oblong; skin dark green, **Ravenscroft.**
faintly striped and marked with green of a *W. D. Brinckle.*
lighter shade, and divided longitudinally by sutures from an inch and a quarter to two inches apart; rind not more than half an inch in thickness; seed cream-color, tipped with brown at the eye, and having a brown stripe around the edge; flesh fine red, commencing abruptly at the rind, and extending to the centre; flavor delicious and sugary; quality "best."

This valuable Watermelon originated with Col. A. G. Sumner of South Carolina.

Souter.
W. D. Brinckle. Size large, sometimes weighing twenty or thirty pounds; form oblong, occasionally roundish; skin peculiarly marked with finely reticulated, isolated gray spots, surrounded by paler green, and having irregular, dark-green, longitudinal stripes extending from the base to the apex; rind thin, about half an inch thick; seed pure cream-white, with a faint russet stripe around the edge; flesh deep red to the centre; flavor sugary and delicious; quality "best." Productiveness said to be unusually great.

This excellent variety originated in Sumter District, S.C.

PRICKLY-FRUITED GHERKIN.

Gherkin. — West-Indian Cucumber. — Jamaica Cucumber. — Cucumis anguria.

This species is said to be a native of Jamaica. The habit of the plant is similar to that of the Globe Cucumber, and its season of maturity is nearly the same. The surface of the fruit is thickly set with spiny nipples, and has an appearance very unlike that of the Common Cucumber. It is comparatively of small size, and of a regular, oval form, — generally measuring about two inches in length by an inch and a third in its largest diameter; color pale green; flesh greenish-white, very seedy and pulpy. The seeds are quite small, oval, flattened, yellowish-white, and retain their vitality five years.

It is somewhat later than the Common Cucumber, and requires nearly the whole season for its full development. Plant in hills about five feet apart; cover the seeds scarcely half an inch deep, and leave three plants to a hill.

The Prickly-fruited Gherkin is seldom served at table sliced in its crude state. It is principally grown for pickling; for which purpose it should be plucked when about half grown, or while the skin is tender and can be easily broken by the nail. As the season of maturity approaches, the rind gradually hardens, and the fruit becomes worthless. In all stages of its growth, the flesh is coarse and spongy, and, in the process of pickling, absorbs a large quantity of vinegar.

THE PUMPKIN.

Cucurbita pepo.

Under this head, on the authority of the late Dr. T. W. Harris, should probably be included "the common New-England Field-pumpkin, the Bell-shaped and Crook-necked winter squashes, the Canada Crook-necked, the Custard squashes, and various others."

The term "pumpkin," as generally used in this country by writers on gardening and agriculture, and as popularly understood, includes only the few varieties of the Common New-England Pumpkin that have been long grown in fields in an extensive but somewhat neglectful manner; the usual practice being to plant a seed or two at certain intervals in fields of corn or potatoes, and afterwards to leave the growing vines to the care of themselves. Even under these circumstances, a ton is frequently harvested from a single acre, in addition to a heavy crop of corn or potatoes.

The Pumpkin was formerly much used in domestic economy; but since the introduction of the Crook-necks, Boston Marrow, Hubbard, and other improved varieties of squashes, it has gradually fallen into disuse, and is now cultivated principally for agricultural purposes.

Varieties. — The following are the principal varieties, although numerous intermediate sorts occur, more or less distinct, as well as more or less permanent in character: —

Canada Pumpkin.
VERMONT PUMPKIN.

The Canada Pumpkin is of an oblate form, inclining to conic, and is deeply and regularly ribbed. When well grown, it is of large size, and often measures thirteen or fourteen inches in diameter, and ten inches in depth. Color fine, deep orange-yellow; skin, or shell, rather thick and hard; flesh yellow, fine-grained, sweet, and well flavored. Hardy and productive.

Compared with the Common Field variety, the Canada is much more flattened in its form, more regularly and deeply ribbed, of a deeper and richer color; and the flesh is generally much sweeter, and less coarse and stringy in its texture. It seems adapted to every description of soil; thrives well in all climates; and is one of the best sorts for agricultural purposes, as well as of good quality for the table.

Cheese Pumpkin.

The plants of this variety are remarkably strong and vigorous, with large, deep-green leaves. The fruit is much flattened, deeply and rather regularly ribbed, broadly dishing about the stem, and basin-like at the opposite extremity. It is of large size, and, when well grown, often measures fifteen or sixteen inches in diameter, and nine or ten inches in depth. Skin fine, deep reddish-orange, and, if the fruit is perfectly matured, quite hard and shell-like; flesh very thick, yellow, fine-grained, sweet, and well flavored. The seeds are not distinguishable from those of the Common Field-pumpkin.

The Cheese Pumpkin is hardy, remarkably productive, and much superior in all respects to most of the field-grown sorts.

Common Yellow Field-pumpkin.

Fruit rounded, usually a little more deep than broad, flattened at the ends, and rather regularly, and more or less prominently, ribbed. Its size is much affected by soil, season, and the purity of the seed. Average specimens will measure fourteen inches in length, and eleven or twelve inches in diameter. Color rich, clear orange-yellow; skin, or rind, if the fruit is well matured, rather dense and hard; flesh variable in thickness, but averaging an inch and a half, of a yellow color, generally coarse-grained, and often stringy, but sometimes of fine texture, dry, and of good quality; seeds of medium size, cream-yellow.

Common Yellow Field-pumpkin.

The cultivation of the Common Yellow Field-pumpkin in this country is almost coeval with its settlement. For a long period, few, if any, of the numerous varieties of squashes, now so generally disseminated, were known; and the Pumpkin was not only extensively employed as a material for pies, but was much used as a vegetable, in the form of squash, at the table. By many it is still highly esteemed, and even preferred for pies to the squash, or the more improved varieties of pumpkins; but its cultivation at present is rather for agricultural than for culinary purposes.

A large, yellow, field variety, not unlike the Common Yellow in form, but with a softer skin, or shell. It is prolific, of fair quality as an esculent, and one of the best for cultivating for stock or for agricultural purposes. *Connecticut Field-pumpkin.*

Fruit oval, much elongated, the length usually nearly twice the diameter. Well- *Long Yellow Field-pumpkin.*

grown specimens measure sixteen to twenty inches in length, and nine or ten inches in diameter; surface somewhat ribbed, but with the markings less distinct than those of the Common Yellow; color bright orange-yellow; skin somewhat tender, generally easily broken by the nail; flesh an inch and a half in thickness, yellow, of good but not fine quality, usually sweet, but watery, and of no great value for the table.

It yields abundantly; is well adapted for planting among corn or potatoes; may be profitably raised for feeding out to stock; keeps well when properly stored; and selected specimens will afford a tolerable substitute for the Squash in the kitchen, particularly for pies.

Between this and the Common Yellow there are various intermediate sorts; and, as they readily hybridize with each other, it is with difficulty that these varieties can be preserved in a pure state. Only one of the sorts should be cultivated, unless there is sufficient territory to enable the cultivator to allow a large distance between the fields where the different varieties are grown.

Nantucket Hard-Shell. "Nigger-Head." Form flattened or depressed, but sometimes oblong or bell-shaped, often faintly ribbed; size medium or rather small; color deep green, somewhat mellowed by exposure to the sun, or at full maturity; skin, or shell, thick and hard, and more or less thickly covered with prominent, wart-like excrescences; flesh quite thick, yellow, sweet, fine-grained, and of excellent flavor, — comparing favorably in all respects with that of the Sugar Pumpkin. It is a productive sort, and its flesh much dryer and more sugary than the peculiar, green, and warty appearance of the fruit would indicate.

When cooked, it should be divided into pieces of convenient size; the seeds, and loose, stringy parts, removed from the inner surface of the flesh, and then boiled or baked in the skin, or shell; afterwards scooping out the flesh, as is practised with the Hubbard Squash, or other hard-shelled varieties of pumpkins. It is an excellent pie-variety, and selected specimens will be found of good quality when served as squash at the table. Season from February to March.

Striped Field-pumpkin. — Fruit similar to the Common Yellow Field-pumpkin. The size, however, will average less; although specimens may sometimes be procured as large as the dimension given for the Common Yellow. Color yellow, striped and variegated with green, — after being gathered, the green becomes gradually softer and paler, and the yellow deeper; flesh yellow, moderately thick, and, though by some considered of superior quality, has not the fine, dry, and well-flavored character essential for table use; seed similar to the foregoing sorts.

The Striped Field-pumpkin is hardy, and yields well. It is, however, exceedingly liable to hybridize with all the varieties of the family, and is with difficulty preserved in an unmixed condition.

Sugar-pumpkin.
SMALL SUGAR-PUMPKIN.

Fruit eight or nine inches at its broadest diameter, and six inches in depth; form much depressed, usually broadest near the middle, and more or less distinctly ribbed; skin bright orange-yellow when the fruit is well ripened, hard and shell-like, and not easily broken by the nail; stem quite long, greenish, furrowed, and somewhat reticulated; flesh of good thickness, light yellow, fine-grained, sweet, and well flavored; seeds of smaller size than, but in other respects similar to, those of the Field-pumpkin.

The variety is the smallest of the sorts usually employed for field cultivation. It is, however, a most

Sugar-pumpkin.

abundant bearer, rarely fails in maturing its crops perfectly, is of first-rate quality, and may be justly styled an acquisition. For pies, it is not surpassed by any of the family; and it is superior for table use to many of the garden squashes. The facility with which it hybridizes, or mixes with other kinds, renders it extremely difficult to keep the variety pure; the tendency being to increase in size, to grow longer or deeper, and to become warty,—either of which conditions may be considered an infallible evidence of deterioration.

Varieties sometimes occur more or less marbled and spotted with green; the green, however, often changing to yellow after harvesting.

THE SQUASH.

All the varieties are tender annuals, and of tropical origin. They thrive well only in a warm temperature; and the seed should not be sown in spring until all danger from frost is past, and the ground is warm and thoroughly settled; as, aside from the tender nature of the plant, the seed is extremely liable to rot in the ground in continued damp and cold weather.

Any good, well-enriched soil is adapted to the growth of the Squash. The hills should be made from eight to ten inches in depth, two feet in diameter, and then filled within three or four inches of the surface with well-digested compost; afterwards adding sufficient fine loam to raise the hill an inch or two above the surrounding level. On this, plant twelve or fifteen seeds, covering three-fourths of an inch deep. Keep the earth about the plants loose and clean, and from time to time remove the surplus vines, leaving the most stocky and vigorous. Three plants are sufficient for a hill, to which number the hills should ultimately be thinned; making the final thinning when all danger from bugs and other vermin is past. The dwarfs may be planted four feet apart; but the running sorts should not be less than six or eight. The custom of cutting or nipping off the leading shoot of the running varieties is now practised to some extent, with the impression that it both facilitates the formation of fruitful laterals and the early maturing of the fruit. Whether the amount of product is increased by the process, is not yet determined.

In giving the following descriptions, no attempt has been made to present them under scientific divisions; but they have been arranged as they are in this country popularly understood : —

Summer Varieties : —

Plant running, not of stocky habit, but healthy and vigorous; fruit obtusely conical, three inches broad at the stem, and two inches and a half in depth; skin yellowish-white, thin and tender while the fruit is young, hard and shell-like when ripe; flesh dry and well flavored in its green state, and often of good quality at full maturity. Apple Squash.
EARLY APPLE.

The fruit is small; and, on this account, the variety is very little cultivated.

Plant dwarfish or bushy in habit, generally two feet and a half in height or length; fruit largest at the blossom-end, and tapering gradually to a neck, which is solid, and more or less curved; average specimens, Bush Summer
Warted
Crookneck.
EARLY SUMMER
CROOKNECK.
YELLOW SUMMER
WARTED CROOK-
NECK.
when suitable for use, measure eight inches in length, and three inches in diameter at the broadest part; color clear, bright yellow; skin very warty, thin, and easily broken by the nail while the fruit is young, and suitable for use. As the season of maturity approaches, the rind gradually becomes firmer, and, when fully ripe, is hard and shell-like; flesh greenish-yellow, dry, and well flavored; seeds small,

broad in proportion to the length, and of a pale-yellow color; four hundred are contained in an ounce.

Bush Summer Warted Crookneck Squash.

The Bush Summer Crookneck is generally esteemed the finest of the summer varieties, but is used only while young and tender, or when the skin can be easily pierced or broken by the nail. After the fruit hardens, the flesh becomes watery, coarse, strong-flavored, and unfit for table use.

On account of the dwarfish character of the plants, the hills may be made four feet apart.

As a class, the summer varieties are greatly inferior to the later sorts in fineness of texture, sweetness and delicacy of flavor.

Early White Bush Scalloped.
WHITE PATTYPAN. CYMLING. WHITE SUMMER SCALLOPED.

This is a sub-variety of the Early Yellow Scalloped. The plant has the same dwarf habit, and the fruit is nearly of the same size and form. The principal distinction between the varieties consists in the difference of color.

By some, the White variety is considered a little inferior in fineness of texture and in flavor to the Yellow; though the White is much the more abundant in the markets. Both of the varieties are hardy and productive; and there is but little difference in the season of their maturity.

In the month of June, large quantities are shipped from the Southern and Middle States to the North and East, where they anticipate from two to three weeks the products of the home-market gardens; the facilities afforded by steam transportation rendering nearly profitless the efforts of gardeners to obtain an early crop. As the variety keeps well, and suffers little from transportation, the squashes are generally found fresh and in good order on their arrival.

Plant dwarf, of rather erect habit, and about two feet and a half in height; fruit somewhat of a hemispherical form, expanded at the edge, which is deeply and very regularly scalloped. **Early Yellow Bush Scalloped. Cymling. Yellow Pattypan. Yellow Summer Scallop.** When suitable for use, it measures nearly five inches in diameter, and three inches in depth; but, when fully matured, the diameter is often ten or twelve inches, and even upwards. Color yellow; skin, while young, thin, and easily pierced, — at maturity, hard and shell-like; flesh pale yellow, tolerably fine-grained, and well flavored, — not, however, quite so dry and sweet as that of the Summer Crookneck; seeds broader in proportion to their length than the seeds of most varieties, and of small size, — four hundred and twenty-five weigh an ounce.

Early Yellow Bush Scalloped.

This variety has been common to the gardens of this country for upwards of a century, during which period the form and general character have been very slightly, if at all, changed. When grown in the vicinity of the Bush Summer Crookneck, the surface sometimes exhibits the same wart-like excrescences; but there is little difficulty in procuring seeds that will prove true to the description above given.

Like the Summer Crookneck, the scalloped squashes are used while young or in a green state. After the hardening of the skin, or shell, the flesh generally becomes coarse, watery, strong flavored, and unfit for the table.

An ornamental variety, generally cultivated for its peculiar egg-like fruit, which usually **Egg Squash.** measures three inches in length, and two inches or two and a half in diameter. Skin, or shell, white. It is seldom used as an esculent; though, in its young state, the flesh is quite similar in flavor and texture to that of the scalloped varieties. "If trained to a trellis, or when allowed to cover a dry branching tree, it is quite ornamental, and, in its ripened state, is quite interesting, and attractive at public exhibitions." Increase of size indicates mixture or deterioration.

Green-striped Bergen. "Plant dwarf, but of strong and vigorous habit; fruit of small size, bell-shaped; colors dark green and white, striped.

"An early but not productive sort, little cultivated at the North or East, but grown to a considerable extent for the New-York market. It is eaten both while green and when fully ripe."

Large Summer Warted Crookneck. A large variety of the Bush or Dwarf Summer Crookneck. Plant twelve feet and upwards in length, running; fruit of the form of the last named, but of much greater proportions,—sometimes attaining a length of nearly two feet; skin clear, bright yellow, and thickly covered with the prominent wart-like excrescences peculiar to the varieties; flesh greenish-yellow, and of coarser texture than that of the Dwarf Summer Crookneck. Hardy, and very productive.

Orange. Fruit of the size, form, and color of an orange. Though generally cultivated for ornament, and considered more curious than useful, "some of them are the very best of the summer squashes for table use; far superior to either the scalloped or warted varieties." When trained as directed for the Egg-squash, it is equally showy and attractive.

Autumn and Winter Varieties:—

Autumnal Marrow.
J. M. Ives.
Boston Marrow. Plant twelve feet or more in length, moderately vigorous; fruit ovoid, pointed at the extremities, eight or nine inches in length, and seven inches in diameter; stem very large, fleshy, and

contracted a little at its junction with the fruit, — the summit, or blossom-end, often tipped with a small nipple, or wart-like excrescence; skin remarkably thin, easily bruised or broken, cream-yellow at the time of ripening, but changing to red after harvesting, or by remaining on the plants after full maturity; flesh rich, salmon yellow, remarkably dry, fine-grained, and in sweetness and excellence surpassed by few varieties. The seeds are large, thick, and pure white: the surface, in appearace and to the touch, resembles glove-leather or dressed goat-skin. About one hundred are contained in an ounce.

In favorable seasons the Autumnal Marrow Squash will be sufficiently grown for use early in August; and, if kept from cold and dampness, may be preserved till March.

Introduced by Mr. John M. Ives of Salem, Mass., in 1831; now universally esteemed and cultivated in almost every section of the United States.

Autumnal Marrow Squash.

A sub-variety of the Vegetable Marrow, with a dwarf, reclining stem, two and a half or three feet in height or length. The fruit has the form and color of the running variety, but is of smaller size, generally measuring six or seven inches in length, and three or four inches in diameter. **Bush, or Dwarf Vegetable Marrow.**

The variety is hardy, productive, comes early into use, and will keep through the winter, though much inferior to the Boston Marrow, Hubbard, and like sorts, as a table vegetable. It is excellent as a pie-squash, and is well suited for cultivation in humid climates or cold latitudes, as the fruit forms early in the season, and is soon ripened.

Canada Crookneck. The plants of this variety are similar in habit to those of the Common Winter Crookneck; but the foliage is smaller, and the growth less luxuriant. In point of size, the Canada Crookneck is the smallest of its class. When the variety is unmixed, the weight seldom exceeds five or six pounds. It is sometimes bottle-formed; but the neck is generally small, solid, and curved in the form of the Large Winter Crooknecks. The seeds are contained at the blossom-end, which expands somewhat abruptly, and is often slightly ribbed. Skin of moderate thickness, and easily pierced by the nail; color, when fully ripened, cream-yellow, but, if long kept, becoming duller and darker; flesh salmon-red, very close-grained, dry, sweet, and fine-flavored; seeds small, of a grayish or dull white color; three hundred are contained in an ounce.

The Canada is unquestionably the best of the Crook-necked sorts. The vines are remarkably hardy and prolific, yielding almost a certain crop both North and South. The variety ripens early; the plants suffer but little from the depredations of bugs or worms; and the fruit, with trifling care, may be preserved throughout the year. It is also quite uniform in quality; being seldom of the coarse and stringy character so common to other varieties of this class.

Cashaw. Cushaw Pumpkin. Somewhat of the form and color of the Common Winter Crookneck. Two prominent varieties, however, occur. The first is nearly round; the other curved, or of the shape of a hunter's horn. The latter is the most desirable. It is not cultivated or generally known in New England, or in the northern portions of the United States; for though well suited to Louisiana and other portions of the South, where it is much esteemed, it is evidently too tender for cultivation where the seasons are short and cool.

Fruit oval, elongated, sixteen to twenty inches in length, eight or ten inches in diameter, and weighing from fifteen to twenty pounds and upwards; skin thin, easily pierced or broken, of an ash-gray color, spotted and marked with light drab and nankeen-brown, — the furrows dividing the ribs, light drab; stem small; flesh deep orange-yellow, of medium thickness; seeds pure white, broader in proportion to their length than those of the Hubbard or Boston Marrow.

Cocoanut Squash.
Cocoa Squash.

The quality of the Cocoanut Squash is extremely variable. Sometimes the flesh is fine-grained, dry, sweet, and of a rich, nut-like flavor; but well-developed and apparently well-matured specimens are often coarse, fibrous, watery, and unfit for table use. The variety ripens in September, and will keep till March or April.

Plant healthy and of vigorous habit, often twenty feet and upwards in length; fruit oblong, gathered in deep folds, or wrinkles, at the stem, near which it

Custard Squash.

Custard Squash.

is the smallest, abruptly shortened at the opposite extremity, prominently marked by large, rounded, lengthwise elevations, and corresponding deep furrows, or depressions; skin, or shell, cream-white; flesh pale yellow, not remarkable for solidity, or fineness of texture, but well flavored; the seeds are yellowish-white, and readily distinguished from those of other varieties by their long and narrow form. Under favorable conditions of soil and season, the Custard Squash attains a large size; often measuring twenty inches and upwards in length, eight or ten inches in diameter, and weighing from eighteen to twenty-five pounds.

It is one of the hardiest and most productive of all varieties. Crops are recorded of fourteen tons from an acre. It is esteemed by some for pies, but, as a table squash, is inferior to most other sorts. Its great yield makes it worthy the attention of agriculturists, as it would doubtless prove a profitable variety to be cultivated for stock.

Honolulu. Plant twelve feet or more in length, remarkably strong and vigorous; leaves very large, — leaf-stems often three feet and upwards in length; fruit large, oblate, depressed about the stem, broadly, and sometimes deeply, but in general faintly ribbed; skin moderately thick, but not shell-like, of an ash-green color, often striped and variegated with drab, or lighter shades of green; flesh reddish-orange, very thick, of good flavor, but less dry and sweet than that of the Hubbard or Boston Marrow; seeds large, white.

This recently introduced variety is hardy, productive, a good keeper, excellent for pies, and by some esteemed for table use.

Specimens frequently occur of a reddish-cream color, striped and marked with drab or pale yellow.

Honolulu Squash.

THE SQUASH.

Hubbard.
J. J. H. Gregory.

Plant similar in character and appearance to that of the Autumnal Marrow; fruit irregularly oval, sometimes ribbed, but often without rib-markings, from eight to ten inches in length, seven or eight inches in diameter, and weighing from seven to nine pounds, — some specimens terminate quite obtusely, others taper sharply towards the extremities, which are frequently bent or curved; skin, or shell, dense and hard, nearly one-eighth of an inch thick, and overspread with numerous small protuberances; stem fleshy, but not large; color variable, always rather dull, and usually clay-blue or deep olive-green,— the upper surface, if long exposed to the sun, assuming a brownish cast, and the under surface, if deprived of light, becoming orange-yellow; flesh rich salmon-yellow, thicker than that of the Autumnal Marrow, fine-grained, sweet, dry, and of most excellent flavor, — in this last respect resembling that of roasted or boiled chestnuts; seeds white, — similar to those of the Autumnal Marrow. Season from September to June; but the flesh is dryest and sweetest during autumn and the early part of winter.

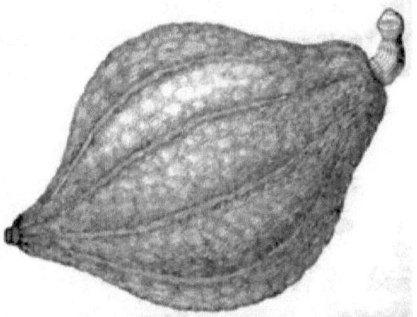

Hubbard Squash.

The Hubbard Squash should be grown in hills seven feet apart, and three plants allowed to a hill. It is essential that the planting be made as far as possible from similar varieties, as it mixes, or hybridizes, readily with all of its kind. In point of productiveness, it is nearly equal to the Autumnal Marrow. The average yield from six acres was five tons of marketable squashes to the acre.

The original squash was green, and the blue sub-variety is believed to have been produced by a cross with the Sweet-potato Squash. In the color of the shell of these hybrids, in the lighter orange tint of the flesh, and sometimes in the form, the old Sweet Potato variety can yet be traced.

Mammoth. This is the largest-fruited variety known. In a very rich compost, and under favorable conditions of climate, it grows to an enormous size. Fruit weighing a hundred and twenty pounds is not uncommon; and instances, though exceptional, are recorded of weights ranging from two hundred to nearly two hundred and fifty pounds.

The leaves are large, and the stems thick, running along the ground to the distance of twenty or thirty feet if not stopped, and readily striking root at the joints.

The fruit is round, or oblate; sometimes flattened on the under side, owing to its great weight; sometimes obtusely ribbed, yellowish, or pale buff, and frequently covered to a considerable extent with a gray netting. Flesh deep yellow; seeds white.

It is used only in its full-grown or ripe state, in which it will keep for several months, and even during the winter, if stored in a dry, warm situation. The flesh is sweet, though generally coarse-grained and watery. It is used in soups and stews, and also for pies, but is seldom served like squash at the table.

Puritan. Plant ten feet and upwards in length; fruit bottle-formed, fourteen or fifteen inches long, and ten inches in diameter at the broadest part; neck solid, four or five inches in diameter; average weight eight to ten pounds; skin thin, usually white, or cream-white, striped and marked with green, though specimens sometimes occur, from unmixed seed, uniformly green; flesh pale yellow, dry, sweet, mild, and well flavored; seeds of medium size, white. Season from August to January.

This variety, long common to gardens in the vicinity

of the Old Colony, retains its distinctive character to a remarkable degree, even when grown under the most unfavorable circumstances. Seeds obtained from a gardener who had cultivated the variety indiscriminately among numerous summer and winter kinds for upwards of twenty years produced specimens uniformly true to the normal form, color, and quality. It is hardy and productive, good for table use, excellent for pies, and well deserving of cultivation. The form of the fruit, its short, fleshy stem, and its peculiar seeds, distinguish the variety from all others.

Puritan Squash.

Sweet-potato Squash.

Plant similar in character to that of the Hubbard and Autumnal Marrow; fruit twelve or fourteen inches long, seven or eight inches thick; sometimes ribbed, but frequently without rib-markings; oblong, tapering to the ends, which are often bent or curved in the manner of some of the types of the Hubbard; stem of medium size, striated; skin ash-green, with a smooth, polished surface; flesh salmon-yellow, thick, fine-grained, dry, and sweet, — if the variety is pure, and the fruit well matured, its quality approaches that of the Hubbard and Autumnal Marrow; seeds white.

The variety is hardy and productive, keeps well, and is deserving of cultivation. When grown in the vicinity of the last-named sorts, it often becomes mixed, and rapidly degenerates. In its purity, it is uniformly of one color, with perhaps the exception of the under surface, which is sometimes paler or yellowish. It has been suggested that this variety and the Hubbard may have originated under similar circumstances.

Turban.
Acorn. Turk's Cap.

Plant running; fruit rounded, flattened, expanding about the stem to a broad, plain, brick-red, or reddish-cream surface, of ten or twelve inches in diameter. At the blossom-end, the fruit suddenly contracts to an irregular, cone-like point, or ter-

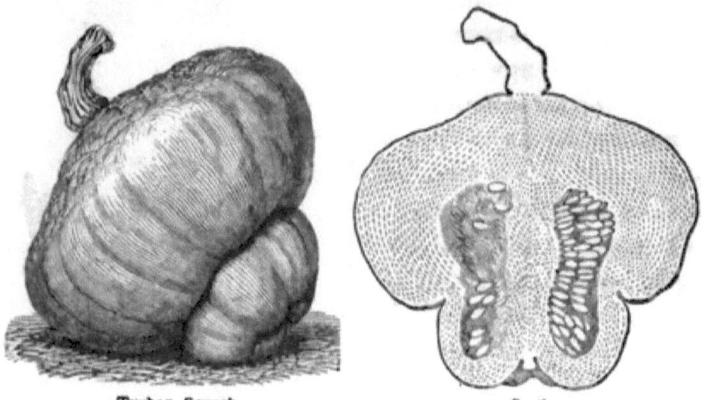

Turban Squash. Section.

mination, usually of a greenish color, striped with white, but sometimes yellowish-white, without the stripes or variegations, and thus in form and color somewhat resembles a turban, whence the name. Flesh orange-yellow, remarkably thick, fine-grained, sugary, and well flavored; seeds white, short, and small.

The Turban Squash is not early, and should have a rich, warm soil, and the advantage of the whole season. Though its keeping properties are not particularly good, it is early fit for the table, and, for use in autumn or early in winter, must be classed as one of the best of all varieties. The weight varies from five to eight pounds, and the specific gravity is said to exceed that of any other known sort.

After harvesting, the fruit should be immediately stored in a dry and warm situation, laid upon the side to avoid injury to the seed or acorn end, which is peculiarly liable to decay, and in this position remain undisturbed till required for use.

In favorable situations, and under high culture, six tons have been obtained from an acre.

A sub-variety — probably the result of acclimation — is known as the Improved Turban. Compared with the original, the plant is hardier, yields more abundantly, and the fruit, besides being quite as sweet and delicate, is a much better keeper, and nearly or quite equal in quality to that of the best Autumnal Marrow.

Improved Turban Squash.

Plant running; fruit oval, sixteen inches in length, ten or eleven inches in diameter, slightly ribbed, and largest at the blossom-end, which often terminates in a wart-like excrescence; skin cream-white, sometimes smooth and polished, but often more or less reticulated, or netted; flesh thick, orange-yellow, generally dry, sweet, and well flavored, but sometimes fibrous and watery; seeds large, nankeen-yellow, smooth, and glossy.

Valparaiso.
Porter's Valparaiso. Commodore Porter.

The variety requires the whole season for its perfection. It hybridizes readily with the Autumnal Marrow and kindred sorts, and is kept pure with considerable difficulty. It is in use from September to spring.

Plant twelve feet and upwards in length; fruit nine inches long, and of an elliptic shape, — but it is sometimes grown to twice that length, and of an oblong form; surface slightly uneven, by irregular, longitudinal, obtuse ribs, which ter-

Vegetable Marrow.
Thomp.

minate in a projecting apex at the extremity of the fruit.

Vegetable Marrow Squash.

When mature, it is of a uniform pale-yellow or straw color. The skin, or shell, is very hard when the fruit is perfectly ripened; flesh white, tender, and succulent, even till the seeds are ripe. It may be used in every stage of its growth. When well ripened, it will keep throughout the winter, if stored in a dry place, out of the reach of frost, and not exposed to great changes of temperature.

Winter Crookneck. Cuckaw. This is one of the oldest and most familiar of the winter varieties. Plant hardy and vigorous; fruit somewhat irregular in form; the neck solid and nearly cylindrical, and the blossom-end more or less swollen. In some specimens, the neck is nearly

Winter Crookneck Squash.

straight; in others, sweeping, or circular; and sometimes the extremities nearly or quite approach each other. The size is very variable, being affected greatly both by soil and season: the weight ranges from six to forty pounds and upwards. Color green, but, when fully mature, often cream-yellow. Flesh salmon-yellow, not uniform in texture or solidity, sometimes close-grained, sweet, and fine flavored, but often coarse, stringy, and nearly worthless for the table. Seeds of medium size, grayish-white, the border darker, or brownish: about two hundred are contained in an ounce.

It is a hardy and productive variety; ripens its crop with great certainty; suffers less from the depredations of insects than most of the winter sorts; and, if protected from cold and dampness during the winter months, will keep the entire year.

Winter Striped Crookneck. This is a sub-variety of the Common Winter Crookneck. Skin pale green, or light cream-white, diversified with lengthwise stripes and plashes of bright green.

Yokohama. A new variety, recently introduced into this country from Japan. Stem running, attaining a length of twelve feet and upwards; fruit roundish, much flattened, strongly ribbed, deeply sunk at the blossom-end and about the stem, eight or ten inches at its largest diameter, and weighing from six to twelve pounds. Skin

Yokohama Squash.

warted, green while the fruit is young, but afterwards gradually changing to yellow, or dull orange; stem long and slender, woody, clavated, and furrowed, like that of the Sugar-pumpkin. Flesh orange-yellow, fine-grained, dry, and sweet. Seeds small, somewhat resembling those of the Scalloped or Warted Crookneck. Season from July to March.

Among other cucurbitaceous plants which are sometimes grown for use, or as objects of curiosity, may be classed the Papanjay, or Sponge Cucumber, the Globe Cucumber, Snake Cucumber, and the Calabash, or Common Gourd, including among its numerous varieties the Hercules Club; full descriptions of which, with modes of culture, are contained in "THE FIELD AND GARDEN VEGETABLES OF AMERICA."

CHAPTER V.

BRASSICACEOUS PLANTS.

Borecole, or Kale. — Broccoli. — Brussels Sprouts. — Cabbage. — Cauliflower. — Kohl Rabi. — Savoy. — Sea-kale.

BORECOLE, OR KALE.

Brassica oleracea sabellica.

MOST of the Borecoles, or Kales, are either annuals or biennials. As a class, they form neither heads as the Common Cabbage, nor eatable flowers like the Broccoli and Cauliflower. Some of the varieties attain a height of six or seven feet; but while a few are compact and symmetrical in their manner of growth, and of good quality for table use, others are "ill-colored, coarse, rambling-growing, unpalatable, and indigestible."

Propagation and Culture. — They are propagated from seeds, which, in size, form, and color, resemble those of the Cabbage, and which are sown at the time of sowing the seeds of the Cabbage or Cauliflower, and in the same manner. Early plants may be started in a hot-bed, or the seeds may be sown in the open ground in April or May. In transplanting, treat the plants like young cabbages, setting them more or less remote, according to the size or habit of the variety.

Though they are extremely hardy, and will endure quite a low temperature, they are generally harvested in autumn, before the closing-up of the ground. If reset in the following spring, they will furnish an abundance of tender sprouts, which resemble Coleworts or Brussels Sprouts in flavor and delicacy.

Use. — "The tender, upper part alone is eaten. They are often, but not always, frozen when cut; and, when this is the case, they should be put into a cool cellar, or in cold water, until the frost is out of them. The beautiful curled leaves are quite ornamental.

Varieties. — The varieties are numerous, but, in many instances, not well marked or defined. Though sometimes found in our gardens, they do not appear to attain that degree of perfection in this country which they are said to possess when grown under the climate of Great Britain.

Of the twenty varieties described in the "FIELD AND GARDEN VEGETABLES OF AMERICA," the Dalmeny Sprouts, Dwarf Green Curled, Green and Red Marrow-stem, Neapolitan, Purple, Thousand-headed, and the Variegated, appear to be the most prominent. The leaves of the latter are lobed, and finely curled. They are also beautifully variegated, sometimes with green and yellowish-white, or green and purple, and sometimes with bright red and green.

It is frequently grown as an ornamental plant, is occasionally employed for garnishing, and is sometimes put into bouquets. It is very good cooked after frost, but is not quite so hardy as the Purple Borecole.

BROCCOLI.

Brassica oleracea var.

In its structure and general habit, the Broccoli resembles the Cauliflower. Between these vegetables, the marks of distinction are so obscure, that some of the white varieties of Broccoli appear to be identical with the Cauliflower. The seeds are similar in the two classes of plants, and their culture is the same.

Use. — The heads, or flowers, are cooked and served in all the forms of the Cauliflower.

Varieties. — These are exceedingly numerous; although the distinctions, in many instances, are neither permanent nor well defined.

The kinds catalogued by seedsmen, and recommended for cultivation, are the following; viz. : —

An excellent kind, of a deep-purple color. When the variety is unmixed, it is close-headed at first; afterwards it branches, but is liable to be too much branched, and to become green. The plant is from two to three feet high, and a strong grower. *Early Purple. Trans.*

A strong-growing, hardy sort, from two to three feet high. The flower is close-headed, and, in the genuine variety, of a rich purple on its first appearance. It is, however, liable to lose its color, and to become greenish. *Early Sprouting. McInt.*

The variety is extensively grown by the market-gardeners in the vicinity of London.

Head pure white, scarcely distinguishable from the finest Cauliflower; size large, — when well formed, measuring from seven to nine inches in diameter. *Frogmore Protecting. Hov. Mag.*

A recently introduced sort, promising to be one of the best. The plants are extremely hardy and vigorous, and rarely fail to develop a large and fine head, having a rich, curdy appearance, and, as before observed, similar to a well-grown Cauliflower. It is of dwarf growth; and the outer leaves, closing over the large head of flowers, protect it from the action of severe weather.

Grange's Early Cauliflower Broccoli.
McInt.

This is an old variety, and, when pure, still stands in high estimation, having a head nearly as large and as white as a Cauliflower. It is not a large grower; and, being upright in habit, may be grown at two feet distant.

Hardy, and well deserving of cultivation. The London market-gardeners cultivate four varieties, of which this is the principal.

Green Cape.
Thomp.

Flower greenish, and generally covered by the leaves.

This variety and the Purple Cape often become intermixed, and are liable to degenerate. They are, however, quite distinct, and, when pure, very beautiful.

Late Dwarf Purple.

This is the latest Purple Broccoli. The plants seldom rise above a foot in height. The flower, at first, shows small and green, but soon enlarges, and changes to a close, conical, purple head. The whole plant presents a singular and beautiful appearance.

Portsmouth.
Thomp.

Flower, or head, buff, or cream-colored. This is a hardy sort; and the flower, which is produced near the ground, is said to exceed in size that of any other variety.

Purple Cape.
Trans.

This variety produces a close, compact head, of a purple color, which, in favorable seasons, comes as large as a Cauliflower. The plants grow from a foot to a foot and a half in height. The head is exposed to view in growing; and, as it enlarges, the projecting parts of the flower show a greenish-white, mixed with the purple color. When boiled, the whole flower becomes green.

Excellent for general culture, as it is not only one of the finest varieties for the table, but the plants form their heads much more generally than many other kinds. It is the earliest of the Purple Broccolis.

A remarkably large, white-flowered variety, recently introduced. It is described as sometimes attaining a weight of seventeen pounds, and measuring, when divested of foliage, four feet in circumference. Though somewhat coarse, and wanting in compactness, it is quite free from fibre, and as tender and delicate as many of the smaller and close-flowered Broccolis.   *Reading Giant.*

This variety is of dwarfish habit. The heads are large, white, compact, well protected by the incurved leaves, and equal in quality to those of the Cauliflower. By many it is considered superior to Grange's Early Cauliflower Broccoli.   *Snow's Superb White Winter. Thomp.*

Leaves with long stems; heads large, compact, somewhat conical, sulphur-colored, sometimes tinged with purple. Hardy.   *Sulphur or Brimstone Broccoli. Trans.*

New, but so closely resembling a Cauliflower as to be scarcely distinguishable from it. The leaves, however, are more curled, and its constitution is of a hardier nature, enduring the cold, and also withstanding heat and drought better. Much esteemed in England, where, by successive sowings, it is brought to the table at every season of the year.   *Walcheren Broccoli. McInt.*

The true Willcove is a variety perfectly distinct from every other of its season. The heads are large, firm, even, and fine, and of a pure whiteness. They are fully exposed, and not protected by the leaves, as most other Broccolis are. On this account, the variety is more liable to be injured by the weather than any other late sort; and therefore, in severe seasons, it must be regarded as deficient in hardiness.   *Willcove. R. Hogg.* LATE WILLCOVE.

BRUSSELS SPROUTS.

Thousand-headed Cabbage. — *Brassica oleracea var.*

In its general character, this vegetable is not unlike some of the varieties of Kale, or Borecole. Its stem is from a foot to four feet in height, and from an inch and a half to upwards of two inches in diameter. It is remarkable for the production of numerous small axillary heads, or sprouts, which are firm and compact "like little cabbages, or rather like hearted Savoys in miniature. A small head, resembling an open Savoy, surmounts the stem of the plant, and maintains a circulation of sap to the extremity. Most of the original side-leaves drop off as these small buds, or heads, enlarge." — *Thomp.*

Brussels Sprouts.

Culture. — The plant is always raised from seeds, which, in size, form, or color, are scarcely distinguishable from the seeds of the Common Cabbage. These should be sown at the time and in the manner of the Cabbage, — either in hot-beds in March or April, or in the open ground in April or May. When three or four inches high, transplant two feet apart in each direction, and cultivate as directed for Cabbages and Cauliflowers.

Use. — The small heads are boiled and served in the manner of Cabbages. They are also often used in the form of the Cauliflower, boiled until soft, then drained, and afterwards stewed with milk, cream, or butter.

Varieties. — Two varieties are enumerated by gardeners and seedsmen; viz. : —

Dwarf Brussels Sprouts. A low-growing sort, usually from eighteen inches to two feet in height. It differs from the following variety principally in size, though it is somewhat earlier. The dwarf stems are said to produce heads which are more tender and succulent when cooked than those obtained from taller plants.

Tall or Giant Brussels Sprouts. Stem nearly four feet in height; plant healthy and vigorous, producing the small heads peculiar to its class in great abundance.
It is somewhat hardier than the foregoing variety, and, on account of its greater length of stalk, much more productive.

There is, however, very little permanency to these sorts. Much of the seed found in the market will not only produce plants corresponding with both of the varieties described, but also numerous intermediate kinds.

THE CABBAGE.

Brassica oleracea capitata.

The Cabbage is a biennial plant, and, though very hardy, — growing at all seasons unprotected in England, — will not withstand the winters of the Northern States in the open ground.

When fully developed, it is from four to five feet in height. The flowers are cruciform, generally yellow, but sometimes white or yellowish-white. The seeds, which ripen in July and August of the second year, are round, reddish-brown or blackish-brown, and retain their vitality five years. About ten thousand are contained in an ounce.

Soil. — Cabbages are best grown in deep, rich, loamy soil. On land that has been long under cultivation, or in dry situations, they rarely succeed well. Ashes, with a mixture of salt, may be advantageously applied, not only for the promotion of growth, but for protection against the attack of the maggot, to which the roots are liable. They may be mixed in the hill at the time of transplanting, or applied about the plant from time to time in the process of cultivation.

Propagation. — All of the varieties are propagated from seed sown annually. For early use, a sowing may be made in a hot-bed in February or March; and, for winter use, the seed may be sown in a nursery-bed, in the open ground, in May or June. When five or six inches high, transplant.

Seed. — American-grown seed is generally considered superior to that of foreign growth; and, when it can be obtained from a reliable seedsman or seeds-grower, the purchaser should not be induced by the difference in price to select the nominally cheaper, as there are few vegetables with which the character of the seed is of greater importance.

Varieties. — The varieties are numerous, and the distinction, in many instances, well-defined and permanent. Between some of the sorts, however, the variations are slight and unimportant.

Champion of America. One of the largest of the recently introduced sorts; the whole plant sometimes attaining a weight of forty pounds and upwards. Head flattened, somewhat resembling the Drumheads; outer leaves very few, succulent, and tender; stalk short; quality tender, mild, and well flavored.

As a market variety, it has few, if any, superiors. It heads with great uniformity, and bears transportation well; but its large size is objectionable when required for the use of families numbering but few members.

Stem dwarfish,—the leaf-stalks coming out quite close to each other; so that scarcely any portion of the stem is to be seen between them. The whole Cabbage measures about three feet in circumference. The heart is shortly conical, with a broad base; near which it is two feet in circumference, when divested of the outside leaves. The ribs boil tender.

Early Battersea.
Thomp.
BATTERSEA.

It is one of the best sorts for the general crop of early cabbages; is not liable to crack; and, when cut close to the stem, often puts forth a number of fresh heads, of fair size and good quality.

This is an intermediate variety, of the size of the Early York, and a little later. The head is round, flattened at the top, firm and well formed, tender in texture, and well flavored.

Early Drumhead.

It is a good sort for the garden, as it heads well, occupies but little space in cultivation, and comes to the table immediately after the earlier sorts.

This well-known and standard variety has a round, medium-sized, solid head, sometimes tinted with brown at its top. The outside and loose leaves are few in number, large, rounded, clasping, blistered, and of a glaucous-green color; the stalk is thick and short.

Early Low Dutch.
EARLY DUTCH DRUMHEAD.

It is early, tender, of good quality, heads well, and one of the best sorts for growing in a small garden for early table use.

Early Sugar-loaf. The color of this variety, and the form of its head, distinguish it from all others. The plant, when well developed, has an appearance not unlike some of the varieties of Cos lettuces; the head being round and full at the top, and tapering thence to the base, forming a regular inverted cone.

Though an early cabbage, it is thought to be more affected by heat than most of the early varieties, and is also said to lose some of its qualities if kept late in the season. Head of medium size, seldom compactly formed, and, when cut and cooked in its greatest perfection, tender and well flavored.

Early Wakefield. Head of medium size, generally somewhat conical, but sometimes nearly round, compact; leaves glaucous-green; stalk small.

A fine, early variety, heading readily. As the plants occupy but little space, it is recommended as a desirable sort for early marketing.

Early York. In this country, the Early York is one of the oldest, most familiar, and, as an early market sort, one of the most popular, of all the kinds now cultivated. The head is of less than medium size, roundish-ovoid, close, and well formed, of a deep or ash-green color, tender and well flavored. The loose leaves are few in number, often revoluted on the border, and comparatively smooth on the service; nerves greenish-white. The plants of the true variety have short stalks, occupy but little space, and seldom fail to produce a well-formed, and, for an early sort, a good-sized head. They require a distance of about eighteen inches between the rows, and fifteen or eighteen inches in the rows.

Its earliness and its unfailing productiveness make it a favorite with market-gardeners; and it still retains its long-established popularity, notwithstanding the introduction of numerous new sorts, represented as being as early, equally prolific, and surpassing it in general excellence.

Head large, loose, and open; stalk long. **Green Glazed.** Its texture is coarse and hard, and the vari- <small>AMERICAN GREEN GLAZED.</small> ety really possesses little merit, though it is somewhat extensively grown in warm latitudes, where it appears to be less liable to the attacks of the cabbage-worm than any other sort.

A distinguishing characteristic of this cabbage is the deep shining-green color; the plants being readily known from their peculiar, varnished, or glossy appearance.

Head large, round, sometimes flattened a **Large Late Drumhead.** little at the top, close and firm; the loose <small>AMERICAN DRUMHEAD.</small> leaves are numerous, broad, round, and full, clasping, blistered, and of a sea-green color; the stem is short. The variety is hardy, seldom fails to form a head, keeps well, and is of good quality,

There are many varieties of this cabbage, introduced by different cultivators and seedsmen under various names, differing slightly, in some unimportant particulars, from the foregoing description, and also differing somewhat from each other, "but agreeing in being large, rounded, cabbaging uniformly, having a short stem, keeping well, and in being tender and good flavored."

This is a larger cabbage than the Early **Large York.** York, which variety it somewhat resembles. The head, however, is broader in proportion to its depth, and more firm and solid. The stalk is also shorter, and it is two or three weeks later.

The Large York seems to be intermediate between the Early York and the Large Late Drumheads, as well in respect to form and general character as to its season of maturity. It is recommended as being less affected by heat than many other kinds, and, for this reason, well adapted for cultivation in warm climates. It seldom fails in forming its head, and is tender and well flavored.

Large Ox-heart.
Large French Ox-Heart.
This is a French variety, of the same form and general character as the Small Ox-heart, but of larger size. The stalk is short; the head firm and close, and of a light-green color; the spare leaves are few in number, generally erect, and concave.

It is a week or ten days later than the Small Ox-heart, forms its head readily, and is of good quality. One of the best of the intermediate sorts.

Little Pixie.
Tom Thumb.
A recent sort, remarkable for its earliness, and for its diminutive size, and generally dwarfish character,— the whole plant, when full grown, being scarcely larger than a colewort, or some varieties of cabbage-lettuce.

It is of tender texture; the flavor is mild and delicate; and as an early variety, particularly where space is limited, is recommended for cultivation.

Marblehead Mammoth Drumhead.
J. J. H. Gregory.
One of the largest of the Cabbage family, produced from the Mason, or Stone-mason, by Mr. Alley, and introduced by Mr. J. J. H. Gregory of Marblehead, Mass.

Heads not uniform in shape,— some being nearly flat, while others are almost hemispherical; size very large, varying from fifteen to twenty inches in diameter,— although specimens have been grown of the extraordinary dimensions of twenty-four inches. In good soil, and with proper culture, the variety is represented as attaining an average weight of thirty pounds. Quality tender and sweet.

Sixty tons of this variety have been raised from a single acre.

The Mason Cabbage, in shape, is nearly hemispherical; the head standing well out from among the leaves, growing on a small and short stalk. Under good cultivation, the heads will average nine inches in diameter, and seven inches in depth. It is characterized for its sweetness, and for its reliability for forming a solid head. It is also an excellent variety for cultivation in extreme Northern latitudes, where, from the shortness of the season, or in those sections of the South, where, from excessive heat, plants rarely cabbage well. Under good cultivation, nearly every plant will set a marketable head.

Mason. *J. J. H. Gregory.*

Mason Cabbage.

Originated by Mr. John Mason of Marblehead, Mass.

This variety is of recent introduction. The head, which is of medium size, has the form of an elongated cone, and is regular and symmetrical. It is quite solid, of a pale or yellowish-green color, tender and well flavored, and remarkable for the peculiar manner in which the leaves are collected, and twisted to a point, at its top. Stalk rather high.

Pomeranian.

It is an intermediate variety, and excellent either as an autumnal or winter cabbage. As it heads promptly, and, besides, is of remarkable solidity, it makes a profitable market cabbage, keeping well, and bearing transportation with little injury.

Head large, bluish-green, round, solid, broad and flat on the top, and often tinted with red or brown. The exterior leaves are few in number, roundish, broad and large, clasping, blis-

Premium Flat Dutch. **LARGE FLAT DUTCH.**

tered on the surface, bluish-green in the early part of the season, and tinged with purple towards the time of harvesting; stalk short.

It is one of the largest of the cabbages, rather late, good for autumn use, and one of the best for winter or late keeping, as it not only remains sound, but retains its freshness and flavor till late in spring. The heads open white and crisp, and, when cooked, are tender and well flavored. It requires a good soil, and should be set in rows not less than three feet apart, and not nearer together than thirty inches in the rows.

As a variety for the winter market, the Premium Flat Dutch has no superior. An acre of land, well set and cultivated, will yield four thousand heads.

Small Ox-heart. Head below medium size, ovate or egg-shaped. The leaves are of the same bright green as those of the York Cabbage; the stalk is short, and the leaves not composing the head few in number.

The Ox-heart cabbages, with respect to character, and period of maturity, are intermediate between the Yorks and Drumheads; more nearly, however, resembling the former than the latter. The Small Ox-heart is ten days later than the Early York.

As not only the heads, but the full-grown plants, of this variety, are of small size, they may be grown in rows two feet apart, and sixteen inches apart in the rows.

Stone-mason. *J. J. H. Gregory.* An improved variety of the Mason, originated by Mr. John Stone, jun., of Marblehead, Mass. Head larger than that of the original, varying in size from ten to fourteen inches in diameter, according to the strength of the soil and the cultivation given it. The form of the head is flatter than that of the Mason, and but little, if any, inferior to it in solidity. Stem short and small. Under good culture, the heads, exclusive of the outer foliage, will weigh nine pounds. Quality exceedingly sweet, tender, and rich. A profitable variety for market-purposes; the gross returns per acre in the vicinity of Boston, Mass., often reaching from two hundred dollars to three hundred and fifty.

The Mason, Stone-mason, and the Marblehead Mammoth, severally originated from a package of seeds received from England, under the name of the " Scotch Drumhead," by Mr. John M. Ives of Salem, Mass.

This variety, though often found upon the cata- **Vanack.** logues of our seedsmen, has not been extensively *Lind.* grown in this country, and perhaps is really but little known.

The head is somewhat irregular in shape, broad at the base, and terminates in a sharp point. The exterior leaves are large, spreading, deep green, and strongly veined.

It is tender in texture, sweet and delicate in flavor, cabbages early and uniformly, and when kept through the winter, and reset in spring, pushes abundant and fine sprouts, forming excellent early coleworts, or greens. Lindley pronounces its quality inferior to none of the best cabbages.

Heads small, but solid, and uniform in **Waite's New** shape. It has little of the coarseness com- **Dwarf.** mon to the larger varieties, and the flavor is *Hov. Mag.* superior.

One of the finest early cabbages, and one of the best sorts for the market. It occupies but little space compared with some of the older kinds, and a large number of plants may be grown upon a small piece of ground.

This is a German variety, somewhat simi- **Winnigstadt.** lar to the Ox-heart, but more regularly **POINTED HEAD.** conical. Head broad at the base, and tapering symmetrically to a point, solid, and of the size of the Ox-heart;

leaves of the head pale or yellowish-green, with large nerves and ribs; the exterior leaves are large, short, and rounded, smooth, and of firm texture; the stalk is short.

It is an intermediate sort, immediately following the Early York. A large proportion of the plants will form good heads; and as these are not only of remarkable solidity, but retain their freshness well during winter, it is a good variety for marketing, though rather hard, and somewhat deficient in the qualities that constitute a good table cabbage.

Red Varieties. — These are few in number, and generally used as salad, or for pickling. When cooked, they are considered less mild and tender than the common varieties, besides retaining a portion of their color, which, by many, is considered an objection.

Early Dwarf Red.
EARLY BLOOD RED. SMALL RED.

Head nearly round, generally of a deep-red or dark-purple color; stalk short.

It is ten days earlier than the Large Red Dutch, and is quite variable in form and color.

Large Red Dutch.

The most familiar, as well as the most popular, of the Red varieties. The head is large, round, hard, and solid; the leaves composing the head are of an intense purplish-red; the outer leaves are numerous, red, with some intermixture or shades of green.

On account of its dark color when cooked, it is seldom used in the manner of the common cabbages, but is chiefly used for pickling, or, like the other Red sorts, cut in shreds, and served as a salad; though any solid, well-blanched, small-ribbed, white-headed sort will answer for the same purpose, and perhaps prove equally tender and palatable.

The Large Red Dutch is one of the latest of cabbages, and should receive the advantage of nearly the entire season.

The heads may be kept fresh and sound until May.

Small, like the Utrecht Red, but of a still deeper color. When pickled, however, the dark coloring matter is greatly discharged, so that the substance is left paler than that of others originally not so dark. It is, therefore, not so good for pickling as other sorts which retain their color and brightness. *Superfine Black. Thomp.*

A small but fine dark-red cabbage. *Utrecht red. Thomp.*

THE CAULIFLOWER.

Brassica oleracea var.

The Cauliflower, like the Broccoli, is strictly an annual plant, as it blossoms and perfects its seed the year in which it is sown. When fully grown, or in flower, it is about four feet in height, and, in character and general appearance, is similar to the Cabbage or Broccoli at a like stage of growth.

The seeds resemble those of the Cabbage in size, form, and color, although not generally so uniformly plump and fair. From ten to twelve thousand are contained in an ounce, and they retain their germinative properties five years.

Soil. — The Cauliflower, like the Cabbage, requires a deep, rich soil, and seldom succeeds well when grown on land long under cultivation. Applications of lime and sulphur have a beneficial effect, not only in preventing the ravages of insects, but in promoting the growth of the plants. The best fertilizers appear to be those of a saline character; and excellent Cauliflowers have been produced by liberal applications of kelp and sea-weed.

Sowing and Culture. — The seed may be sown in a hot-bed in March, at the same time and in the same manner as early cabbages, and the plants set in the open ground late in May; or the seed may be sown in the open air in April or the beginning of May, in a common nursery-bed, in shallow drills six or eight inches apart; and, when sufficiently grown, the plants may be set where they are to remain.

The after-culture should be similar to that bestowed upon the Cabbage. The dry, sunny weather which so often prevails in the summer months is unfavorable to the full development of the Cauliflower; and in such seasons liberal applications of water or liquid manure may be beneficially made, and will often produce fine flowers from plants that would otherwise prove abortive.

The leaves are sometimes gathered, and tied loosely over the tops of the heads, to facilitate the blanching.

Taking the Crop. — Like the Broccoli, Cauliflowers should be cut for use while the head, or what is known as the "curd," is still close and compact. As the plants advance in growth, the head opens, separates into branches, and soon becomes coarse, fibrous, strong-flavored, and unfit for the table.

Use. — The methods of cooking and serving are almost numberless. When well grown and seasonably cut, the flavor is peculiarly mild and agreeable. Few brassicaceous plants are more ornamental, or more generally esteemed.

Varieties. — These are few in number; the distinctions, in many instances, being quite unimportant. In the color, foliage, general habit, and even in the quality, of the entire list, there is great similarity.

Early London Cauliflower.
LONDON PARTICULAR. FITCH'S EARLY LONDON.

Stem tall; leaves of medium size. It has a fine, white, compact "curd," as the unexpanded head is termed, and is the sort grown in the vicinity of London for the early crop. It is hardy, and succeeds well when grown in this country. The plants should be set two feet and a half apart.

Head rather large, white, and compact; leaves large; stalk short. An early sort. In France, it is sown in June, and the heads come to table in autumn. **Early Paris Cauliflower.**

Leaves large, long, waved, and serrated on the borders; stalk of medium height; head large, — measuring from seven to ten inches in diameter, — close, and compact. **Erfurt Early Cauliflower. ERFURT EXTRA EARLY.**

This variety promises to be one of the best for cultivation in this country. Specimens exhibited under this name before the Massachusetts Horticultural Society measured fully ten inches in diameter, the surface being very close, and the heads possessing the peculiar white, curdy character so rarely attained in the climate of the United States. The plants seldom fail to form a good-sized and symmetrical head, or flower.

Stem quite short, and plant of compact habit. The heads are large and close, and their color clear and delicate. Recommended as one of the best for forcing, as well as an excellent sort for open culture. **Frogmore Early Forcing.**

This is a fine, large, white, compact variety, taller and later than the Early London Cauliflower: it has also larger leaves. If sown at the same time, it will afford a succession. **Large Asiatic Cauliflower.** *Thomp.*

Plant fifteen inches high. The leaves are toothed and waved on the margin, and expose a head which is nine inches in diameter, and of a creamy color. **Le Normand.** *R. Hogg.*

It is earlier than the Walcheren, and is readily distinguished from it by the waved and toothed margin of the foliage.

The plants are hardy and vigorous growers, and rarely fail to develop a flower, even in dry and unfavorable seasons.

Mitchell's Hardy Early Cauliflower. A new variety. Bouquet not large, but handsome and compact. It is so firm, that it remains an unusual length of time without running to seed or becoming pithy. A desirable sort for private gardens and for forcing.

New Erfurt Dwarf Mammoth. A recent sort, with large, clear-white flowers, of superior quality.

The plants are low and close, and generally form a head, even in protracted dry and warm weather. It appears to be one of the few varieties adapted to the climate of this country, and is recommended for cultivation.

Stadtholder. A recent variety, introduced from Holland. The plants are strong growers, producing large, compact, pure-white flowers. In the vicinity of London, where it is largely cultivated for the market, it is considered equal, if not superior, to the Walcheren.

Waite's Alma Cauliflower. A new variety, represented as being of large size, and firm; surpassing in excellence the Walcheren.

Walcheren Cauliflower. *Thomp.*
Early Leyden. Legge's Walcheren Broccoli.
Stem short; leaves broad, less pointed and more undulated than those of the Cauliflower usually are. It not only resists the cold in winter, but the drought in summer, much better than other cauliflowers. In hot, dry summers, when scarcely a head of these could be obtained, the Walcheren Cauliflower, planted under similar circumstances,

formed beautiful heads, — large, white, firm, and of uniform closeness.

Messrs. Henderson and Son describe this Cauliflower as the finest kind in cultivation; **Wellington Cauliflower.** bouquet pure white; size of the head over two feet; in growth very dwarfish, — the stem not more than two or three inches from the soil.

It is one of the hardiest varieties known, and is said to withstand the extreme variations of the climate of the United States. An excellent sort for early planting and for forcing.

KOHL RABI.

Turnip Cabbage. — *Brassica caulo-rapa.*

The Kohl Rabi is a vegetable intermediate between the Cabbage and the Turnip. The stem, just above the surface of the ground, swells into a round, fleshy bulb, in form not unlike a turnip. On the top and about the surface of this bulb are put forth its leaves, which are similar to those of the Swede turnips; being either lobed or entire on the borders, according to the variety. The seeds are produced the second year; after the ripening of which, the bulb perishes.

Green Kohl Rabi.

Sowing and Cultivation. — The seeds may be sown in May or June in a nursery-bed, as is practised with the Cabbage, afterwards removing the young plants to rows eighteen inches or two feet apart, and fifteen inches apart in the rows; and they are sometimes sown, like the seeds of the Ruta-baga, in rows where they are to remain.

Seed. — Take up a few plants entire in autumn; preserve them during winter in the manner of cabbages or turnips, and transplant to the open ground in April, two feet apart in each direction. The seeds are not distinguishable from those of the Swede or Ruta-baga Turnip, and retain their vitality from five to seven years.

Use. — The part chiefly used is the turnip-looking bulb, formed by the swelling of the stem. This is dressed, and eaten with sauce or with meat, as turnips usually are. While young, the flesh is tender and delicate, possessing the combined flavor of the Cabbage and Turnip.

They are said to keep better than any other bulb, and to be sweeter and more nutritious than the Cabbage or White Turnip. "In the north of France, they are extensively grown for feeding cattle, — a purpose for which they seem admirably adapted, as they are found not to impart any of that disagreeable taste to the milk which it acquires when cows are fed on turnips."

Varieties. — The following varieties are described in "THE FIELD AND GARDEN VEGETABLES OF AMERICA;" viz., the Artichoke-leaved, Early White, Early Purple, and the Common Green, Purple, and White. The Early White and the Early Purple are the best. Under the influence of the climate of the United States, most of the kinds become so hard, fibrous, and strong flavored, as to be worthless for table use, though the form of the vegetable, and its peculiar manner of growth, often secure for it a place in the field or garden.

SAVOY.

Savoy Cabbage. — *Brassica oleracea, var. bullata.* — *De Cand.*

The Savoys are distinguished from the common head or close-hearted cabbages by their peculiar, wrinkled, or blistered leaves.

Besides this distinction, the Savoys, when compared with the Common Cabbage, are slower in their development, and have more open or less compactly formed heads.

None of the family are hardier or more easily cultivated. So far are they from being injured by cold and frosty weather, that a certain degree of frost is considered necessary for the complete perfection of their texture and flavor.

The seeds, when ripe, in form, size, and color, are not distinguishable from those of the Cabbage. An ounce, which contains ten thousand seeds, will generally produce three thousand plants.

The Savoys require the same soil, and mode of culture, as the Common Cabbage.

Varieties: —

Drumhead Savoy.
Cape Savoy.

Head large, round, compact, yellowish at the centre, and a little flattened, in the form of some of the Common Drumhead cabbages, which it nearly approaches in size. The exterior leaves of the plant are round, sea-green or bluish-green, and are more finely and less distinctly blistered on the surface than the leaves of the Green Globe. Stalk of medium length.

The Drumhead Savoy seldom fails to heart well, affords a good quantity of produce, is hardy, and, when brought to the table, is of very tender substance, and finely flavored. It is considered one of the best of the large kinds, and, wherever cultivated, has become a standard sort. It keeps well during winter, and retains its freshness late into the spring.

As it requires nearly all of the season for its complete development, the seed should be sown early.

Early Dwarf Savoy.
Early Green Savoy.

Head small, flattened, firm, and close; leaves rather numerous, but not large, deep green, finely but distinctly blistered, broad and rounded at the top, and tapering towards the stalk, or stem, of the plant, which is short. It is not quite so early as the Ulm Savoy; but it hearts readily, is tender and of good quality, and a desirable sort for early use.

Early Ulm Savoy.
NEW ULM SAVOY.
EARLIEST ULM SAVOY. *McInt.*

A dwarfish, early sort. Head small, round, solid; leaves small, thick, and fleshy. The loose leaves are remarkably few in number; nearly all of the leaves of the plant contributing to the formation of the head.

It very quickly forms a heart, which, though not of large size, is of excellent quality. It is, however, too small a sort for market-purposes, but for private gardens would, no doubt, be an acquisition. In the London Horticultural Society's garden, it proved the earliest variety in cultivation.

Green Globe Savoy.
GREEN CURLED SAVOY. LARGE GREEN SAVOY.

One of the best and one of the most familiar of the Savoys, having been long in cultivation, and become a standard sort. The head is of medium size, round, bluish or sea-green on the outside, yellow towards the centre, and loosely formed. Stalk of medium height.

Savoy Cabbage.

The variety possesses all the qualities of its class: the texture is fine, and the flavor mild and excellent. On account of its remarkably fleshy and tender character, the inner loose leaves about the head will be found good for the table, and to possess a flavor nearly as fine as the more central parts of the plant.

It is remarkably hardy, and attains its greatest perfection only late in the season, or under the influence of cool or frosty weather. As the plants develop much less rapidly than those of the Common Cabbage, the seed should be sown early.

Transplant in rows two and a half or three feet apart, and allow a space of two feet and a half between the plants in the rows.

SEA-KALE.

Crambe maritima.

Of Sea-kale there is but one species cultivated; and this is perennial, and perfectly hardy. The leaves are large, thick, oval or roundish, sometimes lobed on the borders, smooth, and of a peculiar bluish-green color; the stalk, when the plant is in flower, is solid and branching, and measures four feet in height; the flowers, which are produced in groups, or clusters, are white, and have an odor very similar to that of honey. The seed is enclosed in a yellowish-brown shell, or pod, which, externally and internally, resembles a pit, or cobble, of the common cherry. Six hundred seeds, or pods, are contained in an ounce; and they retain their germinative powers three years. "They are large and light, and, when sold in the market, are often old, or imperfectly formed; but their quality is easily ascertained by cutting them through the middle: if sound, they will be found plump and solid." They are usually sown without being broken.

Preparation of the Ground, and Sowing. — The ground should be trenched to the depth of from a foot to two feet, according to the depth of the soil, and well enriched throughout. The seeds may be sown in April where the plants are to remain; or they may be sown at the same season in a nursery-bed, and transplanted the following spring. They should be set or planted out in rows three feet apart, eighteen inches apart in the rows, and the crowns covered three inches deep.

Culture. — Keep the plants clear of weeds; nip off the shoots of such as tend to run to flower; and in the autumn, when the leaves have decayed, add a liberal dressing of compost, or stable manure. Very early in spring, stir or rake over the bed, being careful not to injure the crowns of the roots; and cover eight or ten inches deep with the material intended for blanching. This may be beach-sand, dry peat, common gravel, or whatever of like character can be conveniently obtained.

In England, the plants are blanched by inverting over them pots made for the purpose, and known as "sea-kale pots," and sometimes by using as a substitute ten or twelve inch flower-pots.

Cutting. — The sprouts are cut for use when they are from three to six inches high, and the season continues about six weeks. Like Asparagus, the roots are injured by excessive cutting; and some of the shoots should be allowed to make their natural growth, that strength may be secured for the crop of the following spring. A plantation, with good culture and moderate use, will continue from seven to ten years.

Seeds. — The seeds, which are best preserved in the pods, may be obtained plentifully by allowing a few strong plants to make their natural growth.

Use. — The blanched sprouts are used cooked as Asparagus, or as Broccoli and the Cauliflower.

CHAPTER VI.

SPINACEOUS PLANTS.

Leaf-beet, or Swiss Chard.—New-Zealand Spinach.—Spinach.—Orach.

LEAF-BEET, OR SWISS CHARD.
Sicilian Beet.—White Beet.—Beta cicla.

THE Leaf-beet is a native of the sea-coasts of Spain and Portugal. It is a biennial plant, and is cultivated for its leaves and leaf-stalks. The roots are much branched or divided, hard, fibrous, and unfit for use.

Propagation and Cultivation.—It is propagated, like other beets, from seeds sown annually, and will thrive in any good garden soil. The sowing may be made at any time in April or May, in drills eighteen inches apart, and an inch and a half deep. When the plants are well up, thin them to ten or twelve inches apart, and treat during the season as the common Red Beet, stirring the surface frequently, and keeping clear of weeds. The excellence of this vegetable consists in the succulent character of the stems and nerves of the leaves; and these properties are best acquired in moist and warm seasons, or by copious watering in dry weather.

The seed, or fruit, has the appearance peculiar to the family; although those of the different varieties, like the seeds of the Red Beet, vary somewhat in size, and shade of color.

An ounce of seed will sow a hundred feet of drill, or be sufficient for a nursery-bed of fifty square feet.

Use. — " This species of Beet is cultivated exclusively for its leaves; whereas the Red Beet is grown for its roots. These leaves are boiled like Spinach, and also put into soups. The midribs and stalks, which are separated from the lamina of the leaf, are stewed and eaten like Asparagus, under the name of " Chard." As a spinaceous plant, the White Beet might be grown to great advantage in the vegetable-garden, as it affords leaves fit for use during the whole summer." — *McInt.*

The varieties are as follow : —

Large-ribbed Curled.
Curled Leaf-Beet.
Stalks white; leaves pale yellowish-green, with broad midribs, large nerves, and a blistered surface, like some of the Savoys. It may be grown as a substitute for Spinach.

Large-ribbed Scarlet Brazilian.
Red Stalk Leaf-Beet.
Leaf-stalks bright purplish-red; leaves green, blistered on the surface; nerves purplish-red. A beautiful sort, remarkable for the rich and brilliant color of the stems and nerves of the leaves.

Large-ribbed Yellow Brazilian.
Yellow-Stalked Leaf-Beet.
A variety with bright yellow leaf-stalks and yellowish leaves. The nerves of the leaves are yellow, like the leaf-stalks; the color is peculiarly rich and clear; and the stalks are quite attractive, and even ornamental. Quality tender and good.

Silver-leaf Beet.
Swiss Chard.
Sea-Kale Beet.
Large-Ribbed Silver-Leaf Beet.
Stalks large; leaves of medium size, erect, with strong, white ribs and veins. The leaf-stalks and nerves are cooked and served like Asparagus, and somewhat resemble it in texture and flavor. It is considered the best of the Leaf-beets.

NEW-ZEALAND SPINACH.—*Loud.*

Tetragonia expansa.

This plant, botanically considered, is quite distinct from the common garden Spinach; varying essentially in its foliage, flowers, seeds, and general habit.

It is a hardy annual. The leaves are of a fine green color, large and broad, and remarkably thick and fleshy; the flowers, which are produced in the axils of the leaves, are quite inconspicuous; the fruit is of a dingy-brown color, three-eighths of an inch deep, three-eighths of an inch in diameter at the top or broadest part, hard and wood-like in texture, somewhat urn-shaped, with four or five horn-like points at the top. Three hundred and twenty-five of these fruits are contained in an ounce; and they are generally sold and recognized as the seeds. They are, however, really the fruit, — six or eight of the true seeds being contained in each. They retain their germinative powers five years.

Propagation and Culture. — It is always raised from seed, which may be sown in the open ground from April to July. Make the drills three feet apart, and an inch and a half or two inches deep; and sow the seed thinly, or so as to secure a plant for each foot of row. In five or six weeks from the planting, the branches will have grown sufficiently to allow the gathering of the leaves for use. They grow vigorously, and in good soil will extend, before the end of the season, three feet in each direction.

Gathering. — The leaves, which are the parts of the plant used, are gathered as they are developed, leaving the ends of the young shoots uninjured. If not cut to excess, the plants will yield abundantly till destroyed by frost. No one of the family of spinaceous plants is more easily raised, and few, if any, are more productive.

Use. — It is cooked and served in the same manner as Common Spinach.

There are no described varieties.

SPINACH.

Spinacia oleracea.

Spinach is a hardy annual, of Asiatic origin. When in flower, the plant is from two to three feet in height. The fertile and barren flowers are produced on separate plants, — the former in groups, close to the stalk at every joint; the latter in long, terminal bunches, or clusters.

The seeds vary in a remarkable degree in their form and general appearance, — those of some of the kinds being round and smooth, while others are angular and prickly: they retain their vitality five years. An ounce contains twenty-four hundred of the prickly seeds, and twenty-seven hundred of the round or smooth.

Soil and Cultivation. — Spinach is best developed, and most tender and succulent, when grown in rich soil. For the winter sorts, the soil can hardly be made too rich.

It is always raised from seeds, which are sown in drills twelve or fourteen inches apart, and three-fourths of an inch in depth. For a succession, a few seeds of the summer varieties may be sown, at intervals of a fortnight, from April till August.

Taking the Crop. — "When the leaves are two or three inches broad, they will be fit for gathering. This is done either by cutting them up with a knife wholly to the bottom, drawing and clearing them out by the root, or only cropping the large outer leaves, — the root and heart remaining to shoot out again. Either method can be adopted, according to the season or other circumstances." — *Rogers.*

Use. — The leaves and young stems are the only parts

of the plant used. They are often boiled and served alone; and sometimes, with the addition of sorrel-leaves, are used in soups, and eaten with almost every description of meat. Of itself, Spinach affords little nourishment. It should be boiled without the addition of water, beyond what hangs to the leaves in rinsing them; and, when cooked, the moisture which naturally comes from the leaves should be pressed out before being sent to the table. The young leaves were at one period used as a salad. — *McInt.*

Varieties: —

Flanders Spinach. *Trans.* — This is a winter Spinach, and is considered superior to the Prickly or Common Winter Spinach, which is in general cultivation during the winter season in our gardens. It is equally hardy, perhaps hardier.

The lower leaves measure from twelve to fourteen inches in length, and from six to eight in breadth. They are not only larger, but thicker and more succulent, than those of the Prickly Spinach. The whole plant grows more bushy, and produces a greater number of leaves from each root; and it is sometimes later in running to seed. The seeds are like those of the Round or Summer Spinach, but larger: they are destitute of the prickles which distinguish the seeds of the Common Winter Spinach.

For winter use, sow at the time directed for sowing the Large Prickly-seeded, but allow more space between the rows than for that variety: subsequent culture, and treatment during the winter, the same as for the Prickly-seeded.

Large Prickly-seeded Spinach. LARGE WINTER SPINACH. — Leaves large, rounded at the ends, thick and succulent. In foliage and general character, it is similar to some of the round-seeded varieties, but is much hardier, and slower in running to seed.

It is commonly known as "Winter Spinach," and principally cultivated for use during this portion of the year. The seeds are planted towards the last of August, in drills a foot apart, and nearly an inch in depth. When well up, the plants should be thinned to four or five inches apart in the drills; and, if the weather is favorable, they will be stocky and vigorous at the approach of severe weather. Before the closing-up of the ground, lay strips of joist, or other like material, between the rows, cover all over with clean straw, and keep the bed thus protected until the approach of spring, or the crop has been gathered for use.

Lettuce-leaved Spinach. Leaves large, on short stems, rounded, deep-green, with a bluish tinge. The variety is neither so early nor so hardy as some others; but it is slow in the development of its flower-stalk, and there are few kinds more productive or of better quality. The seeds are round and smooth. For a succession, a sowing should be made at intervals of two weeks.

Sorrel-leaved Spinach. Leaves of medium size, halberd-formed, deep-green, thick, and fleshy. A hardy and productive sort, similar to the Yellow or White Sorrel-leaved, but differing in the deeper color of its stalks and leaves.

Summer or Round-leaved Spinach. Round Dutch. Leaves large, thick, and fleshy, rounded at the ends, and entire, or nearly entire, on the borders.

This variety is generally grown for summer use; but it soon runs to seed, particularly in warm and dry weather. Where a constant supply is required, a sowing should be made every fortnight, commencing as early in spring as the frost leaves the ground. The seeds are round and smooth. Plants from the first sowing will be ready for use the last of May, or early in June.

Leaves seven or eight inches long, halberd-shaped, deep green, thin in texture, and nearly erect on the stalk of the plant; seeds prickly. *Winter or Common Prickly Spinach.*

From this variety, most of the improved kinds of Prickly Spinach have been obtained; and the Common Winter, or Prickly-seeded, is now considered scarcely worthy of cultivation.

The leaves of this variety are similar in form and appearance to those of the Garden Sorrel. They are of medium size, entire on the border, yellowish-white at the base, greener at the tips, and blistered on the surface. *Yellow Sorrel-leaved Spinach. White Sorrel-Leaved Spinach.*

New. Represented as being hardy, productive, slow in the development of its flower-stalk, and of good quality.

ORACH.

Arrach. — French Spinach. — Mountain Spinach. — Atriplex hortensis.

Orach is a hardy annual plant, with an erect, branching stem, from three to four feet in height. The leaves are variously shaped, thin in texture, and slightly acid to the taste. The seeds are small, black, and surrounded by a thin, pale-yellow membrane: their vitality is retained three years.

Sowing and Culture. — The seeds are sown in drills eighteen inches apart, and three-fourths of an inch in depth; the plants afterwards being thinned to twelve inches apart in the drills. It requires high culture: when grown in dry, arid soil, it is nearly worthless.

Use. — Orach is rarely found in the vegetable gardens of this country. The leaves have a pleasant, slightly acid taste, and, with the tender stalks, are used boiled in the same manner as Spinach or Sorrel, and are often mixed with the latter to reduce the acidity.

A few plants will afford an abundant supply.

Varieties : —

Green Orach. The leaves of this variety are of a dark
Trans. grass-green color, slightly toothed, and bluntly pointed; the stalk of the plant and the leaf-stems are strong and sturdy, and of the same color as the leaves. It is the lowest growing of all the varieties.

Lurid Orach. Leaves pale purple, tinged with dark green;
Trans. the stalk of the plant and the stems of the
PALE-RED ORACH. leaves are bright red, slightly streaked with white; height three feet and upwards.

Purple Orach. Plant from three to four feet in height;
Trans. leaves dull, dark purple, more wrinkled and more deeply toothed than those of any other variety. The stalk of the plant and the stems of the leaves are deep red, and slightly furrowed. The leaves change to green when boiled.

Red Orach. Upper surface of the leaf very dark, inclin-
Trans. ing to a dingy purple: the under surface is of a much brighter color. The stems are deep red; height three feet and upwards.

This is an earlier but a less vigorous sort than the White. The leaves of this variety, as also those of most of the colored sorts, change to green in boiling.

White Orach. Leaves pale-green or yellowish-green, much
Trans. wrinkled: the stalk of the plant and the stems of the leaves are of the same color as the foliage. It is of low growth.

CHAPTER VII.

CORN.

Zea mays.

GARDEN AND TABLE VARIETIES.

A DISTINCT and well-marked table variety. Ears seven to eight inches in length, two inches in diameter, twelve or fourteen rowed, and rather abruptly contracted at the tips; kernel white, rounded, somewhat deeper than broad, and indented at the exterior end, which is whiter and less transparent than the interior or opposite extremity. The depth and solidity of the kernel give great comparative weight to the ear; and, as the cob is of small size, the proportion of product is unusually large.

<small>Adams's Early White.</small>

In its general appearance, the ear is not unlike some descriptions of Southern or Western field-corn, from which, aside from its smaller dimensions, it would hardly be distinguishable. In quality it cannot be considered equal to some of the shrivelled-kernelled, sweet descriptions, but will prove acceptable to those to whom the peculiar sugary character of these may be objectionable. It is a good garden variety, though not so early as the Jefferson or Darling's Early.

Much grown for the market in the Middle States, but less generally known or cultivated in New England.

Plant, in height and general habit, similar to Darling's Early; ears six to eight inches in length, uniformly eight-rowed; kernels

<small>Black Sweet, or Mexican. SLATE SWEET.</small>

roundish, flattened, deep slate-color, much shrivelled at maturity. Early.

The variety is sweet, tender, and well flavored, remains a long period in condition for use, and, aside from its peculiar color (which by some is considered objectionable), is well worthy of cultivation.

Burr's Improved.
Burr's Sweet.
An improved variety of the Twelve-rowed Sweet. The ears are from twelve to sixteen rowed, rarely eighteen, and, in good soils and seasons, often measure eight or ten inches in length, nearly three inches in diameter, and weigh, when in condition for the table, from eighteen to twenty-two ounces; cob white; kernel rounded, flattened, pure white at first, or while suitable for use, — becoming wrinkled, and changing to dull, yellowish, semi-transparent white, when ripe.

The variety is hardy and productive, and, though not early, usually perfects its crop. For use in its green state, plantings may be made to the 20th of June.

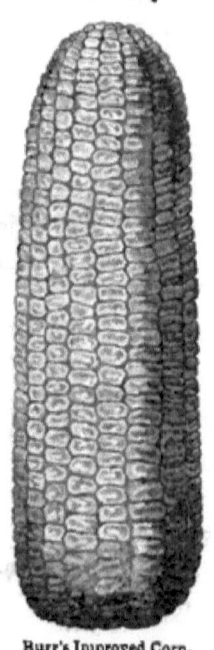

Burr's Improved Corn.

The kernel is tender, remarkably sugary, hardens slowly, is thin-skinned, and generally considered much superior to the Common Twelve-rowed.

It is always dried or ripened for seed with much difficulty; often moulding or decaying before the glazing, or hardening, of the kernel takes place. If in the milk, or still soft and tender, at the approach of freezing weather, it should be gathered, and suspended, after being husked, in a dry and airy room or building, taking care to keep the ears entirely separate from each other.

GARDEN AND TABLE VARIETIES. 163

Stalk five feet in height, and of slender habit; the ears are from six to eight inches in length, an inch and a half in diameter, and, when the variety is unmixed, uniformly eight-rowed; the kernels are roundish, flattened, pure white, when suitable for boiling, — much shrivelled or wrinkled, and of a dull, semi-transparent yellow, when ripe; the cob is white.

*Darling's Early.
DARLING'S EARLY SWEET.

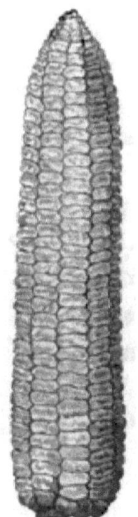

Darling's Early Corn.

The variety is early, tender, and sugary, yields well, produces little fodder, ears near the ground, and is one of the best sorts for planting for early use, as it seldom, if ever, fails to perfect its crop. In the Middle States, and in the milder sections of New England, it may be planted for boiling until near the beginning of July.

Early Dwarf Sugar.
EXTRA EARLY DWARF.

Plant three or four feet high, and very slender; the ears, of which from one to three are produced on a stalk, are put forth near the ground, and are eight-rowed, — they are six inches long, and in their general form resemble Darling's Early, though of smaller size; the kernels are white before maturity, dull yellowish-white and much shrivelled when ripe.

Like Darling's Early, it is a valuable sort for early use, and also for planting for a succession. The kernel is sweet and tender, and, with others of the class known as " Sugar " varieties, is slow in ripening, and thus for a long season continues in good condition for table use.

Early Jefferson.

Stalk five to six feet high, producing one or two ears, which are of small size, eight-rowed, and measure six or eight inches in length, and an inch and a half in diameter at the largest part; cob white; kernel white, roundish, flattened, — the surface of a portion of the ear, especially near its tip, often tinged with a delicate shade of rose-red. The kernel retains its color, and never shrivels or wrinkles in ripening.

The variety is hardy and productive, but is principally cultivated on account of its early maturity; though, in this respect, it is little, if at all, in advance of Darling's. The quality is tender and good, but much less sugary than the common shrivelled varieties; on which account, however, it is preferred by some palates. It remains but a short time tender, and in good condition for boiling, soon becoming hard, glazed, and unfit for use.

Golden Sweet.
GOLDEN SUGAR.
Stalk and general habit similar to Darling's Early; ears six to eight inches long, an inch and a half or an inch and three-fourths in diameter, regularly eight-rowed; the kernel, when ripe, is semi-transparent yellow.

The variety is apparently a hybrid between the Common Yellow, or Canada Corn, and Darling's Early. In flavor, as well as appearance, both of these varieties are recognized. It does not run excessively to stalk and foliage, yields well, is hardy, and seldom fails to ripen perfectly in all sections of New England. For boiling in its green state, plantings may be made until the last week of June, or first of July.

Mammoth Eight-rowed Sugar.
Stalk from six to seven feet high, producing one or two ears, which are uniformly eight-rowed, and measure ten or twelve inches in length; the kernel is broader than deep, pure white when fit for boiling, and yellowish-white and shrivelled when ripe; the cob is white.

Narraganset.
Am. Agr.
With Figure.
The plants of this variety are of slender habit, and produce but little forage. The ears, which are put forth low on the stalk,

are eight or ten rowed, and quite small, seldom measuring more than five inches in length; the kernel is large, and, like other Sugar varieties, shrivelled or wrinkled at maturity; the cob is red.

It is tender, and of excellent quality, and, as a first early, is recommended for cultivation. It is also a good sort for a succession, for which a planting should be made at intervals of two weeks until the last of June. In warm and light soil, it not only thrives better, but is much earlier, than when grown in soil naturally strong or highly enriched. The hills should be two feet and a half apart.

Narraganset Corn.

Old Colony.
Hov. Mag.

This variety was originated by the late Rev. A. R. Pope, of Somerville, Mass. At the time of its production, he was a resident of Kingston, Plymouth County, Mass.; and, in consequence of the locality of its origin, it received the name above given. Mr. Pope describes it as follows: —

"It is a hybrid, as any one can readily perceive by inspection, between the Southern White and the Common Sweet Corn of New England, and exhibits certain characteristics of the two varieties, combining the size of the ear and kernel and productiveness of the Southern with the sweetness and tenderness of the Northern parent."

The stalks are from ten to twelve feet in height, and of corresponding circumference. The ears are from five to seven inches in length, and the number of rows varies from twelve to twenty; the kernels are very long, or deep; and the cob, which is always white, is quite small compared with the size of the ear. When ripe, the kernels are of a dull, semi-transparent, yellowish-white, and much shrivelled. The ears are produced on the stalk, four or five feet from the ground. Very productive, but late.

For cultivation in the Southern States and tropical climates it has been found to be peculiarly adapted, as it not only possesses there the sweetness and excellence that distinguish the Sweet Corn of the temperate and cooler sections, but does not deteriorate by long cultivation, as other sweet varieties almost invariably are found to do.

Parching Corn (White Kernel).
Pop-Corn.
Stalk six feet high, usually producing two ears, which are from six to eight inches long, quite slender, and uniformly eight-rowed; cob white; kernel roundish, flattened, glossy, flinty, or rice-like, and of a dull, semi-transparent, white color. When parched, it is of pure snowy whiteness, very brittle, tender, and well flavored, and generally considered the best of all the sorts used for this purpose.

In many parts of New England, the variety is somewhat extensively cultivated for commercial purposes. Its peculiar properties seem to be most perfectly developed in dry, gravelly, or silicious soils, and under the influence of short and warm seasons. In field culture, it is either planted in hills three feet apart, or in drills three feet apart, and eighteen inches apart in the drills. The product per acre is usually about the same number of bushels of ears that the same land would yield of shelled corn of the ordinary field varieties.

Increase of size is a sure indication of deterioration. The cultivator should aim to keep the variety as pure as possible by selecting slender and small-sized but well-filled ears for seed, and in no case to plant such as may have yellow or any foreign sort intermixed. The value of a crop will be diminished nearly in a relative proportion to the increase of the size of the ears.

Parching Corn (Yellow).
A Yellow variety of the preceding. It retains its color to some extent after being parched; and this is considered an objection. It is tender,

GARDEN AND TABLE VARIETIES. 167

but not so mild flavored as the White, and is little cultivated. The size and form of the ears are the same, and it is equally productive.

Red-cob Sweet. — Ears about eight inches in length by a diameter of two inches, — usually twelve, but sometimes fourteen, rowed; kernels roundish, flattened, white when suitable for boiling, — shrivelled, and of a dull, semi-transparent white, when ripe; the cob is red, which may be called its distinguishing characteristic. Quality good, the kernel being tender and sweet. It remains long in good condition for the table, and is recommended for general cultivation. Season intermediate.

Rhode-Island Asylum.
Am. Agr.
With Figure.

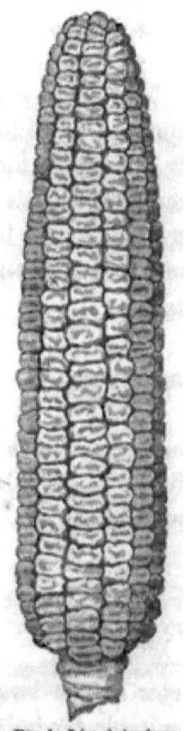

Rhode-Island Asylum Corn.

So named from its origin on the grounds of this institution. The plant is of medium size, producing one or two ears; foliage abundant; the ears are rather large, and eight or ten rowed; kernel yellowish-white at maturity, shrivelled and indented.

The variety is not early, but is recommended for productiveness, and for the tender, sugary character of the kernel.

Like most of the later and larger descriptions of sugar-corn, the plants attain a greater size, the ears are more fully developed, and the sweet, succulent character of the kernel is greatly increased, when grown in soil under a high state of cultivation.

A sub-variety occurs with eight rows, the form and size of the ear and kernel resembling Darling's Early.

Rice (Red Kernel). — This is a variety of the White Rice, with deep purplish-red or blood-red kernels. The ears are of the same size and form. Its quality, though inferior to the White, is much superior to the Yellow. Productiveness, and season of maturity, the same. The varieties of Rice Corn rapidly intermix, and rapidly degenerate, especially when grown in the vicinity of common field corn.

Rice (White Kernel). Stalk six feet or more in height; ears five or six inches long, an inch and a half in diameter, broadest at the base, and tapering to the top, which is often more or less sharply pointed; the cob is white; the kernels are long and slender, angular, sharply pointed at the outward extremity, as well as, to some extent, at the opposite, and extremely hard and flinty. They are not formed at right angles on the cob, as in most varieties of corn, but point upward, and rest, in an imbricated manner, one over the other.

The variety is hardy and prolific, and, though not late, should have the benefit of the whole season. For parching, it is inferior to the common Parching Corn before described, though it yields as much bulk in proportion to the size of the kernel, and is equally as white; but the sharp points often remain sound; and it is, consequently, less crisp and tender.

Rice (Yellow Kernel). Another sub-variety of the White Rice, the ear and kernel being of the same form and size. It is equally productive, and matures as early, but, when parched, is inferior to the White both in crispness and flavor.

Stowell's Evergreen.
STOWELL'S EVERGREEN SWEET. Stalk from six to seven feet in height; ears of a conical form, six or seven inches long, and two inches and a quarter in diameter at the base; kernels long, or deep, pure white when suitable for boiling, — of a dull yellowish-white, and much

shrivelled, when ripe; cob white, and, in consequence of the depth of the kernels, small in comparison to the diameter of the ear.

The variety is intermediate in its season, and if planted at the same time with Darling's, or equally early kinds, will keep the table supplied till October. It is hardy and productive, very tender and sugary, and, as implied by the name, remains a long period in a fresh condition, and suitable for boiling.

Tuscarora.
Turkey Wheat.

Tuscarora Corn.

Plant five to six feet in height, moderately strong and vigorous; ears eight-rowed, and of remarkable size,—exceeding in this respect almost every sort used for the table in the green state. In good soil, they are often a foot and upwards in length, and from two inches and three-fourths to three inches in diameter at the base. The kernel, which is much larger than that of any other table variety, is pure white, rounded, flattened, and, when divided in the direction of its width, apparently filled with fine flour of snowy whiteness; the cob is red, and of medium size.

In point of maturity, the Tuscarora is an intermediate variety. In its green state it is of fair quality, and considered a valuable sort by those to whom the sweetness of the Sugar varieties is objectionable. In their ripened state, the kernels, to a great extent, retain their fresh and full appearance, not shrivelling in the manner of the Sugar sorts, though often indented at the ends, like some of the Southern Horse-toothed field varieties.

When ground, in the ripe state, it is much less farinaceous, and valuable for cooking, or feeding stock, than the fine, white, floury appearance of the kernel, when cut or broken, would seem to indicate.

Twelve-rowed Sweet. A large, late variety. Stalk seven feet high; the ears are from ten to fourteen rowed, seven to nine inches long, often two inches and a half in diameter in the green state, and taper slightly towards the top, which is bluntly rounded; cob white; the kernels are large, round, or circular, sometimes tooth-shaped, pure white when suitable for the table, dull white and shrivelled when ripe.

The variety is hardy, yields a certain crop, and is sweet, tender, and of good quality. It is the parent of one or two varieties of superior size and excellence, to which it is now gradually giving place.

Field Varieties.

Canada Yellow.
Early Canada. Ear seven inches in length, symmetrical, broadest at the base, and tapering to the tip, uniformly eight-rowed, in four double rows; kernel roundish, smooth, and of a rich, glossy, orange-yellow color; cob small, white; stalk four to five feet high, slender; the leaves are not abundant, and the ears, of which the plant rarely produces more than two, near the ground.

On account of the small size of the ear, the yield per acre is much less than that of almost any other field variety; twenty-five or thirty bushels being an average crop. The dwarfish character of the plants, however, admits of close culture, — three feet in one direction by two or two and a half in the opposite affording ample space for their full development; four plants being allowed to a hill.

Its chief merit is its early maturity. In ordinary seasons, the crop will be fully ripened in August. If cultivated for a series of years in the Eastern or Middle States, or in a latitude much warmer than that of the Canadas, the plant increases in size, the ears and kernels grow larger, and it is slower in coming to maturity.

Ears nine or ten inches long, broadest at the base, tapering slightly towards the tip, ten or twelve rowed, and rarely found with the broad clefts or longitudinal spaces which often mark the divisions into double rows in the eight-rowed varieties, — the outline being almost invariably smooth and regular; kernel as broad as deep, smooth, and of a rich, clear, glossy, yellow color; cob large, white; stalk of medium height and strength, producing one or two ears.

Dutton.
EARLY DUTTON.

Dutton Corn.

It is one of the handsomest of the field varieties, nearly as early as the King Philip, and remarkable for the uniformly perfect manner in which, in good seasons, the ears are tipped out, or filled out. In point of productiveness, it compares favorably with the common New-England Eight-rowed; the yield per acre varying from fifty to seventy bushels, according to soil, culture, and season.

It is also much prized for mealing, both on account of its quality, and its peculiar, bright, rich color. In cultivation, the hills are made three feet and a half apart in each direction, and five or six plants allowed to a hill.

A sub-variety, known as the Early Dutton, is common to many localities. The ears are ten or twelve rowed, well filled at the tips, and the kernel has the bright color of the common Dutton. The plant, however, is less stocky, the ears are smaller, and the yield, particularly in strong soil, generally less. On light land, it succeeds better than the old variety, — compared with which, it is also about two weeks earlier.

Hill Corn.

Hill.
WHITMAN. WHITMAN'S IMPROVED.
WEBSTER. SMUTTY WHITE. OLD-COLONY PREMIUM.

Stalk six feet or more in height, moderately strong at the ground, but slender above the ear; foliage not abundant; the ears are produced low on the stalk, often in pairs, are uniformly eight-rowed, well filled at the tips, and, when fully grown, ten or eleven inches in length; cob white and small; kernel dusky, transparent-white, large and broad, but not deep.

The Hill Corn is nearly of the season of the common New-England Eight-rowed, and is, unquestionably, the most productive of all field varieties. In Plymouth County, Mass., numerous crops have been raised of a hundred and fifteen bushels and upwards to the acre; and, in two instances, the product exceeded a hundred and forty.

This extraordinary yield is in a degree attributable to the small size of the plant and the relative large size of the ear. The largest crops were obtained by planting three kernels together, in rows three feet asunder, and from fifteen to eighteen inches apart in the rows.

No variety is better adapted for cultivation for farm consumption; but for market, whether in the kernel or in the form of meal, its dull-white color is unattractive; and it commands a less price than the Yellow descriptions.

From the most reliable authority, the variety was originated by Mr. Leonard Hill, of East Bridgewater, Plymouth County, Mass.; and was introduced to public notice in 1825-6. Though at present almost universally known as "The Whitman," it appears to have been originally recog-

FIELD VARIETIES.

nized as "The Hill;" and, of the numerous names by which it has since been called, this is, unquestionably, the only legitimate one.

Illinois Yellow. Western Yellow.

Stalk ten feet or more high; foliage abundant; ears high on the stalk, single or in pairs, twelve to sixteen rowed, eleven to thirteen inches long, broadest at the base, and tapering gradually towards the tip, which is bluntly rounded; kernel bright yellow, long and narrow, or tooth-formed, paler at the outer end, but not indented; cob white.

The variety ripens perfectly in the Middle States, but is not suited to the climate of New England.

Illinois White. Western White.

Similar in its general character to the Illinois Yellow. Kernel rice-white; cob generally white, but sometimes red.

King Philip, or Brown. Improved King Philip.

Ears ten to twelve inches in length, uniformly eight-rowed when the variety is pure or unmixed; kernel copper-red, rather large, somewhat broader than deep, smooth and glossy; cob small, pinkish-white; stalk six feet in height, producing one or two ears, about two feet and a half from the ground.

In warm seasons, it is sometimes fully ripened in ninety days from the time of planting, and may be considered as a week or ten days earlier than the Common New-England Eight-rowed, of which it is apparently an improved variety.

King Philip Corn.

Very productive, and recommended as one of the best field sorts now in cultivation. In good soil and favorable seasons, the yield per acre is from seventy-five to ninety bushels, although crops are recorded of a hundred and ten, and even of a hundred and twenty bushels.

As grown in different localities, and even in the product of the same field, there is often a marked variation in the depth of color, arising either from the selection of paler seed, or from the natural tendency of the variety towards the clear yellow of the New-England Eight-rowed. A change of color from yellowish-red to paler red or yellow should be regarded as indicative of degeneracy.

Said to have originated on one of the islands in Lake Winnipiseogee, N.H.

New-England Eight-rowed. Stalk six or seven feet high, producing one or two ears, which are from ten to eleven inches long, and uniformly eight-rowed; kernel broader than deep, bright yellow, smooth, and glossy; cob small, white.

The variety is generally grown in hills three feet and a half apart in each direction, and five or six plants allowed to a hill, the yield varying from fifty to seventy bushels to the acre, according to season, soil, and cultivation. It is a few days later than the King Philip, but ripens perfectly in the Middle States and throughout New England, except, perhaps, at the extreme northern boundary, where the Canada Yellow would probably succeed better.

It often occurs with a profuse intermixture of red, sometimes streaked and spotted, sometimes copper-red, like the King Philip, and occasionally of a rich, bright, clear blood-red. As the presence of this color impairs its value for marketing, and particularly for mealing, more care should be exercised in the selection of ears for seed; and this, continued for a few seasons, will restore it to the clear yellow of the Dutton, or Early Canada.

Many local sub-varieties occur, the result of selection and cultivation, differing in the size and form of the ear, size, form, and color of the kernel, and also in the season of maturity. The Dutton, Early Canada, King Philip, and numerous other less important sorts, are but improved forms of the New-England Eight-rowed.

White Horse-tooth. SOUTHERN WHITE. Stalk twelve feet or more in height, with large, luxuriant foliage; ears single, often in pairs, short and very thick, sixteen to twenty-two rowed; kernel remarkably large, milk-white, wedge-formed, indented at the outer end; cob red.

Yellow Horse-tooth. SOUTHERN YELLOW. Plant similar to that of the White Horse-tooth; kernel very large, bright yellow, indented; cob red.

Extensively cultivated throughout the Southern States, but not adapted to the climate of the Middle or Northern. Other varieties of the Horse-tooth Corn occur, differing principally in color. One of these is of the copper-red peculiar to the King Philip; and there is also a variety with the bright blood-red, found occasionally in the New-England Eight-rowed.

Baden. An improved variety of the White Gourd-seed. The plant often produces five or six, and sometimes seven or eight ears.

Long White Flint. Ears frequently fourteen inches in length, very slender, and uniformly eight-rowed; kernel nearly as deep as broad, rice white; cob white.

Succeeds well in the Middle States, but not suited for cultivation at the North.

White Gourd-seed. Stalk ten feet and upwards in height; foliage abundant; ears short and thick, containing from eighteen to thirty-two rows; kernal long and narrow, indented at the end.

The variety is not adapted to the climate of New England, or the cooler portions of the Middle States; but under the long, warm seasons of the Southern States, it is grown in great perfection, and yields abundantly.

White Flint. Ear of the size and form of the Yellow or Golden Flint; kernel small, rice-white; cob large, white.

Yellow, or Golden Flint. Ears ten to twelve inches long, and ten or twelve rowed; kernel small, bright glossy yellow; cob large, white.

The plant is a strong grower, and the variety is quite productive, but requires a strong soil, and a long, warm season, for its full perfection.

CHAPTER VIII.

SALAD PLANTS.

Celery. — Celeriac, or Turnip-rooted Celery. — Chiccory, or Succory. — Cress, or Peppergrass. — Endive. — Horse-radish. — Lettuce. — Mustard.

CELERY.

Smallage.—Apium graveolens.

CELERY, or SMALLAGE, is a hardy, umbelliferous biennial. The plant flowers the second year, and then measures from two to three feet in height; the seeds are small, somewhat triangular, of a yellowish-brown color, aromatic when bruised, and of a warm, pleasant flavor. They are said to retain their germinative powers ten years, but by seedmen are not considered reliable when more than five years old. An ounce contains nearly seventy thousand seeds.

Soil. — Any good garden soil, in a fair state of cultivation, is adapted to the growth of Celery.

Propagation. — It is always propagated by seed, a fourth of an ounce of which is sufficient for a seed-bed five feet wide and ten feet long. The first sowing is usually made in a hot-bed in March; and it may be sown in the open ground in April or May, but, when so treated, vegetates slowly, often remaining in the earth several weeks before it comes up.

Sufficient plants for any family may be started in a large

flower-pot or two, placed in the sitting-room, giving them plenty of light and moisture.

Cultivation.— As soon as the young plants are three inches high, prepare a small bed in the open air, and make the ground rich and the earth fine. Here set out the plants for a temporary growth, placing them four inches apart. This should be done carefully; and they should be gently watered once, and protected for a day or two against the sun. A bed ten feet long and four feet wide will contain three hundred and sixty plants.

Corbett directs that the plants should remain in this nursery-bed till the beginning or middle of July, when they should be removed into trenches. Make the trenches a foot or fifteen inches deep, a foot wide, and not less than five feet apart; and lay the earth into the middle of the space between the trenches, so that it may not be washed into them by heavy rains; for it will, in such case, materially injure the crop by covering the hearts of the plants. At the bottom of the trench, put some good, rich, but well-digested compost manure; for, if too fresh, the Celery will be rank and pipy, or hollow, and will not keep nearly so long or so well. Dig this manure in, and make the earth fine and light; then take up the plants from the temporary bed, and set them out carefully in the bottom of the trenches, six or eight inches apart.

Blanching. — "When the plants begin to grow (which they will quickly do), hoe on each side and between them with a small hoe. As they grow up, earth their stems; that is, put the earth up against them, but not too much at a time, and always when the plants are dry; and let the earth put up be finely broken, and not at all cloddy. While this is being done, keep the stalks of the outside leaves close up, to prevent the earth getting between the stems of the outside leaves and inner ones; for, if it gets there, it checks the plant, and makes the Celery bad. When the earthing is commenced, take first the edges of the trenches, working backwards, time after time, till the earth is reached that was taken from the trenches; and by this time the earth against the plants will be above the level of the land. Then take the earth out of the middle, till at last the earth against the plants forms a ridge, and the middle of each interval a sort of gutter. Earth up very often, not putting up much at a time, every week a little; and by the last of September, or beginning of October, it will be blanched sufficiently for use."

Some allow the plants to make a natural growth, and earth up at once, about three weeks before being required for use. When so treated, the stalks are of remarkable whiteness, crisp, tender, and less liable to russet-brown spots than when the plants are blanched by the more common method.

Taking the Crop.— Before the closing-up of the ground, the principal part of the crop should be carefully taken up (retaining the roots, and soil naturally adhering), and removed to the cellar, where they should be packed in moderately moist earth or sand, without covering the ends of the leaves.

A portion may be allowed to remain in the open ground; but the hearts of the plants must be protected from wet weather. This may be done by placing boards lengthwise, in the form of a roof, over the ridges. As soon as the frost leaves the ground in spring, or at any time during the winter when the weather will admit, Celery may be taken for use directly from the garden.

Use.— The stems of the leaves are the parts of the plant used. These, after being blanched, are exceedingly crisp and tender, with an agreeable and peculiarly aromatic flavor. They are sometimes employed in soups, but are more generally served crude, with the addition of oil, mustard, and vinegar, or with salt only. The seeds have the taste and odor of the stems of the leaves, and are often used in their stead for flavoring soups.

With perhaps the exception of Lettuce, Celery is more generally used in this country than any other salad plant. It succeeds well throughout the Northern and Middle States, and, in the vicinity of some of our large cities, is produced of remarkable size and excellence.

Varieties. —

Boston-market Celery. A medium-sized, white variety; hardy, crisp, succulent, and mild flavored. Compared with the White Solid, the stalks are more numerous, shorter, not so thick, and much finer in texture. It blanches quickly, and is recommended for its hardiness and crispness, — the stalks rarely becoming stringy or fibrous, even at an advanced stage of growth. Much grown by market-gardeners in the vicinity of Boston, Mass.

Cole's Superb Red. *McInt.* This is a new sort, of much excellence, and of remarkable solidity. It is of medium size, and well adapted for cultivation in the kitchen-garden and for family use, but not so well suited for marketing or for exhibition purposes. It has the valuable property of not piping, or becoming hollow or stringy, and remains long without running to seed. The leaf-stalks are of a fine purple color, tender, crisp, and fine flavored. A well-grown plant will weigh six pounds.

Cole's Superb White. Much like Cole's Superb Red; differing little, except in color. It is an excellent sort, hardy, runs late to seed, and is one of the best of the White varieties. Stalks short and thick.

Early Dwarf Solid White. *Thomp.* Rather dwarf, but thick-stemmed. The heart is remarkably full; the leaf-stalk solid, blanching promptly. There is, in fact, much more blanched substance in a plant of this variety than in one of the tall sorts; and the quality is excellent. It comes into use early, and is one of the hardiest of the White varieties.

This is considered the largest variety yet produced: specimens have been grown in England of the extraordinary weight of eight or ten pounds, and at the same time perfectly solid. Color bright red; flavor excellent.

Laing's Improved Mammoth Red Celery.

This variety scarcely differs from the Red Solid. It has, however, a coarser habit, with a somewhat rounder stalk; and, this being the case, the heart is not so compact. It is grown largely for marketing, and is excellent for soups and stewing.

Manchester Red Celery. *Thomp.* MANCHESTER RED GIANT.

The plant grows to a large size, full-hearted, with a thick stem. Leaf-stalks thick, deeply furrowed, and remarkably solid, of a dark red or purplish hue where exposed, and rose-colored where partially blanched; but the perfectly blanched portion is pure white, more so than the blanched part of the White varieties of Celery. It is also crisp, of excellent flavor, and unquestionably the best variety of Red Celery.

Red Solid. *Thomp.* NEW LARGE RED, NEW LARGE PURPLE. TOURS PURPLE.

A large, vigorous-growing variety; in good soils, often attaining a height of nearly three feet. The stalks are solid; flat at the base, where they overlap, and form a compact, crisp, and, with ordinary care, a well-blanched heart of excellent quality. It succeeds best, as most other sorts do, in rich, moist soil; and when so grown, and properly blanched, will yield a large proportion of Celery, of a pure white color, and of excellent quality.

Seymour's Superb White. *Thomp.* SEYMOUR'S SUPERB WHITE SOLID.

It is one of the best sorts for extensive culture for the markets, as it is also one of the best varieties for small gardens for family use. It blanches readily, and, with little care, will supply the table from the last of September through most of the winter.

Seymour's White Champion. A variety represented as being superior to Seymour's Superb White. The stalks are broad, flat at the base, and form a compact, well-blanched, crisp heart.

Shepherd's Red. *Thomp.*
SHEPHERD'S GIANT RED. Much like the Manchester Red, but has flatter stems; consequently it is more compact, and blanches sooner and more perfectly, than that variety; to which, for these reasons, it is preferred by growers for competition.

Turkey or Prussian Celery.
GIANT WHITE. TURKISH GIANT SOLID. A remarkably large variety, resembling the Common White Solid. Leaf-stalks long, large, erect, fleshy, and solid; leaves large, with rounded serratures, and of a glossy green color.

It is one of the largest of the White sorts, and is considered superior to the Common White Solid.

Wall's White Celery. *Thomp.* An improved variety of the Italian, esteemed by growers for competition, where quantity, not quality, is the principal consideration.

White Lion's-paw Celery. *McInt.*
LION'S PAW. A short, broad, flat-stalked variety, of excellent quality; crisp and white. Its short, flat, spreading habit gave rise to its name.

White Solid. *Thomp.*
FINE WHITE SOLID. This variety is of strong and rather tall growth; the leaf-stalks are generally solid, but when grown in rich, highly manured soil, they sometimes become slightly hollow; the leaves are large,

smooth, and bright green; serratures large and obtuse. It blanches readily, is crisp, of excellent quality, and comes into use earlier than the Red sorts. It is generally cultivated in the Northern States, not only on account of its hardiness, but for its keeping qualities. As a market variety, it is one of the best.

CELERIAC, OR TURNIP-ROOTED CELERY.

This variety forms at the base of the leaves, near the surface of the ground, a brownish, irregular, rounded root, or tuber, measuring from three to four inches in diameter. The leaves are small, with slender, hollow stems. In favorable exposures and rich soil, the roots sometimes attain a weight of more than three pounds. It is much hardier than the common varieties of Celery.

Propagation. — It is propagated from seeds, which may be sown in the open ground in April or May, in shallow drills six or eight inches apart. As soon as the seedlings are three or four inches high, take them up, remove the small side-shoots, or suckers, and set the plants in rows eighteen inches or two feet apart, and a foot apart in the rows.

Subsequent Cultivation. — The growing crop will require no peculiar treatment. When the bulbs are two-thirds grown, they are earthed over for the purpose of blanching, and to render the flesh crisp and tender.

Taking the Crop. — Some of the bulbs will be ready for use in September; from which time, till the last of November, the table may be supplied directly from the garden. Before severe weather, the quantity required for winter should be drawn, packed in damp earth or sand, and stored in the cellar.

Use. — The root, or bulb, is the part of the plant eaten; the flesh of this is white and tender, with the flavor of the stalks of Common Celery, though generally less mild and delicate. Where the common varieties of Celery are grown or preserved with difficulty, this might be successfully cultivated, and afford a tolerable substitute. The bulbs are sometimes eaten boiled, and the leaves are occasionally used in soups.

Curled-leaved Celeriac. This is a variety of the Common Celeriac, or Turnip-rooted Celery; like which, it forms a sort of bulb, or knob, near the surface of the ground. It is, however, of smaller size, usually measuring about three inches in diameter. The skin is brown, and the flesh white and fine grained; leaves small, spreading, curled.

It is in no respect superior to the Common Turnip-rooted, and possesses little merit aside from the peculiarity of its foliage.

CHICCORY, OR SUCCORY.
Wild Endive. — Cichorium intybus.

A hardy, perennial plant, introduced into this country from Europe, and often abounding as a troublesome weed in pastures, lawns, and mowing-lands. The stem is erect, stout, and branching, and, in its native state, usually about three feet in height, — under cultivation, however, it sometimes attains a height of five or six feet; the flowers are large, of a fine blue color, and generally produced in pairs; the seeds somewhat resemble those of Endive, though ordinarily smaller, more glossy, and of a deeper brown color. They will keep ten years. The plants continue in blossom from July to September; and the seeds ripen from August to October, or until the plants are destroyed by frost.

Soil, Sowing, and Cultivation. — As the roots of Chiccory are long and tapering, it should be cultivated in rich, mellow soil, thoroughly stirred, either by the plough or spade, to the depth of ten or twelve inches. The seed should be sown in April or May, in drills fifteen inches apart, and three-fourths of an inch deep. When the young plants are two or three inches high, thin them to eight inches apart in the rows; and, during the summer, cultivate frequently, to keep the soil light, and the growing crop free from weeds.

Blanching. — Before using as a salad, the plants are blanched, either by covering with boxes a foot in depth, or by strips of boards twelve or fourteen inches wide, nailed together at right angles, and placed lengthwise over the rows. They are sometimes blanched by covering with earth, the leaves being first gathered together, and tied loosely at the top, which should be left exposed to the light.

Taking the Crop. — When the leaves are properly blanched, they will be of a delicate, creamy white; and, when they are a foot high, they will be ready for use. As soon as they are cut, the roots should be removed, and others brought forward to succeed them.

Use. — It is used as Endive, its flavor and properties being much the same. Though rarely grown in this country, it is common to the gardens of many parts of Europe, and is much esteemed. The blanched leaves are known as *Barbe de Capucin*, or "Friar's Beard."

Varieties: —

Improved Chiccory, or Succory.
Leaves larger than those of the Common Chiccory, and produced more compactly, forming a sort of head, or solid heart, like some of the Endives.

The plant is sometimes boiled and served in the manner of Spinach.

Variegated or Spotted Chiccory. *Vil.*
This is a variety of the preceding, distinguished by the color of the leaves, which are veined, and streaked with red. In blanching, the red is not changed, but retains its brilliancy; while the

green becomes nearly pure white, the two colors blending in rich contrast. In this state they form a beautiful as well as tender and well-flavored salad.

Large-rooted or Coffee Chiccory.
Turnip-Rooted Chiccory.
This variety is distinguished by its long, fleshy roots, which are sometimes fusiform, but generally much branched or divided: when well grown, they are twelve or fourteen inches in length, and about an inch in their largest diameter. The leaves have the form of those of the Common Chiccory, but are larger and more luxuriant.

Though the variety is generally cultivated for its roots, the leaves, when blanched, afford a salad even superior to some of the improved sorts before described.

Vilmorin mentions two sub-varieties of the Large-rooted or Coffee Chiccory; viz.:—

Brunswick Large-rooted. Roots shorter than those of the Magdeburg, but of greater diameter; leaves spreading.

Magdeburg Large-rooted. Roots long and large; leaves erect.

After several years' trial, preference was given to this variety, which proved the more productive.

Sowing and Cultivation. — For raising Coffee Chiccory, the ground should first be well enriched, and then deeply and thoroughly stirred by spading or ploughing. The seeds should be sown in April or May, in shallow drills a foot apart, and the young plants thinned to three or four inches apart in the rows. Hoe frequently; water, if the weather is dry; and in the autumn, when the roots have attained sufficient size, draw them for use. After being properly cleaned, cut them into small pieces, dry them thoroughly in a kiln or spent oven, and store for use or the market. After being roasted and ground, Chiccory is mixed with coffee in various proportions, and thus forms a pleasant beverage; or, if used alone, will be found a tolerable substitute for genuine coffee.

The roots of any of the before-described varieties may be used in the same manner, but as they are much smaller, and consequently less productive, are seldom cultivated for the purpose.

It is an article of considerable commercial importance, and large quantities are annually imported from the south of Europe to different seaports of the United States. As the plant is perfectly hardy, of easy culture, and quite productive, there appears to be no reason why the home demand for the article may not be supplied by home production. Of its perfect adaptedness to the soil and climate of almost any section of this country, there can scarcely be a doubt.

CRESS, OR PEPPERGRASS.

Lepidium sativum.

The Common Cress of the garden is a hardy annual, and a native of Persia. When in flower, the stem of the plant is smooth and branching, and about fifteen inches high. The flowers are white, small, and produced in groups, or bunches; the seeds are small, oblong, rounded, of a reddish-brown color, and of a peculiar, pungent odor. About fourteen thousand are contained in an ounce, and they retain their germinative properties five years.

Soil and Cultivation. — Cress will flourish in any common garden-soil, and is always best when grown early or late in the season. The seed vegetates quickly, and the plants grow rapidly. As they are milder and more tender while young, the seed should be sown in succession, at intervals of a fortnight; making the first sowing early in April. Rake the surface of the ground fine and smooth, and sow the seed rather thickly, in shallow drills six or eight inches apart. Half an ounce of seed will be sufficient for fifty feet of drill.

Use. — The leaves, while young, have a warm, pungent taste, and are eaten as a salad, either separately, or mixed with lettuce or other salad plants. The leaves should be cut or plucked before the plant has run to flower, as they then become acrid and unpalatable. The curled varieties are also used for garnishing.

Varieties : —

Broad-leaved Cress. A coarse variety, with broad, spatulate leaves. It is sometimes grown for feeding poultry, and is also used for soups; but it is less desirable as a salad than most of the other sorts.

Common or Plain-leaved Cress. This is the variety most generally cultivated. It has plain leaves, and consequently is not so desirable a sort for garnishing. As a salad kind, it is tender and delicate, and considered equal, if not superior, to the Curled varieties.

Curled Cress. GARNISHING CRESS. Leaves larger than those of the Common Plain variety, of a fine green color, and frilled and curled on the borders in the manner of some kinds of Parsley. It is used as a salad, and is also employed as a garnish.

It is very liable to degenerate by becoming gradually less curled. To keep the variety pure, select only the finest curled plants for seed.

Golden Cress. *Trans.* This variety is of slower growth than the Common Cress. The leaves are of a yellowish-green, flat, oblong, scalloped on the borders, sometimes entire, and of a much thinner texture than any of the varieties of the Common Cress. It is very dwarf, and is consequently short when cut as a salad herb for use. It has a mild and delicate flavor. When run to flower, it does not exceed eighteen inches in height.

It deserves more general cultivation, as affording a pleasant addition to the varieties of small salads.

The seeds are of a paler color, or more yellow, than those of the other sorts.

An excellent variety, introduced by Mr. Charles McIntosh, and described as being remarkable hardy, and therefore better adapted for sowing early in spring or late in summer. **Normandy Curled Cress.** *McInt.*

The leaves are finely cut and curled, and make not only a good salad, but a beautiful garnish.

It is difficult to procure the seed true; the **Common Curled** being, in general, substituted for it.

ENDIVE.

Chicorium endivia.

Endive is a hardy annual, and, when fully developed, is from four to six feet in height. The leaves are lobed and cut upon the borders; the flowers are usually of a blue color, and rest closely in the axils of the leaves; the seeds are small, long, angular, and of a grayish color; their germinative properties are retained for ten years. Nearly twenty-five thousand are contained in an ounce.

Soil. — All of the varieties thrive well in any good, mellow, garden soil. Where there is a choice of situations, select one in which the plants will be the least exposed to the effects of drought and heat.

Propagation. — The plants can be raised only from seed, which may be sown where the plants are to remain, or in close drills in a nursery-bed for transplanting. If sown where the plants are to remain, sow in shallow drills a foot apart for the smaller, curled varieties, and fifteen inches for the larger, broad-leaved sorts; afterwards thinning out the plants to a foot asunder in the rows.

If sown in a nursery-bed, transplant when the young plants have eight or ten leaves, setting them at the distances before directed.

The first sowing may be made as early in spring as the weather will permit; and a sowing may be made a month or six weeks after, for a succession: but as it is for use late in autumn, or during the winter and spring, that Endive is most required, the later sowings are the most important. These are usually made towards the end of July.

Blanching. — Before using, the plants must be blanched, which is performed in various ways. The common method is as follows: When the root-leaves have nearly attained their full size, they are taken when entirely dry, gathered together into a conical form, or point, at the top, and tied together with matting, or any other soft, fibrous material, by which means the large, outer leaves are made to blanch the more tender ones towards the heart of the plant.

After being tied in this manner, the plants are sometimes blanched by earthing, as practised with Celery or Cardoons. Blanching-pots, or, in the absence of these, common flower-pots, inverted over the plants, will be found a safe and effectual means of rendering them white, crisp, and mild flavored.

Time required for Blanching. — In summer weather, when vegetation is active, the plants will blanch in ten days; but in cool weather, when the plants have nearly attained their growth, or are slowly developing, three weeks will be required to perfect the operation.

Harvesting, and Preservation during Winter. — " Before frost sets in, take them up with a ball of soil to each, and put them into light earth in a cellar or some warm building. Put only the roots into the earth. Do not suffer the plants to touch each other, and pour a little water round the roots after they are placed in the earth. If they are perfectly dry when tied up, they will keep till spring." — *Corb.*

Use. — " The leaves are the parts used, and these only when blanched to diminish their natural bitterness of taste. It is one of the best autumn, winter, and spring salads." — *McInt.*

Varieties. — The different sorts are divided into two classes, — the " Batavian " and the " Curled-leaved."

Batavian Endives. — Under the Batavian Endives are included all the varieties with broad leaves, generally rounded at the points, with the margin slightly ragged or torn, but not curled. As most of the sorts require more room than the Curled-leaved kinds, the rows should be fourteen or fifteen inches apart, and the plants thinned out from nine to twelve inches in the rows.

The Batavian Endives are inferior to the Curled for garnishing, as well as for salad; and their cultivation in this country is quite limited.

The principal kinds are the Broad-leaved, Curled, Large, Lettuce-leaved or White, and the Small. Of these, the Broad-leaved and the Lettuce-leaved are considered the best.

Curled Endives. — Curled Endives are those with narrow leaves, more or less divided, and much curled. They are usually full in the heart.

Many of the varieties afford a fine garnish, and make a tender salad. In some parts of Europe, Endive is grown in great perfection, and is much esteemed. In this country, though found to some extent in our markets during the winter and early in spring, it is less generally used as a salad plant than Lettuce or Celery.

The prominent curled sorts are the Dutch Green, Large Green, Green Summer, Italian Green, Long Italian Green, Triple-curled Moss, Staghorn or Rouen, and the White Curled. Of these, the Green, Long Italian, and the Staghorn are perhaps the best. For detailed descriptions, the cultivator is referred to " THE FIELD AND GARDEN VEGETABLES OF AMERICA."

HORSE-RADISH.

Cochlearia armoracia.—*Nasturtium* armoracia.

Horse-radish is a hardy perennial, introduced from Europe, and growing naturally along old roads, and about gardens and waste places in long-settled towns. The root is white within and without, long, nearly cylindrical, and from an inch to two inches and a half in diameter; the flowers are white, and are put forth in June; the seed-pods are globular, but are very rarely formed, the flowers being usually abortive.

There are no varieties.

Soil, Propagation, and Culture. — Horse-radish will not thrive in dry, gravelly soil; neither will it succeed well where the subsoil is of a hard, clayey character. The finest roots are obtained from a deep, naturally rich, mellow soil; and it is only in such situations that the yield will repay the cost of planting and cultivation.

It is always propagated by planting the crowns of the roots, which may be set either in spring or autumn. Trench the ground eighteen inches or two feet deep, and set the crowns or leading buds of old roots (cut off about three inches in length) in rows eighteen inches apart, and nine inches from each other in the rows; cover six inches deep, and cultivate in the usual manner during the summer. The shoots will soon make their appearance, and the large leaves of the plant completely occupy the surface of the bed. After two seasons' growth, the roots will be fit for use.

Taking the Crop. — Its season of use is from October till May; and, whenever the ground is open, the table may be supplied directly from the garden.

For winter use, take up the requisite quantity of roots in November, pack them in moist sand or earth, and store in the cellar, or in any situation out of reach of frost.

Use. — The root shredded or grated, with the addition of vinegar, is used as a condiment with meats and fish. It has an agreeable, pungent flavor, and, besides aiding digestion, possesses other important healthful properties.

It has been truthfully remarked, that "there is scarcely another culinary vegetable, of equal importance, in which cultivation is, in general, so greatly neglected as in this. It is often found planted in some obscure corner of the garden, where it may have existed for years, and is only visited when needed for the proprietor's table. The operation of hastily extracting a root or two is too often all that is thought of; and the crop is left to fight its way amongst weeds and litter as best it may."

LETTUCE.

Lactuca sativa.

Lettuce is a hardy, annual plant, and, when fully developed, from two to three feet in height, with an erect, branching stem. The flowers are compound, yellow, usually half an inch in diameter; the seeds are oval, flattened, and either white, brown, or black, according to the variety. Nearly thirty thousand are contained in an ounce, and their vitality is retained five years.

Soil. — Lettuce succeeds best in rich, moist soil, and is also best developed, and most crisp and tender, if grown in cool, moist weather. A poor soil, and a hot, dry exposure, may produce a small, tolerable lettuce early in spring, or late in autumn; but, if sown in such situations during the summer months, it will soon run to seed, and prove nearly, if not entirely, worthless for the table. The richer the soil may be, and the higher its state of cultivation, the larger and finer will be the heads produced; and the more rapidly the plants are grown, the more tender and brittle will be their quality.

Propagation.— It is always grown from seeds, which are small and light; half an ounce being sufficient to sow a nursery-bed of nearly a hundred square feet. It is necessary that the ground should be well pulverized and made smooth before it is sown, and the seeds should not be covered more than a fourth of an inch deep.

Cultivation.— Some recommend sowing where the plants are to remain, in drills from ten to fifteen inches apart, and thinning the plants to nearly the same distance in the lines. Others recommend sowing in a small nursery-bed, and transplanting. The process of transplanting unquestionably lessens the liability of the plants to run to seed, and produces the largest and finest heads. The first sowing in the open ground may be made as soon in March or April as the frost leaves the ground; and, if a continued supply is desired, a sowing should afterwards be made, at intervals of about four weeks, until September.

Forcing.— Lettuce is now served at table the year round; not, of course, of equal excellence at all seasons. Sowings are consequently required for each month: those intended for the spring supply are made from December to February, — twelve weeks being required for its full development when reared in the winter months. The seed is sown rather thinly, broadcast, in a hot-bed; and, when the plants have made two or three leaves, they are pricked out to three or four inches apart in another portion of the bed, — thus affording them more space for growth, and opportunity to acquire strength and hardiness. When two or three inches high, they are finally transplanted into yet another part of the bed, at distances corresponding with the size of the variety, varying from ten to fourteen inches in each direction. As the plants increase in size, the quantity of air should be increased; and water should be given whenever the surface of the bed becomes dry. In severe cold or in cloudy weather, and almost always at night, straw-matting (made thick and heavy for the purpose), woollen carpeting, or a similar substitute, should be extended over the glass, for the retention of heat.

Some practise transplanting directly from the nursery-bed to where the plants are to remain; but the finest Lettuce is generally obtained by the treatment above described.

Use. — "Lettuce is well known as one of the best of all salad plants. It is eaten raw in French salads, with cream, oil, vinegar, salt, and hard-boiled eggs. It is also eaten by many with sugar and vinegar; and some prefer it with vinegar alone. It is excellent when stewed, and forms an important ingredient in most vegetable soups. In lobster and chicken salads, it is indispensable; and some of the varieties furnish a beautiful garnish for either fish, flesh, or fowl.

"In a raw state, Lettuce is emollient, cooling, and in some degree laxative and aperient, easy of digestion; but it contains no nourishment."

Varieties. — These are exceedingly numerous, though the number of kinds grown to any considerable extent in this country is quite limited.

They are generally divided into two classes; viz., Cabbage Lettuces and Cos Lettuces.

Cabbage Lettuces : —

Head of medium size, rather long and loose; the leaves, which coil or roll back a little on the borders about the top of the head, are yellowish-green, washed or stained with brownish-red; diameter twelve to fourteen inches; weight eight ounces.

Brown Dutch.
Black-Seeded.
Vil.

This Lettuce cabbages readily, forms a good-sized head, is tender, of good quality, hardy, and tolerably early. It does not, however, retain its head well in dry and warm weather, and, as it is little affected by cold, seems best adapted to winter or very early culture. It resembles the Yellow-seeded Brown Dutch, but is not so early; and the head is looser and larger.

Brown Silesian or Marseilles Cabbage. *Vil.* **BROWN BATAVIAN.** Head green, tinted with brown, remarkably large, — not compactly, but regularly formed. The diameter of a well-grown plant is eighteen inches, and its weight twenty-eight ounces. The seeds are white.

This Lettuce, though somewhat hard, is brittle and mild-flavored, but is better when cooked than when served in its crude state as a salad. It is a hardy, late sort, succeeds well in winter, and retains its head a long period, but is rarely employed for forcing, on account of its size, — one of the plants occupying, in a frame or hot-bed, the space of two plants of average dimensions.

Early or Summer Cape. ROYAL CAPE. Head roundish, usually well formed, and moderately close and firm: when divided, it is yellowish to the centre. The plants, when fully grown, measure nearly a foot in diameter, and weigh from six to ten ounces.

The variety is not well adapted for forcing, or for early culture in the open ground. As a summer Lettuce, it is one of the best, enduring the heat well, and not running soon to seed. Though not so crisp and brittle as some of the winter or spring grown varieties, it is well flavored and of good quality. It is similar to the Summer or Royal Cabbage.

Early White Spring or Black-seeded Gotte. *Trans.* A small spring Cabbage Lettuce, growing close to the ground. Its heart is hard and firm, and measures four inches in diameter when stripped of its outer leaves; color pale green; weight rarely above four ounces.

This Lettuce comes early into use, and, besides, is of excellent flavor; but its chief merit is that it remains longer than almost any other sort before running to seed, and even sometimes bursts before the flower-stem is formed. It is one of the smallest of the Cabbage Lettuces, and somewhat resembles the Tennis-ball.

The variety has black seeds; and this fact should be particularly attended to in obtaining it from seedsmen, as the White-seeded Gotte Lettuces run much sooner to flower.

This variety forms no head. The leaves are finely frilled and curled, and spread regularly from a common centre in the form of a rosette. A well-developed plant resembles Curled Endive. It appears to be nearly identical with the Green Curled Lettuce.

Endive-leaved. VII.

The seeds are black, and smaller than those of any other variety.

The Green Curled strongly resembles, if it is not identical with, the Endive-leaved. When well grown, the plant measures ten inches in diameter, and is one of the most beautiful of all the Lettuces. The exterior leaves are finely frilled and curled, and of a rich, golden-green color; the central leaves are smaller, but frilled and curled like those of the exterior. When in perfection, the plants have the form of a rosette, and make an excellent garnish. The seeds are white.

Green Curled. CURLED. ENDIVE-LEAVED. BOSTON CURLED.

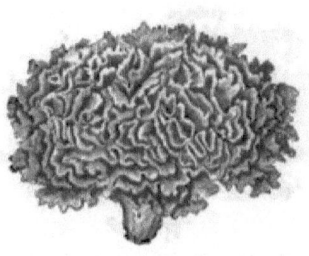

Green Curled Lettuce.

It is hardy, well adapted for forcing, and is extensively grown in the vicinity of Boston, Mass., for early marketing.

As respects its value for the table, it cannot be considered equal to many of the Cabbage varieties, as it is deficient in crispness, and tenderness of texture, — qualities essential in all salad plants. Its recommendations are its hardiness, its adaptation to early culture and forcing, and particularly its beautiful appearance.

Market-gardeners and cultivators make three sub-varieties, which are known as "Single-curled," "Double-curled," and "Triple-curled;" the difference consisting in the finer frilling, or curling, of the last named. A well-grown plant resembles some varieties of Endive; whence the term "Endive-leaved."

Green Winter Cabbage.
Hardy Winter Cabbage. Head pale green, of medium size, round and regular, firm and solid. Winter-grown plants will measure twelve inches in their full diameter, and weigh from fourteen to sixteen ounces. Seeds white.

The Green Winter Cabbage Lettuce is tender, and of excellent flavor, particularly if cultivated in cool weather. It is hardy, forms its head promptly and uniformly, is slow in the development of its flowers, and must be classed as one of the best of the hardy, winter varieties.

Hammersmith Hardy. *McInt.*
Hardy Green Hammersmith. A popular, old variety, with a small, dark-green head. The leaves are much wrinkled, concave, thick, and fleshy; the seeds are white.

It is considered the hardiest sort in cultivation, and is one of the best for growing in winter, or for forcing. When raised in spring, late in autumn, or in cool, moist weather, the plants attain a diameter of nearly ten inches, and weigh from six to eight ounces; but summer-grown specimens are much smaller, rarely measuring more than six or seven inches in diameter, or weighing above three or four ounces. In warm, dry weather, it soon runs to seed.

Ice Cabbage. *Trans.* This variety belongs to the division of the Silesian or Batavian Lettuces, and must not be confounded with the White Cos. The leaves are of a light shining green, nearly erect, eight inches long, and five or six inches broad: the outer leaves spread a little at the top, but grow close at the heart. It blanches without tying up, and becomes white, crisp, and tender.

The Ice Cabbage Lettuce comes into use with the White Silesian, from which it differs, as it also does from any other of its class, in being much more curled, having a lucid, sparkling surface (whence probably its name), and not turning in so much at the heart. It lasts as long in crop as the White Silesian.

A large and excellent variety, but inferior to the Versailles or the Ice Cabbage. Head large, regular, a little oblong, of a dull, pale-green color, and not compactly formed; diameter fourteen inches; weight twelve to fifteen ounces; seeds white. Imperial Head.
Turkey Cabbage.

This is a crisp and tender Lettuce, though sometimes slightly bitter. It is not early, and soon shoots up to seed; but is quite hardy, and well adapted for winter cultivation.

The Imperial Head, or Imperial Cabbage Lettuce, with white seeds, was at one period more generally cultivated in small gardens than any other variety; and though some of the recently introduced sorts excel it, not only in size, but in tender consistency and flavor, the Imperial is still extensively cultivated and much esteemed.

With the exception of the color of its seeds, it resembles the Turkey Cabbage.

This variety somewhat resembles the White Silesian or White Batavian. The plants attain a large size, frequently measuring sixteen or eighteen inches in diameter. The heads are not remarkable for solidity, but are white within, crisp and tender, with little of the bitter flavor common to many other varieties. The seeds are white. India.
Large India.

The India Lettuce, like the White Silesian, withstands heat and drought, and is a favorite market sort in various parts of the Middle States. It is one of the best for summer culture, and, aside from its large size, one of the best for forcing.

Large Brown Cabbage or Mogul.
MAMMOTH.

Head remarkably large, round, regularly formed, grayish-green, tinted or washed with reddish-brown at the top. The diameter of a well-grown plant is fourteen inches, and its weight nearly a pound. Seeds black.

The Large Brown Cabbage Lettuce is crisp and tender, but is sometimes slightly bitter. Its season is near that of the Versailles; but it is slower in forming its head, and sooner runs to flower. It is hardy, good for forcing, and well adapted for cultivation during winter. In summer, the heads are small, and loosely formed.

Large Red Cabbage.
Vil.

Head green, washed with red, of medium size, regularly but loosely formed; diameter thirteen or fourteen inches; weight twelve ounces; seeds black.

Its season is near that of the Large Brown Cabbage. When grown in warm weather, the head is small, and the plant soon runs to seed: in winter, the head is much larger, more solid, and longer retained. It resembles the Brown Dutch, but differs in the deeper color of the leaves.

Large Winter Cabbage or Madeira.

Head of medium size, regular, but not compact, green, washed with red at the top. When grown in winter, or in cool, moist weather, the plants will measure a foot in diameter, and weigh nearly a pound. The seeds are white.

It is quite brittle, though not remarkable for tenderness of texture; hardy; succeeds well when grown in cold-weather, and remains long in head before shooting up to seed. Season, the same with that of the Green Winter Cabbage.

Malta or Ice Cabbage.
ICE COS. DRUM-HEAD. WHITE CABBAGE.

In its general character, this variety resembles the White Silesian. The head is remarkably large, somewhat flattened, compact, pale green without, and white at the centre. The extreme diameter of a full-grown plant is sixteen inches, and the weight from twenty to twenty-four ounces. The seeds are white.

The variety heads readily, blanches naturally, and is crisp, tender, and well flavored. It is hardy, but not early, and remains long in head without running to seed.

It is extensively cultivated in England, and in some localities succeeds better, and is of finer quality, than the White Silesian or Marseilles Cabbage. The name is derived from the glazed or polished surface of the leaves.

Neapolitan. NAPLES CABBAGE.

Plant dwarfish; head of large size, round, regularly formed, solid, — when in perfection, resembling a well-developed cabbage. If well grown, the plants will measure sixteen inches in diameter, and weigh from twenty to twenty-four ounces. Seeds white.

The Neapolitan Lettuce blanches naturally, is well flavored, and so slow in the development of its flower-stalk, that the heads are sometimes artificially divided at the top to facilitate its growth, and to secure the seeds, a supply of which is always obtained with difficulty, as, aside from the tardiness of the plant in flowering, the yield is never abundant.

It is not so good for forcing as many others, and must be classed as a summer rather than as a winter variety.

Palatine. *Vil.* BROWN CABBAGE.

A variety of medium size, with a round, somewhat depressed head, stained with red about the top. Extreme diameter of the plant, ten or eleven inches; weight twelve ounces. The seeds are black.

It is quite brittle; of excellent flavor; yields a large quantity of salad in proportion to its size; flourishes well at all seasons, even during winter; and must be classed as one of the best, and recommended for general cultivation.

Stone Tennis-ball. *Vil.* Plant quite small, with a uniformly green, regular, solid head, all of the leaves to the heart being strongly wrinkled and coarsely blistered. Summer-grown plants measure six or seven inches in diameter, and weigh three ounces. When grown early or late in the season, or under the influence of cool and moist weather, the plants attain a larger size, often measuring nine or ten inches in diameter, and weighing eight ounces. The seeds are black.

The Stone Tennis-ball hearts well, is of excellent quality, and, in proportion to its size, yields a large quantity of salad. It retains its head a long period, even in warm weather, without shooting up to seed; and, as most of the leaves of the plant are embraced in the head, it occupies but a small space of ground in cultivation. Hardy and early.

Summer Cabbage.
LARGE WHITE CABBAGE. ROYAL CABBAGE. *Vil.*
Foliage pale yellowish-green; head of medium size, round, somewhat flattened, firm, and close. The entire diameter of a well-grown plant is twelve inches, and the weight from ten to twelve ounces. The seeds are white.

It is one of the best sorts for summer cultivation, as it not only forms its head readily in warm and dry weather, but remains long in head before running to flower. For forcing, or for sowing early in the season, some other varieties would succeed better. Though sometimes slightly bitter, it is crisp, tender in texture, appears to be adapted to our climate, and is recommended for cultivation.

Tennis-ball.
GREEN BALL. BUTTON. CAPUCHIN. HARDY HAMMERSMITH. *Vil.*
One of the oldest and most esteemed of the Cabbage Lettuces. The head is below medium size, dark green, very solid if grown in cool weather, but often loose and open-hearted if cultivated during the summer months. The seeds of the genuine variety are black.

The Tennis-ball Lettuce is remarkable for its extreme hardiness. Winter-grown plants, or those raised in cool, moist weather, will measure ten inches in diameter, and weigh eight ounces; while those raised under opposite conditions rarely exceed seven or eight inches in diameter, or weigh more than four or five ounces.

It is slow in running to seed, and the head blanches white and tender. " It requires little room in frames in winter, and yields a great return in spring, as almost the whole plant is eatable." A large Cabbage Lettuce, tinted with brown about the head, is erroneously known in some localities as the " Tennis-ball."

Similar to the Imperial Head; the principal if not only difference consisting in the color of the seeds, which are black. **Turkey Cabbage.**

Head pale yellowish-green, large, long, and compactly formed. When in its greatest perfection, the extreme diameter of the whole plant is fourteen inches, and its weight twelve or fourteen ounces. The seeds are white. **Versailles.** *Vil.* Sugar Lettuce.

This variety forms its head quickly and uniformly; cabbages white and crisp; is slow in shooting up to seed; flourishes in almost every description of soil, and at all seasons, except perhaps in extreme cold; and, though sometimes slightly bitter, is tender, and of good quality.

With the exception of its paler color, it resembles the Neapolitan. It is one of the best of all varieties for summer cultivation.

An excellent early and hardy variety. The head is of medium size, tinted or washed with red at the top, round and compact; the leaves are large, yellowish-green, wrinkled, and blistered. If grown in summer, the plants measure eight or nine inches **Victoria or Red-bordered.** *Vil.*

in diameter, and weigh four ounces. In cool weather, the plants attain a diameter of twelve inches, and weigh from ten to twelve ounces. The seeds are white.

The Victoria Lettuce is larger than the Tennis-ball, heads freely, and is crisp and well flavored. When sown in summer, it soon runs to flower; but, in cool weather, the heads are well retained.

White Gotte, (Black-seeded.) *Vil.* A small, low-growing, yellowish-green cabbage-lettuce, with a loose, open head. The plants rarely measure more than six inches in their full diameter, or weigh above four ounces.

It is one of the earliest of all the lettuces; crisp, of good flavor, and well adapted for forcing, or for frame culture. Besides the distinction in the color of the seeds, it differs from the White-seeded White Gotte in its smaller and more loosely formed heads.

White Gotte, (White-seeded.) *Vil.* **White Tennis-ball.** This variety has a small, long, firm, and close head, and is uniformly of a yellowish-green color. The plant is of small dimensions, and rarely measures more than six or seven inches in diameter, or weighs above three ounces. The variety is early, crisp, and well flavored, but soon runs to seed, and is much better adapted for growing in winter, or for forcing, than for cultivation in the summer months.

White Silesian, or White Batavian. *Vil.* **Drumhead Cabbage. Large Drumhead. Spanish.** One of the largest of the cabbage-lettuces. Head golden-green, tinted with brownish-red about the top, regularly, but not compactly formed. The exterior leaves are large and broad, yellowish-green bordered with brown, wrinkled, and coarsely blistered. When well grown, the entire diameter of the plant is eighteen inches, and its weight twenty ounces. The seeds are white.

This variety appears to be adapted to all seasons, is hardy, retains its head well, withstands heat and drought, blanches white and crisp, and is of excellent flavor. It succeeds well in frames, but, on account of its large size, is not a profitable sort for forcing.

White Silesian Lettuce.

A variety known as the "Tennis-ball" in some localities much resembles this; and the "Boston Cabbage" of New England, if not identical, seems to be but an improved form of the White Silesian.

Head of medium size, yellowish-green, stained with brownish-red, firm and solid. **White Stone Cabbage.** When fully developed, the entire diameter of the plant is fourteen inches, and its weight sixteen ounces. The seeds are white.

This Lettuce is brittle, of tender texture and good quality, though it is sometimes slightly bitter. It is hardy, heads readily, is slow in running to flower, succeeds well in warm and dry weather, and is also well adapted for frame culture or for forcing.

Head of medium size, yellowish-green variegated with red, rounded at the top, and tapering to a point at the base; compact; seeds yellow. **Yellow-seeded Brown Dutch.** *Vil.* **White Dutch. American Brown Dutch.**

A half-early sort, of good quality, hardy, and well adapted for winter culture, or for sowing early in spring. It somewhat resembles the Black-seeded Brown Dutch; but, apart from the difference in the color of the seeds, its foliage is more blistered, and more colored with red, and the plant produces numerous sprouts, or shoots, about the base of the head.

Cos Lettuces. — These are quite distinct from the cabbage-lettuces before described. The heads are long, erect, largest at the top, and taper towards the root, — the exterior leaves clasping or coving over and around the head in the manner of a hood, or cowl. As a class, they are remarkable for hardiness and vigor; but the midribs and nerves of the leaves are coarse and hard, and most of the kinds will be found inferior to the cabbage-lettuces in crispness and flavor. They are ill adapted for cultivation in dry and hot weather, and attain their greatest perfection only when grown in spring or autumn, or in cool and humid seasons.

Varieties: —

Alphange or Florence Cos, (Black-seeded.) *Vil.* In the form of the head, and in its general character, this variety resembles the White-seeded. Both of the sorts are remarkable for size, for hardiness, and healthy habit, for the length of time they remain in head before running to seed, and for the brittle and tender character of the ribs and nerves of the leaves.

Besides the difference in the color of the seeds, the head of this variety is smaller, and the foliage paler, than that of the White-seeded.

Alphange or Florence Cos, (White-seeded.) *Vil.* **Magnum Bonum Cos.** Head large, long, not compact, and forming well only when the exterior leaves are tied loosely together. The midribs and nerves of the leaves are large, but brittle, and of tender texture. A well-grown plant will weigh twelve ounces.

It is ten or twelve days later than the Green Paris Cos, retains its head well, is hardy and of healthy habit, but is deficient in flavor, and inferior to either of the Paris sorts.

This variety has much merit as a hardy, **Bath Green**
winter, green sort, and is nearly related to the   Cos. *McInt.*
Brown Cos. It is, however, less brown on the outer leaves;
and, while that has white seeds, the seeds of this variety are
black. Hence there are found, upon the catalogues of seedsmen, Black-seeded Bath, or Brown Cos, and White-seeded
Bath, or Brown Cos; the latter seeming to be the hardiest,
while the former appears to be the best.

This is one of the oldest of the Cos Lettuces, **Brown Cos.**
and considered the hardiest of the class. The   BATH COS.
head is of large size, pointed, not compact, and requires to
be tied in order to obtain it in its greatest perfection; the
leaves are of a copper-green color, stiff and firm, toothed and
blistered; the seeds are white.

The Brown Cos blanches white and tender, and is exceedingly crisp and well flavored; but the dark, brownish
color of the exterior leaves is deemed an objection, and it is
often displaced by really inferior varieties. In weight and
measurement, it differs little from the Green Paris Cos.
Extensively cultivated and much esteemed in England.

Head of the form of an inverted cone; green, **Gray Paris**
with a grayish tone about the top; compact,   Cos. *Vil.*
and forming well without tying. The exterior leaves are
numerous, deep green, erect, firm, and prominently blistered.
The full diameter of the plant is nearly twelve inches, and
its weight twenty ounces. The seeds are white.

The Gray Paris Cos is brittle, and of tender texture, but
is considered inferior to the other Paris Cos sorts, and is
but little cultivated.

Head inversely conical, compact; leaves **Green Paris**
deep green, erect, firm, hooded or cowl-formed   Cos. *Vil.*
towards the ends, and serrated on the margin;   KENSINGTON COS. SUTTON'S SUPERB GREEN COS. WELLING-
the ribs and nerves are large and prominent.   TON. ADY'S FINE LARGE.

When full grown, the entire diameter of the plant is fifteen or sixteen inches, and its weight twenty-four ounces. The seeds are white.

It is considered one of the best of the Cos Lettuces, and, though not so hardy as the Brown Cos, is a good variety for forcing, and furnishes a tender, well-flavored head during summer. Whether for spring, summer, or autumn, it is an excellent sort. It attains a large size, is of a fine green color, and, " from the manner in which the outer leaves cove over the interior ones, blanches well without having to be tied together."

It has a tender, brittle leaf; is some days earlier than the White Paris; and is the principal variety employed by the market-gardeners of Paris for cultivating under glass.

Green Winter Cos. *Vil.* Head elongated, somewhat of the form of the preceding variety; deep green, and not forming well, unless the exterior leaves are tied together at the tips. The seeds are black.

It blanches well; but the ribs and nerves of the leaves are somewhat coarse and hard. Well adapted to winter culture, but, as a summer lettuce, of little value.

White Paris Cos. *Vil. McInt.* **London White Cos. Sutton's Superb White Cos.** The head of this variety has the form of the Green Paris, and blanches well without tying. The extreme diameter of the entire plant, when well grown, is fourteen inches, and its weight nearly twenty-four ounces. The seeds are white.

This is the sort most generally grown by the London market-gardeners, millions of it being produced annually within a few miles of London alone; and it has been adopted almost exclusively by the gardeners of Paris for cultivation in the open air. Next to the Green Paris Cos, this is the best, the largest, and the longest in running to seed, of all the summer lettuces. It is tender, brittle, and mild flavored, less hardy, and a few days later, than the Green Paris Cos.

MUSTARD.

Black Mustard. — Brown Mustard. — Red Mustard. —
Sinapis nigra.

Black Mustard is a hardy, annual plant, introduced from Europe. In some localities, it grows naturally in great abundance, and is regarded as a troublesome weed. The seeds — which furnish the common table mustard — are small, round, brownish-black, and retain their germinative powers many years. Nearly eighteen thousand are contained in an ounce.

Propagation and Cultivation. — It is raised from seeds, four quarts of which will be required for sowing an acre. It is sometimes grown in the vegetable garden, but is generally cultivated in fields for its seeds, which, as before remarked, furnish the common table mustard. The sowing is usually made from the middle of April to the middle of May. After making the surface of the ground fine and smooth, sow broadcast, or thinly in shallow drills fourteen or fifteen inches apart; cultivate during the season in the usual manner, and in August the crop will be ready for harvesting. Cut the stalks at the ground before the pods shed their seeds, and spread in a light and airy situation till they are sufficiently dried for threshing.

When grown for salad in the vegetable garden, it should be sown, and cut for use, as directed for White Mustard.

Use. — Besides the use of the flour of the seeds as a condiment, the seed-leaves are used as salad in the manner of those of the White species; and the young plants, cut to the ground, are used as spring greens, either boiled alone or mixed with Spinach.

White Mustard.
SINAPIS ALBA.

White Mustard is a hardy annual, introduced from Europe, and occasionally found growing spontaneously in the vicinity of fields and gardens where it has been once cultivated. The stem is three feet and upwards in height; the leaves are large, deeply lobed, and of a rich deep-green color; the flowers are large, yellow, produced in loose, terminal spikes; the seeds are yellow, much larger than those of the preceding species, and retain their vitality five years. Seventy-five hundred are contained in an ounce.

Propagation.—White Mustard is always raised from seeds, four quarts of which will be necessary for seeding an acre. When grown for salad, an ounce will sow forty feet of drill.

Cultivation.—When cultivated in the vegetable garden for salad or greens, the first sowing may be made as early in the season as the frost will admit. Sow the seeds thickly, in drills eight or ten inches apart, and cover half an inch deep with fine mould.

The plants should be cut for use while in the seed-leaf: when much developed, they become strong, rank, and ill-flavored.

For a succession, a small sowing may be made every week until September.

In field-culture, the seeds are sometimes sown broadcast; but the more common method is to sow in drills fifteen or eighteen inches apart. When the crop is ready for harvesting, the plants are cut to the ground, and stored and threshed as directed for Black Mustard.

Use.—The plants, before the development of the rough leaves, are used as salad: when more advanced, they are boiled and eaten as Spinach. The flour of the seeds furnishes a table mustard of good quality, though the seeds of the Black species possess greater piquancy, and are generally employed for the purpose. The seeds of both species are much used in medicine, and are considered equally efficacious.

CHAPTER IX.

OLERACEOUS PLANTS.

Balm. — Basil. — Caraway. — Coriander. — Lavender. — Marjoram. — Parsley. — Rosemary. — Sage. — Savory. — Spearmint. — Thyme.

BALM.

Melissa officinalis.

A HARDY, perennial plant, from the south of Europe. The stalk is four-sided, branching, and from two to three feet high; leaves opposite, in pairs, ovate, toothed on the borders; the flowers are small, nearly white, produced in spikes, or clusters, at or near the top of the plant. The seeds are quite small, and retain their variety two years.

Soil, Propagation, and Culture. — Any warm, mellow, garden soil is suited to its growth. It is generally propagated by dividing the roots, which may be done either in spring or in autumn. After thoroughly stirring the soil, set the roots in rows fifteen inches apart, and a foot apart in the rows. Under good management, the plants will soon completely cover the surface of the ground, and the bed will not need renewal for many years.

Gathering. — If required for drying, the plants should be cut as they come into flower, separating the stems at the surface of the ground. They should not be exposed to the sun in drying, but spread in an airy, shady place, and allowed to dry gradually. The leaves, in their green state, may be taken directly from the plants as they are required for use.

Use. — The plant has a pleasant, lemon-like odor, an agreeable, aromatic taste, and, in flavoring certain dishes, is used as a substitute for Lemon Thyme. It is beneficial in hemorrhage, and other diseases of the lungs; and, in the form of tea, constitutes a cooling and grateful diluent in fevers. A mixture of balm and honey, or sugar, is sometimes applied to the interior of beehives, just previous to receiving the swarm, for the purpose of "attaching the colony to its new settlement."

BASIL.

Ocymum.

There are two species of Basil cultivated in gardens; viz., the Common Sweet Basil (*O. basilicum*) and the Small Bush Basil (*O. minimum*). Of the Common Sweet Basil, there are three varieties; and of the Bush Basil, two varieties. They are all annuals, and are grown from seeds, which are black, small, oblong, and retain their vitality from six to ten years.

Common Sweet Basil. LARGE SWEET BASIL. OCYMUM BASILICUM. Stem from a foot to a foot and a half in height; leaves green, ovate, sharply pointed; flowers white, in whorls at the extremities of the stems and branches. The whole plant, when bruised, is highly aromatic, having the odor and flavor of cloves.

Varieties : —

Purple Basil. Leaves and flowers purple. When grown in sunny situations, the leaf-stems and young branches are also purple. In other respects, the variety is similar to the Common Sweet Basil. Its properties and uses are the same.

The leaves of this variety are large, pale green, wrinkled and blistered like those of some kinds of lettuce; whence the name. It resembles the foregoing varieties in taste and odor, and is used for the same purpose.

Lettuce-leaved Basil. Vil.

The Bush Basils are small, low-growing, branching plants, and are propagated and cultivated like the Common Sweet Basil.

Bush Basil. Ocymum Minimum.

Stem eight inches high; leaves small, green, oval; flowers white, produced in whorls about the upper portion of the principal stalk and towards the extremities of the branches.

Green Bush Basil. Vil.

Leaves purple. In other respects, similar to the Green Bush Basil.

Purple Bush Basil. Vil.

Use. — The leaves and young branches have a strong, clove-like taste and odor, and are used in highly-seasoned soups and meats. They are also sometimes added to salads. For winter use, the stalks are cut while in flower, dried, powdered, and preserved, like other pot-herbs.

CARAWAY.

Carum carui.

The Common Caraway is a hardy, biennial plant; a native of various parts of Europe, and, to a considerable extent, naturalized in this country. The flower-stalks are about two feet and a half in height. The flowers are small, white, and produced in umbels at the ends of the branches; the seeds, which ripen quite early in the season, are of a clear olive-brown color, and pleasant, aromatic flavor and odor. Nearly eight thousand five hundred seeds are contained in an ounce, and they retain their vitality three years.

Soil and Cultivation. — Caraway is one of the hardiest of plants, and succeeds well in almost any soil or situation. In the coldest parts of the United States, and even in the Canadas, it is naturalized to such an extent about fields and mowing-lands, as to be obtained in great abundance for the mere labor of cutting up the plants as the ripening of the seeds takes place.

When cultivated, the sowing may be made in April or May; but, if sown just after ripening, the seeds not only vegetate with greater certainty, but the plants often flower the ensuing season, thus saving a summer's growth. Sow in drills twelve or fifteen inches apart, cover half an inch deep, and, when the plants are well up, thin to six or eight inches apart.

Use. — It is principally cultivated for its seeds, which constitute an article of some commercial importance; a large proportion, however, of the consumption in this country is supplied by importation from Europe. They are extensively employed by confectioners, and for distillation. They are also mixed in cake, and, by the Dutch, introduced into cheese.

It is sometimes cultivated for its young leaves, which are used in soups and salads, or as a pot-herb, like Parsley. The roots are boiled in the manner of the Carrot or Parsnip, and by some are preferred to these vegetables, the flavor being considered pleasant and delicate.

There are no described varieties.

CORIANDER. — *Law.*

Coriandrum sativum.

A hardy annual, supposed to have been introduced from the south of Europe, but now naturalized in almost all temperate climates where it has once been cultivated.

Stem two feet in height, generally erect, but, as the seeds approach maturity, often acquiring a drooping habit. The flowers are white; the seeds are globular, an eighth of an inch in diameter, of a yellowish-brown color, with a warm, pleasant, aromatic taste: they become quite light and hollow by age, and are often affected by insects in the manner of seed-peas. Though they will sometimes vegetate when kept for a longer period, they are not considered good when more than two years old.

Propagation and Cultivation. — Like all annuals, it is propagated from seed, which should be sown in April or May. Sow in drills made fourteen or sixteen inches asunder, and three-fourths of an inch in depth, and thin to nine inches in the rows. It soon runs to flower and seed, and will be ready for harvesting in July or August.

Use. — It is generally cultivated for its seeds, which are used to a considerable extent by druggists, confectioners, and distillers. In the garden, it is sometimes sown for its leaves, which are used in soups and salads; but, when so required, a sowing should be made at intervals of three or four weeks.

There are no varieties.

LAVENDER.

Lavendula spica.

Lavender is a hardy, low-growing, shrubby plant, originally from the south of Europe. There are three varieties; and they may be propagated from seeds by dividing the roots, or by slips, or cuttings.

The seeds are sown in April or May. Make the surface of the soil light and smooth, and sow the seeds in very shallow drills six inches apart. When the seedlings are two or three inches high, transplant them in rows two feet apart, and a foot apart in the rows.

The slips, or cuttings, are set in April, two-thirds of the length in the soil, and in rows, as directed for transplanting seedlings. Shade them for a few days, until they have taken root; after which, little care will be required beyond the ordinary form of cultivation.

The roots may be divided either in spring or autumn. Though Lavender grows most luxuriantly in rich soil, the plants are more highly aromatic, and less liable to injury from severe weather, when grown in light, warm, and gravelly situations.

Use. — Lavender is sometimes used as a pot-herb, " but is more esteemed for the distilled water which bears its name, and which, together with the oil, is obtained in the greatest proportion from the flower-spikes which have been gathered in dry weather, and just before the flowers are fully expanded. The oil of lavender is obtained in the ratio of an ounce to sixty ounces of dried flowers." — *Law.*

In the neighborhood of Mitcham, in Surrey, England, upwards of two hundred acres are occupied with Lavender alone.

Varieties : —

Broad-leaved Lavender. *Mill.*
SPIKE LAVENDER.

Compared with the Common Lavender, the branches of this variety are shorter, more sturdy, and thicker set with leaves; the latter being short and broad.

The Broad-leaved Lavender rarely blossoms; but, when this occurs, the leaves of the flower-stalk are differently formed from those of the lower part of the plant, and somewhat resemble those of the Common variety. The stalks are taller, the spikes lower and looser, and the flowers smaller, than those of the last named.

The plant is very fragrant, but inferior to the Blue-flowering, particularly for distillation.

A shrubby, thickly branched plant, from a foot to upwards of three feet high, according to the depth and quality of the soil in which it is cultivated. The leaves are opposite, long, and narrow; flowers blue or purple, in spikes. *Common or Blue-flowering Lavender.* NARROW-LEAVED BLUE-FLOWERING.

The whole plant is remarkably aromatic; but the flowers have this property in a greater degree than the foliage or branches. The plants are in perfection in July and August, and are cut for drying or distillation close to the stem, as the blossoms on the lower part of the spikes begin to change to a brown color.

There is a variety with white flowers; but it is more tender than the Blue-flowering, and is not so generally cultivated. Its properties and uses are the same.

MARJORAM.

Origanum.

A perennial species, with a shrubby, four-sided stem a foot and a half high; the leaves somewhat resemble those of the Sweet Marjoram; the flowers are pale red, or flesh-colored, and produced in rounded, terminal spikes; the plants blossom in July and August, and the seeds ripen in September. *Common Marjoram.* ORIGANUM VULGARE.

Propagation and Culture. — It may be grown from seeds, but is generally propagated by dividing the roots, either in spring or autumn. Set them in a dry and warm situation, in rows fifteen inches apart, and ten or twelve inches from plant to plant in the rows.

There is a variety with white flowers, and another with variegated foliage.

Use. — The young shoots, cut at the time of flowering, and dried in the shade, are used as Sweet Marjoram for seasoning soups and meats. The whole plant is highly aromatic.

Sweet Marjoram.
KNOTTED MARJORAM. ORIGANUM MAJORANA.

Sweet Marjoram is a native of Portugal. Though a biennial, it is always treated as an annual, as it is not sufficiently hardy to withstand the winters of the Middle or Northern States in the open ground. The plant is of low growth, with a branching stem, and oval or rounded leaves. The flowers, which appear in July and August, are of a purplish color, and produced in compact clusters, or heads, resembling knots; whence the term "Knotted Marjoram" of many localities. The seeds are brown, exceedingly small, and retain their germinative properties three years.

Sowing and Cultivation. — Sweet Marjoram is raised from seeds sown annually in April, May, or June. Its propagation, however, is generally attended with more or less difficulty, arising from the exceeding minuteness of the seeds, and the liability of the young seedlings to be destroyed by the sun before they become established. The seeds are sown in drills ten or twelve inches apart, and very thinly covered with finely pulverized loam. Coarse, light matting is often placed over the bed immediately after sowing, to facilitate vegetation, and, if allowed to remain until the plants are well up, will often preserve a crop which would otherwise be destroyed.

The seeds are sometimes sown in a hot-bed, and the plants set out in May or June, in rows twelve inches apart, and six inches apart in the rows.

Gathering. — The plants, when in flower or fully developed, are cut to the ground, and for winter use are dried and preserved as other pot-herbs.

Use. — Sweet Marjoram is highly aromatic, and is much used, both in the green state and when dried, for flavoring broths, soups, and stuffings.

Pot Marjoram.
ORIGANUM ONITES.

A perennial species, from Sicily; stem a foot or more in height, branching; leaves oval, smooth; the flowers are small, of a purplish color, and produced in spikes.

It is much inferior to Sweet Marjoram.

A half-hardy perennial, from the south of Europe. Stem eighteen inches high, purplish; the leaves resemble those of Sweet Marjoram; the flowers are white, and are put forth in July and August, in spikelets two inches in length; the seeds ripen in September.

<small>Winter Sweet Marjoram. *Corb.* ORIGANUM HERACLEOTICUM.</small>

Propagation and Culture. — It is propagated, cultivated, and used as Common Marjoram.

There is a variety with variegated leaves, but differing in no other respect from the foregoing.

PARSLEY.

Apium petroselinum.

Parsley is a hardy, biennial plant from Sardinia. The leaves of the first year are all radical, compound, rich, deep green, smooth, and shining. When fully developed, the plant measures three or four feet in height; the flowers are small, white, in terminal umbels; the seeds are ovoid, somewhat three-sided, slightly curved, of a grayish-brown color, and aromatic taste. Seven thousand are contained in an ounce, and they retain their vitality three years.

Soil and Propagation. — Parsley succeeds best in rich, mellow soil, and is propagated from seeds sown annually; an ounce of seed being allowed to a hundred and fifty feet of drill.

Sowing. — As the seed vegetates slowly, — sometimes remaining in the earth four or five weeks before the plants appear, — the sowing should be made as early in spring as the ground is in working condition. Lay out the bed of a size corresponding to the supply required, spade it deeply and thoroughly, level the surface (making it fine and smooth), and sow the seeds in drills fourteen inches apart, and half an inch deep. When the plants are two or three inches high, thin them to eight or ten inches apart, being careful in the thinning to leave only the best curled plants.

The finest Curled Parsley is obtained by repeated transplantings. When the seedlings are two inches high, they are set in rows ten inches apart, and six inches apart in the rows. In about four weeks, they should be again transplanted to where they are to remain, in rows eighteen inches apart, and fourteen inches apart in the rows. When thus treated, the plants become remarkably close, of a regular, rosette-like form, and often entirely cover the surface of the ground. When grown for competition or for exhibition, this process of transplanting is thrice, and often four times, repeated.

Use. — The leaves of the Curled varieties afford one of the most beautiful of garnishes: they are also used for flavoring soups and stews. If properly dried, and excluded from air, they retain their odor and taste a long period. The seeds are aromatic, and are sometimes used as a substitute for the leaves, though the flavor is much less agreeable.

Varieties : —

Dwarf Curled Parsley.
CURLED PARSLEY. SUTTON'S DWARF CURLED. USHER'S DWARF CURLED.

A fine, dwarfish, curled variety, long cultivated in England. In some gardens it is grown in such perfection as to resemble a tuft of finely curled green moss.

It is hardy, and slow in running to seed, but liable to degenerate, as it constantly tends to increase in size, and to become less curled.

From the Dwarf Curled Parsley, by judicious cultivation and a careful selection of plants for seed, have originated many excellent sorts of stronger growth, yet retaining its finely curled and beautiful leaves.

A fine, curled sort, larger than the Dwarf Curled, and, on account of its remarkable hardiness, recommended as one of the best for winter culture.

Mitchell's Matchless Winter. *Thomp.*

The leaves of this variety are large and spreading, bright green above, paler beneath. When true, the foliage is nearly as finely curled as that of the Dwarf, though the plant is much larger and stronger in its habit.

Myatt's Triple Curled. MYATT'S GARNISHING. MYATT'S EXTRA FINE CURLED. WINDSOR CURLED.

The leaves of this sort are plain, or not curled, and the plant produces them in greater quantity than the Curled sorts. It is also somewhat hardier.

Plain Parsley. *Thomp.* COMMON PARSLEY.

For many years it was the principal variety grown in the gardens of this country, but has now given place to the Curled sorts, which, if not of better flavor, are generally preferred on account of their superior excellence for garnishing.

A variety of the Dwarf Curled, of larger size, the leaves being as finely curled, and equally beautiful.

Rendle's Treble Garnishing. *Trans.*

A variety of the Common Plain Parsley, with stronger foliage. Though the leaves are sometimes used in the manner of those of the Common Parsley, it is generally cultivated for its fusiform, fleshy roots.

Hamburg or Large-rooted Parsley. *McInt.* TURNIP-ROOTED PARSLEY.

To obtain these of good size and quality, the soil should not be too rich, but deeply and thoroughly trenched. Sow the seeds in April or May, in drills a foot or fourteen inches apart, and three-fourths of an inch deep; thin the plants to eight inches apart in the rows; cultivate during the season as carrots or parsnips; and in October the roots will have attained their growth, and be suitable for use. Take them up before the ground closes, cut off the tops within an inch or two of the crowns, pack in earth or sand, and store in the cellar for winter.

Use. — The roots are eaten boiled as carrots or parsnips. In connection with the leaves, they are also mixed in soups and stews, to which they impart a pleasant, aromatic taste and odor.

ROSEMARY.

Rosmarinus officinalis.

Rosemary is a half-hardy, shrubby plant, from three to six feet in height. The leaves vary in form and color in the different varieties; the flowers are small, generally blue, and produced in axillary clusters; the seeds are brown, or blackish-brown, and retain their vitality four years.

Propagation and Cultivation. — Like most aromatic plants, Rosemary requires a light, dry soil, and, as it is not perfectly hardy, should have a sheltered situation. The Common Green-leaved and the Narrow-leaved are best propagated by seeds; but the variegated sorts are propagated only by cuttings, or by dividing the roots. The seeds are sown in April, in a small nursery-bed, and the seedlings, when two or three inches high, transplanted in rows two feet apart, and eighteen inches apart in the rows.

When propagated by cuttings, they should be taken off in May or June, six inches long, and set two-thirds of the length in the earth, in a moist, shady situation; when well rooted, transplant as directed for seedlings. The roots may be divided in spring or autumn.

Use. — It is sometimes employed, like other pot-herbs, for flavoring meats and soups. It is used in the manufacture of "eau de Cologne;" and its flowers and calyxes form a principal ingredient in the distillation of "Hungary Water." Infusions of the leaves are made in some drinks, and the young stems are used as a garnish.

Varieties: —

Leaves narrow, rounded at the ends, — the upper and under surface green; the flowers are comparatively large, and deep colored.   Common or Green-leaved.

The plant is of spreading habit, and in all its parts is more strongly aromatic than the Narrow-leaved. It is decidedly the best sort for cultivation.

The plants of this variety are smaller and less branched than those of the Common or   Narrow-leaved.
Green-leaved, and are also less fragrant; the leaves are hoary beneath, and the flowers are smaller and of a paler color.

It is used in all the forms of the Common or Green-leaved, but is less esteemed.

SAGE.

Salvia.

Sage is a low-growing, hardy, evergreen shrub, originally from the south of Europe. Stem from a foot and a half to two feet high, — the leaves varying in form and color in the different species and varieties; the flowers are produced in spikes, and are white, blue, red, purple, or variegated; the seeds, of which seven thousand are contained in an ounce, are round, of a blackish-brown color, and retain their power of germination three years.

Soil and Propagation. — Sage thrives best in light, rich, loamy soil. Though easily grown from slips or cuttings, it is, in this country, more generally propagated from seeds.

These may be sown on a gentle hot-bed in March, and the plants set in the open ground in June, in rows eighteen inches apart, and a foot asunder in the rows; or the seeds may be sown in April, where the plants are to remain, thinly, in drills eighteen inches apart, and three-fourths of an inch deep. When the plants are two inches high, thin them to a foot apart in the rows, and, if needed, form fresh rows by resetting the plants taken up in thinning.

Gathering and Use. — Sage should be gathered for drying before the development of the flowering-shoots; and, when cultivated for its leaves, these shoots should be cut out as they make their appearance. When thus treated, the product is largely increased, as the leaves are put forth in much greater numbers, and attain a larger size.

It is sometimes treated as an annual; the seeds being sown in April, in drills fourteen inches apart, and the plants cut to the ground when they have made sufficient growth for use.

The leaves are employed, both in a green and dried state, for seasoning stuffings, meats, stews, and soups. Sage is also used for flavoring cheese, and, in the form of a decoction, is sometimes employed for medical purposes.

Varieties : —

Common or Red-leaved. PURPLE-TOP. RED-TOP. SALVIA OFFICINALIS. This is the Common Sage of the garden, and with the Green-leaved, which is but a sub-variety, the most esteemed for culinary purposes. The young stalks, the leaf-stems, and the ribs and nerves of the leaves, are purple; the young leaves are also sometimes tinged with the same color, but generally change by age to clear green.

The Red-leaved is generally regarded as possessing a higher flavor than the Green-leaved, and is preferred for cultivation; though the difference, if any really exists, is quite unimportant. The productiveness of the varieties is nearly the same. The leaves of the Green Sage are larger than those of the Red; but the latter produces them in greater numbers.

A variety of the preceding; the young shoots, the leaf-stalks, and the ribs and nerves of the leaves, being green.   **Green-leaved.** Green-Top.

There appears to be little permanency in the characters by which the varieties are distinguished. Both possess like properties, and are equally worthy of cultivation. From seeds of either of the sorts, plants answering to the description of the Red-leaved and Green-leaved would probably be produced, with almost every intermediate shade of color.

SAVORY.

Saturjea.

The cultivated species are as follow:—

An annual species, from the south of Europe. Stem twelve or fifteen inches high, erect, rather slender, and producing its branches in pairs; the leaves are opposite, narrow, rigid, with a pleasant odor, and warm, aromatic taste; the flowers are pale pink, or flesh-colored, and are produced at the base of the leaves, towards the upper part of the plant,—each stem supporting two flowers; the seeds are quite small, deep brown, and retain their vitality two or three years.   **Summer Savory.** Saturjea Hortensis.

Propagation and Cultivation.— Summer Savory is always raised from seeds, sown annually in April or May. It thrives best in light, mellow soil, and the seed should be sown in shallow drills fourteen or fifteen inches apart. When the plants are two or three inches high, thin them to five or six inches apart in the rows, and cultivate in the usual manner during the summer.

When the plants have commenced flowering, they should be cut to the ground, tied in small bunches, and dried in an airy, shady situation.

For early use, the seeds are sometimes sown in a hot-bed on a gentle heat, and the seedlings afterwards transplanted to the open ground in rows, as directed for sowing.

Use. — The aromatic tops of the plant are used, green or dried, in stuffing meats and fowl. They are also mixed in salads, and sometimes boiled with pease and beans. It is sold in considerable quantities, at all seasons of the year, in a dried and pulverized state, packed in hermetically-sealed bottles or boxes.

Winter Savory. *Thomp.* SATUREJA MONTANA. A hardy, evergreen shrub, with a low, branching stem about a foot in height. The leaves are opposite, narrow, and rigid, like those of the preceding species; the flowers resemble those of the Summer Savory, but are larger and of a paler color; the seeds, which ripen in autumn, are small, dark brown, and retain their vitality three years.

Propagation and Culture. — It may be raised from seed, or increased by a division of the roots. The seeds are sown in April or May, in shallow drills, fifteen inches apart; and the roots may be divided in spring or autumn. The plants should be set one foot apart in the rows, to which distance the seedlings should also be thinned as soon as they are well up.

After they are established, the shrubs are treated as Sage, — trimmed in September or October, and replanted once in three or four years.

Use. — It is used for the same purposes as Summer Savory. The leaves and tender parts of the young branches are mixed in salads; they are also boiled with pease and beans, and, when dried and powdered, are used in stuffings for meats and fowl.

SPEARMINT.

Green Mint. — Mentha viridis.

A hardy, perennial plant, generally cultivated in gardens, but growing naturally in considerable abundance about springs of water, and in rich, wet localities. The stem is erect, four-sided, smooth, and two feet or more in height; the leaves are opposite, in pairs, stemless, toothed on the margin, and sharply pointed; the flowers are purple, and are produced in August, in long, slender, terminal spikes; the seeds are small, oblong, of a brown color, and retain their vitality five years.

Soil, Propagation, and Culture. — It may be grown from seed, but is best propagated by a division of the roots, which are long and creeping, and readily establish themselves wherever they are planted. Spearmint thrives best in rich, moist soil, but may be grown in any good garden loam. The roots may be set either in the autumn or spring.

Use. — Mint is sometimes mixed in salads, and is used for flavoring soups of all descriptions. It is often boiled with green pease, and, with the addition of sugar and vinegar, forms a much-esteemed relish for roasted lamb. It has also much reputed efficacy as a medicinal plant.

Curled-leaved Spearmint.
A variety with curled foliage. It is a good sort for garnishing, but, for general use, is inferior to the Common or Plain-leaved species before described. Propagated by dividing the roots.

THYME.

Thymus.

Two species of Thyme are cultivated for culinary purposes, — the Common Garden Thyme (*T. vulgaris*) and the Lemon or Evergreen Thyme (*T. citriodorus*).

They are hardy, perennial plants, of a shrubby character,

and low growth. They are propagated from seeds, and by dividing the roots; but the finest plants are produced from seeds.

Broad-leaved. The Broad-leaved or Common Garden
<small>THYMUS VULGARIS.</small> Thyme is more cultivated in this country than any other species or variety. The stem is ten or twelve inches high, shrubby, of a brownish-red color, and much branched; the leaves are small, narrow, green above, and whitish beneath; flowers purple, in terminal spikes; the seeds are black, and exceedingly small. Two hundred and thirty thousand are contained in an ounce, and they retain their vitality two years.

Propagation and Cultivation. — The seeds are sown in April or May, thinly, in shallow drills ten or twelve inches apart. If propagated by dividing the roots, the old plants should be taken up in April, and divided into as many parts as the roots and tops will admit. They may be cut for use in August and September.

Use. — The leaves have an agreeable, aromatic odor, and are used for flavoring soups, stuffings, and sauces.

Lemon Thyme. *Loud.* A low, evergreen shrub, with a somewhat
<small>THYMUS CITRIODORUS.</small> trailing stem, rarely rising more than six or eight inches high. It is readily distinguished from the Common or Broad-leaved by the soft, pleasant, lemon-like odor of the young shoots and leaves.

It is used for flavoring various dishes, and by some is preferred to the Broad-leaved.

Seedling plants are said to vary in fragrance; and, when a choice stock can be obtained, it is better to propagate by dividing the plants.

Additional Oleraceous plants, including Anise, Borage, Clary, Costmary, Cumin, Dill, Fennel, Lovage, Nigella, Peppermint, and Marigold, with modes of sowing, culture, and using, will be found in "THE FIELD AND GARDEN VEGETABLES OF AMERICA."

CHAPTER X.

EGG-PLANT, PEPPER, AND TOMATO.

EGG-PLANT.
Solanum melongena.

THE Egg-plant is a tender annual, with an erect, branching stem, and oblong, bluish-green, powdered leaves. The fruit is often somewhat oblong, but exceedingly variable in form, size, and color; the seeds are small, yellowish, reniform, flattened, and retain their germinative properties seven years.

Sowing and Culture. — The seed should be sown in a hot-bed in March, at the time and in the manner of sowing tomato-seed. The seedlings should not be transplanted into the open ground until the commencement of summer weather, when they may be set out in rows two feet apart, and two feet asunder in the rows. The fruit will be fit for use the last of August, or beginning of September.

If no hot-bed is at hand, sufficient plants for a small garden may be easily raised by sowing a few seeds in March in common flower-pots, and placing them in the sunny window of the sitting-room or kitchen.

In favorable seasons, a crop may be obtained by sowing the seeds in May in the open ground, and transplanting the seedlings, when two or three inches high, in a warm and sheltered situation.

Use. — "It is used, both boiled and stewed, in sauces, like the Tomato. A favorite method among the French is to scoop out the seeds, fill up the cavity with sweet herbs, and fry the fruit whole." — *McInt.*

A common method of cooking and serving is as follows: Cut the fruit in slices half an inch thick; press out as much of the juice as possible, and parboil; after which, fry the slices in batter, or in fresh butter in which grated bread has been mixed; season with pepper, salt, and sweet herbs, to suit; or, if preferred, the slices may be broiled as steaks or chops.

Varieties: —

American Large Purple. Fruit remarkably large, — often measuring eight inches in depth, seven inches in diameter, and weighing four or five pounds; skin deep purple, with occasional stripes of green about the stem; plant hardy and stocky.

The American Large Purple is more generally cultivated in this country than any other variety. The plants produce two (rarely three) fruits; but the first formed are usually the best developed.

American Large Purple Egg-plant.

It is similar to, if not identical with, the Round Purple of English and French authors.

Quite distinct from the Common White or **Chinese Long White.** *Vil.*
the Purple. Plant of low growth, with pale
foliage; fruit white, eight or nine inches long, two inches
and a half in diameter, and often more or less curved, particularly when the end is in contact with the ground.

It is later than the White or Purple varieties, and nearly
of the season of the Scarlet-fruited. To obtain the fruit
in full perfection, the plants must be started in a hot-bed.

Fruit nearly ovoid, smaller than the Round **Guadaloupe Striped.** *Vil.*
or Long Purple; skin white, streaked and
variegated with red.

The plants of this variety resemble those **Long Purple.** *Trans.*
of the Round Purple. The fruit is oblong,
somewhat club-shaped, six or eight inches in length, sometimes straight, but often slightly bent. At maturity, the skin
is generally deep purple; but the color varies much more
than the Large Round: it is sometimes pale purple, slightly
striped, sometimes variegated with longitudinal yellowish
stripes, and always more deeply colored on the exposed
side.

It is early, of easy culture, hardy and productive, excellent for the table, thrives well in almost any section of the
Northern States, and, if started in a hot-bed, would perfect
its fruit in the Canadas.

A sub-variety of the Large Round, producing **New-York Improved.**
the same number of fruits, which are
generally of a deeper color, and average of larger size.
The leaves are often spiny; and, if the variety is genuine,
the plants will be readily distinguished from those of the
last named by their more dense or compact habit of growth.

It is not early, and appears to be better suited to the
climate of the Middle States than to that of New England;
though it is successfully cultivated in the vicinity of Boston,

Mass., by starting the plants in a hot-bed, and setting them in a warm and sheltered situation.

Round Purple.
Trans.
LARGE ROUND PURPLE.
Plant from two to three feet high. The fruit is obovate, four or five inches in diameter, six or seven inches deep, slightly indented at the apex, and of a fine deep purple when well matured, though specimens sometimes occur slightly striped or rayed with yellowish-green.

The American Large Purple, if not the same, is but an improved form of this variety.

Scarlet-fruited Egg-plant.
Hov. Mag.
A highly ornamental variety, introduced from Portugal. The plant attains the height of three feet, with leaves six inches long. In general appearance, it resembles the Common Egg-plant; but the fruit, which is of the size of a hen's egg, is of a beautiful scarlet.

It is rarely if ever used for food, but is principally cultivated for its peculiar, richly colored, and ornamental fruit, which makes a fine garnish.

The variety is late, and not hardy. The seeds should be started early in a hot-bed, and the plants grown in a warm and sheltered situation.

White Egg-plant.
Fruit milk-white, egg-shaped, varying from three to five inches in length, and from two inches and a half to three inches and a half in diameter.

It is the earliest, hardiest, and most productive of all varieties. The plants frequently produce five or six fruits each; but the first formed are generally the largest.

If sown in the open ground early in May, the plants will often perfect a portion of their fruit; but they are most productive when started in a hot-bed.

The fruit is sometimes eaten cooked in the manner of the Purple varieties, but is less esteemed.

PEPPER.

Capsicum. — *Capsicum annuum.*

The *Capsicum annuum*, or Common Garden-pepper, is a native of India. The stalks vary in height from a foot to nearly three feet; the flowers are generally white or purple; the pods differ in a remarkable degree in size, form, color, and acridness; the seeds are yellow, nearly circular, flattened, and, like the flesh or rind of the fruit, remarkable for their intense piquancy. Nearly forty-five hundred are contained in an ounce, and their vitality is retained five years.

Propagation and Cultivation. — The plants are always propagated from seeds. Early in April, sow in a hot-bed, in shallow drills six inches apart, and transplant to the open ground when summer weather has commenced. The plants should be set in warm, mellow soil, in rows sixteen inches apart, and the same distance apart in the rows; or, in ordinary seasons, the following simple method may be adopted for a small garden, and will afford an abundant supply of peppers for family use: When all danger from frost is past, and the soil is warm and settled, sow the seeds in the open ground, in drills three-fourths of an inch deep, and fourteen inches apart; and, while young, thin out the plants to ten inches apart in the rows. Cultivate in the usual manner, and the crop will be fit for use early in September.

Use. — "The pod, or fruit, is much used in pickles, seasonings, and made dishes, as both the pod and seeds yield a warm, acrid oil, the heat of which, being imparted to the stomach, promotes digestion, and corrects the flatulency of vegetable aliments. The larger and more common sorts are raised in great quantities, by market-gardeners in the vicinity of populous towns, for the supply of pickle warehouses."

Species and Varieties. — Bell-Pepper. Plant two feet and upwards in height, stocky and branching; LARGE BELL. BULL-NOSE. flowers white, sometimes measuring nearly an inch and a half in diameter.

The pods, which are remarkably large, and often measure nearly four inches deep and three inches in diameter, are pendent, broadest at the stem, slightly tapering, and generally terminate in four obtuse, cone-like points. At maturity, the fruit changes to brilliant, glossy, coral-red.

Bell-pepper.

The Bell-pepper is early, sweet, and pleasant to the taste, and much less acrid or pungent than most of the other sorts. In many places, it is preferred to the Squash-pepper for pickling, not only because of its mildness, but for its thick, fleshy, and tender rind.

In England, they are pickled as follows: The pods are plucked while green, slit down on one side, and, after the seeds are taken out, immersed in salt and water for twenty-four hours, changing the water at the end of the first twelve. After soaking the full time, they are laid to drain an hour or two, put into bottles or jars, and boiled vinegar, after being allowed to cool, poured over them till they are entirely covered. The jars are then closely stopped for a few weeks, when the pods will be fit for use. In this form, they have been pronounced the best and most wholesome of all pickles.

Bird-pepper. Stem fifteen to eighteen inches high; pods
Vil. erect, sharply conical, an inch and three-quarters long, half an inch in diameter, and of a brilliant coral-red when ripe.

The variety is late. If sown in the open ground, some of the pods, if the season be favorable, will be fit for use before the plants are destroyed by frost; but few will be fully perfected unless the plants are started under glass.

The Bird-pepper is one of the most piquant of all varieties, and is less valuable as a green pickle than many milder and thicker-fleshed sorts. It is cultivated in rows fourteen inches apart, and ten or twelve inches asunder in the rows.

The pods of this species are quite small, **Cayenne Pepper.** cone-shaped, coral-red when ripe, intensely **C. Frutescens.** acrid, and furnish the Cayenne Pepper of commerce. Like others of the family, it is of tropical origin, and being a perennial, and of a shrubby character, will not succeed in open culture at the North.

Both the green and ripe pods are used as pickles, and also for making Chili vinegar, or pepper-sauce, which is done by simply putting a handful of the pods in a bottle, afterwards filled with the best vinegar, and stopping it closely. In a few weeks, it will be fit for use.

The process of preparing Cayenne Pepper is as follows: The pods are gathered when fully ripe. "In India, they are dried in the sun; but, in cooler climates, they should be dried on a slow hot-plate, or in a moderately heated oven: they are then pulverized, and sifted through a fine sieve, mixed with salt, and, when dried, put into close, corked bottles, for the purpose of excluding the air. This article is subject to great adulteration, flour being often mixed with it, and, still worse, red lead, which is much of the same color, and greatly increases the weight.

"A better method is to dry the pods in a slow oven, split them open, extract the seeds, and then pulverize them (the pods) to a fine powder; sifting the powder through a thin muslin sieve, and pulverizing the parts that do not pass through, and sifting again until the whole is reduced to the finest possible state. Place the powder in air-tight glass bottles, but add no salt or other ingredient whatever." — *McInt.*

The pods of either of the long-fruited sorts, or those of the Cherry-pepper, prepared as above, will furnish a quality of Cayenne Pepper greatly superior to that ordinarily sold by grocers, or even by apothecaries and druggists.

The larger and milder kinds, powdered in the same manner, make a wholesome and pleasant grade of pepper, of sufficient pungency for a majority of palates.

Cherry-pepper.
Capsicum Cerasi-forme.

Stem twelve to fifteen inches high, strong and branching; pod, or fruit, erect, nearly globular or cherry-form, and, at maturity, of a deep, rich, glossy scarlet color. It is remarkable for its intense piquancy, exceeding in this respect nearly all the annual varieties.

Cherry-pepper.

It is not so early as some of the larger sorts, but in favorable seasons will perfect a sufficient portion of its crop in the open ground, both for seed and pickling. For the latter purpose, the peppers should be plucked while still green, put into a common jar or wide-mouthed bottle, and vinegar added to fill the vessel. In a few weeks, they will be fit for use.

When in perfection, the plants are very ornamental, the glossy, coral-red of the numerous pods presenting a fine contrast with the deep-green foliage surrounding them.

A variety occurs with larger, more conical, and pendent pods; and there is also a variety with yellow fruit.

Chili Pepper. *vu.* Pods pendent, sharply conical, nearly two inches in length, half an inch in diameter, of a brilliant scarlet when ripe, and exceedingly piquant; plant eighteen inches high. Requires a long, warm season.

Long Red Pepper. Fruit brilliant coral-red, generally pendulous, sometimes erect, conical, often curved towards the end, nearly four inches in length, and from an inch to an inch and a half in diameter; skin, or flesh, quite thin, and exceedingly piquant.

Long Red Pepper. Stalk two feet high; foliage of medium size, blistered and wrinkled.

The variety yields abundantly, but attains its greatest perfection when started in a hot-bed. The ripe pods, dried and pulverized as directed for Cayenne Pepper, make an excellent substitute for that article.

The plants, with ripe fruit, are very ornamental.

Long Yellow.

Pods pendent, long, and tapering, three to four inches in length, and an inch in their greatest diameter. At maturity, they assume a lively, rich, glossy yellow, and the plants are then showy and ornamental.

Stem two feet and upwards in height. The flowers are white, and nearly an inch in diameter. Like the Long Red, it is very piquant. It is also late; and, to obtain the fruit in perfection, the seed should be started in a hot-bed in April.

Round or Large Red Cherry-pepper.

This is but a sub-variety of the common Red Cherry-pepper, differing only in its larger size.

It is quite late, and should be started in a hot-bed.

Squash-pepper. TOMATO-SHAPED.

Fruit compressed, more or less ribbed, two inches and three-quarters in diameter, and two inches in depth; skin smooth and glossy,— when ripe, of a brilliant coral-red; flesh thick, mild, and pleasant to the taste, though possessing more piquancy than the Large Bell or Sweet Spanish.

Plant two feet high, stout and branching; leaves broad and large; fruit drooping; fruit-stem short and thick.

The Squash-pepper is extensively grown for the market, and is most in use in the pickle warehouses of the Eastern and Middle States. In field-culture, the plants are started in hot-beds in April, and, after the beginning of summer weather, transplanted to the open ground, fourteen to eighteen inches apart, according to the quality of the soil. The fruit is generally sold by weight; and an acre of land, in a fair state of cultivation, will yield three tons, — a bushel of the thick-fleshed sort weighing nearly thirty-two pounds. An excellent pickle may be made by preparing the peppers in the manner directed for the Bell variety.

As grown by different market-men and gardeners, there are several sub-varieties of the Squash-pepper, differing both in form and in the thickness of the flesh; the latter quality, however, being considered of the greater importance, as the thick-fleshed sorts not only yield a greater weight to the acre, but are more esteemed for the table.

The Squash-pepper succeeds well when sown in the open ground in May, in drills fourteen inches apart. The plants should be ten or twelve inches apart in the rows. When grown too closely, they are liable to draw up, making a weakly, slender growth, and yield much less than when allowed sufficient space for their full development. Low-growing, stocky, and branching plants are the most productive.

Sweet Mountain Pepper. This variety resembles the Large Bell, if it is not identical. The Sweet Mountain may be somewhat larger; but, aside from this, there is no perceptible difference in the varieties.

Sweet Spanish. Fruit obtusely conical, often four inches in length, and nearly three inches in diameter, — brilliant glossy scarlet at maturity; stem strong and sturdy, two feet or more in height; fruit sometimes erect, but generally drooping.

Though one of the largest varieties, the Sweet Spanish is also one of the earliest. The flesh is sweet, mild, and pleasant, and the variety is much esteemed by those to whom the more pungent kinds are objectionable. When prepared in the same form, it makes a pickle equally as fine as the Large Bell.

TOMATO.

Love-apple. — *Solanum lycopersicum.*

When fully grown, the Tomato-plant is from four to seven feet and upwards in height or length, with a branching, irregular, recumbent stem, and dense foliage. The flowers are yellow, in branching groups or clusters; the fruit is red, white, or yellow, and exceedingly variable in size and form; the seeds are lens-shaped, yellowish-white, or pale gray. Twenty-one thousand are contained in an ounce, and they retain their vitality five years.

Propagation. — The Tomato is raised from seeds, which should be sown in a hot-bed in March, or in the open ground as soon as the frost will permit. As the plants, even in the most favorable seasons, seldom perfectly mature their full crop, they should be started as early and forwarded as rapidly as possible, whether by hot-bed or open-air culture. If the seeds are sown in a hot-bed, the drills should be made five inches apart, and half an inch deep. When the plants are two inches high, they should be removed to another part of the bed, and pricked out four or five inches apart, or removed into small pots, allowing a single plant to a pot. They are sometimes twice transplanted, allowing more space or a larger pot at each removal, by which process the plants are rendered more sturdy and branching than they become by being but once transplanted.

As early in May as the weather is suitable, the plants may be set in the open ground where they are to remain, and should be three feet apart in each direction; or, if against a wall or trellis, three feet from plant to plant. Water freely at the time of transplanting, shelter from the sun for a few days or until they are well established, and cultivate in the usual form during summer.

If sown in the open ground, select a sheltered situation, pulverize the soil finely, and sow a few seeds in drills, as directed for the hot-bed. This may be done in November (just before the closing-up of the ground), or the last of March, or first of April. In May, when the plants are three or four inches high, transplant to where they are to remain, as before directed.

In gardens where tomatoes have been cultivated, young plants often spring up abundantly from the seeds of the decayed fruit of the preceding season. These are generally hardy and stocky, and, when transplanted, often succeed as well, and frequently produce fruit as early, as plants from the hot-bed or nursery-bed.

Sufficient plants for the garden of a small family may be started with little trouble by sowing a few seeds in a garden-pan or large flower-pot, and placing it in a sunny window of the sitting-room or kitchen. If the seed is sown in this manner about the middle or 20th of March, the plants will be of good size for setting by the time the weather will be suitable for their removal.

Hoop-training of the Tomato.

Forcing the Crop. — "The ripening of the fruit may be hastened by setting the plants against a south wall or close fence. As the plants increase in size, they must be nailed or otherwise attached to the wall or fence, and, if the weather be dry, liberally watered. When the two first trusses of bloom have expanded, the shoot should be stopped by pinching off the portion which is beyond the leaf above the second truss, and no more lateral shoots should be suffered to grow; but the leaves must be carefully preserved, especially those near the trusses of bloom. The number of shoots on each plant will vary according to the strength and vigor of the particular plant; but three or four will be quite enough, leaving about half a dozen trusses of fruit.

Culture and Training. — A convenient, simple, and economical support for the plants may be made from three narrow hoops, — one twelve, another fifteen, and the third eighteen or twenty inches in diameter, — and attaching

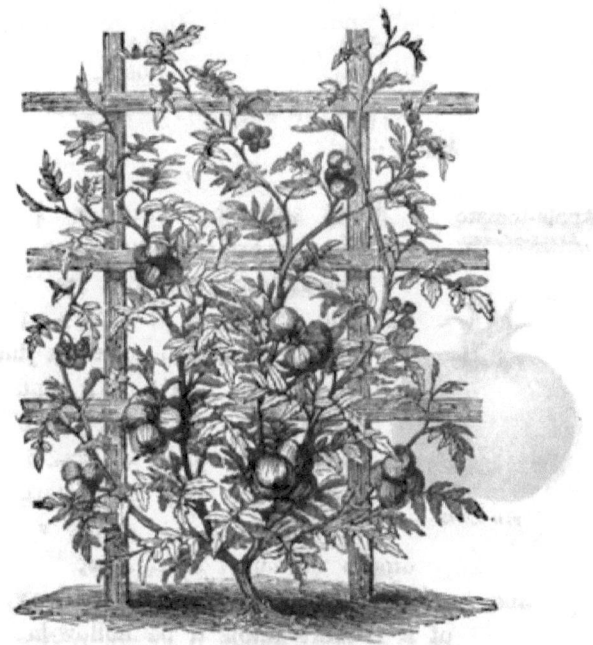

Trellis-training.

them a foot from each other to three stakes, four feet in length; placing the lower hoop so that it may be ten inches from the surface of the ground after the stakes are driven.

EGG-PLANT, PEPPER, AND TOMATO.

The figure on the preceding page illustrates this method of training. It secures abundance of light, free access of air, and, in skilful hands, may be made quite ornamental.

Or a trellis may be cheaply formed by setting common stakes, four feet in length, four feet apart, on a line with the plants, and nailing laths, or narrow strips of deal, from stake to stake, nine inches apart on the stakes; afterwards attaching the plants by means of bass, or other soft, fibrous material, to the trellis, in the manner of grape-vines or other climbing plants. By either of these methods, the plants not only present a neater appearance, but the ripening of the fruit is facilitated, and the crop much more conveniently gathered when required for use.

Varieties. — These are quite numerous. Some are merely nominal, many are variable or quite obscure, and a few appear to be distinct, and, in a degree, permanent. The principal are as follow : —

Apple-tomato.
APPLE-SHAPED.

Apple-tomato.

Fruit somewhat flattened, inclining to globular, depressed about the stem, but smooth and regular in its general outline. The size is quite variable; but, if well grown, the average diameter is two inches and a half, and the depth two inches. Skin deep, rich crimson; flesh bright pink, or rose-color, — the rind being thick and hard, and not readily reduced to a pulp when cooked.

The Apple-tomato is early, hardy, productive, keeps well, and, for salad and certain forms of cookery, is much esteemed; but it is more liable to be hollow-hearted than any other of the large varieties.

In form, as well as in the thick, tough character of its rind, it resembles the Bermuda.

Bermuda.

This is a red or rose-colored, apple-formed sort, extensively imported from Bermuda into the Middle and Northern States in May and the early summer months.

Like the preceding variety, it varies considerably in size, — some specimens measuring little more than an inch in diameter, while others from the same plant, matured at nearly the same season, frequently exceed a diameter of two inches and a half.

It possesses a thick, rather tough rind, which rarely becomes pulpy in the process of cooking, and, besides, is quite light and hollow-hearted. In size and form, it somewhat resembles the Apple-tomato. When cultivated in New England or the Middle States, it has little merit, either for its productiveness or early maturity.

Extra Early. White's Extra Early. EARLY RED.

A medium-sized Red variety, generally round, but frequently of an oval form, flattened, sometimes ribbed, but generally smooth, and, when fully matured, of a deeper color than the later Red sorts. Average specimens measure two inches and a half in diameter, and an inch and a half in depth. The plants are moderately vigorous, and readily distinguished by their peculiar curled and apparently withering foliage.

Flesh pale red, quite firm, mild, not very seedy, and well filling the fruit, which is considerably heavier than the Apple-shaped. When cooked, it yields a much greater product, in proportion to its size, than the last-named and similar hollow-hearted varieties. Productive, and of good quality.

Planted at the same time with the Common Red varieties, it will ripen two weeks earlier. An excellent sort for the garden, and recommended for general cultivation.

In order to retain this or any other early variety in its purity, seed for planting should be saved from the smoothest, best-formed, and earliest-ripened fruit. Few of the numerous kinds now cultivated possess much permanency of character, and rapidly degenerate if raised from seed taken from the scattered, irregular, and often immature tomatoes remaining upon the plants at the close of the season.

Fejee. Fruit quite large, red, often blushed or tinged with pinkish-crimson, flattened, sometimes ribbed, often smooth, well filled to the centre; flesh pink, or pale red, firm, and well flavored; plant hardy, healthy, and a strong grower.

Seeds received from different reliable sources, and recommended as being strictly true, produced plants and fruit in no respects distinguishable from the Perfected.

Fig-tomato.
RED PEAR-
SHAPED TOMATO.
A small, red, pyriform or pear-shaped sort, measuring from an inch and a quarter to an inch and a half in length, and nearly an inch in its broadest diameter. Flesh pale red, or pink, very solid and compact, and generally completely filling the centre of the fruit.

Like the Plum-tomato, it is remarkably uniform in size, and also in shape; but it is little used, except for preserving, — other larger varieties being considered more economical for stewing, making catchup, and like purposes.

Fig-tomato.

The variety is usually employed for making tomato-figs, which are thus prepared: —

"Pour boiling water over the tomatoes in order to remove the skin; after which, weigh, and place in a stone jar, with as much sugar as tomatoes, and let them stand two days; then pour off the sirup, and boil and skim it till no scum rises; pour it over the tomatoes, and let them stand two days as before; then boil and skim again. After the third time, they are fit to dry, if the weather is good;

if not, let them stand in the sirup until drying weather. Then place them on large earthern plates, or dishes, and put them in the sun to dry, which will take about a week; after which, pack them down in small wooden boxes, with fine, white sugar between every layer. Tomatoes prepared in this manner will keep for years." — *Mrs. Eliza Marsh, in Hov. Mag.*

An improved variety of the Common Large Red, attaining a much larger size. Fruit solid, bright red, sometimes smooth, but generally ribbed, and often exceedingly irregular; some of the larger specimens seemingly composed of two or more united. The fruit is frequently produced in masses or large clusters, which clasp about the stem, and rest so closely in the axils of the branches as to admit of being detached only by the rending asunder of the fruit itself; flesh pale pink, and well flavored.

Giant Tomato.
Hov. Mag.
MAMMOTH. MAMMOTH CHIHUAHUA.

Like most varieties, the amount of product is in a great degree dependent on soil, culture, and season. Under favorable conditions, twenty-five pounds to a plant is not an unusual yield. Single specimens of the fruit sometimes weigh four, and even five or six pounds.

The Giant Tomato is not early, and, for the garden, perhaps not superior to many other kinds; but for field-culture, for market, for making catchup in quantities, or for the use of pickle-warehouses, it is recommended as one of the best of all the sorts now cultivated.

In size and form, this variety differs little from the common Apple-tomato. Its superiority consists in its much greater solidity, in the absence of the tough rind common to the old variety, and in the less seedy and much more pulpy character of its flesh. The color also is somewhat deeper, and it ripens nearly two weeks earlier.

Improved Apple-tomato.
EARLY APPLE-TOMATO.

The Improved Apple-tomato is remarkable for its uniform size and smoothness, and must be classed as being decidedly one of the best. Recommended for general cultivation.

Large Red Tomato. Fruit sometimes smooth, often irregular, flattened, more or less ribbed; size large, but varied much by soil and cultivation,—well-grown specimens are from three to four inches in diameter, two inches and a half in depth, and weigh from eight to twelve ounces;

Large Red Tomato.

skin smooth, glossy, and, when ripe, of a fine red color; flesh pale red, or rose color,—the interior of the fruit being comparatively well filled; flavor good.

Not early, but one of the most productive of all the varieties; the plants, when grown in rich soil, and properly treated, producing from twelve to fifteen pounds each.

From the time of the introduction of the Tomato to its general use in this country, the Large Red was almost the only kind cultivated, or even commonly known. The numerous excellent sorts now almost everywhere disseminated, including the Fejee, Seedless, Giant, and Lester's Perfected, are but improved sub-varieties, obtained from the Common Large Red by cultivation and selection.

Large Yellow. Plant, in its general character, not distinguishable from the Large Red. The fruit also is quite similar in form and size, the principal mark of distinction being its color, which is a fine, clear, semi-transparent yellow. Flesh yellow, well filling the centre, and perhaps a little sweeter or milder than the Red, though generally not distinguishable when stewed or otherwise prepared for the table.

The variety is hardy, yields abundantly, and comes to perfection with the Large Red. It is, however, not generally cultivated, the Red descriptions being more commonly used, and consequently better adapted for cultivation for the market.

Mexican. Fruit large, smooth, frequently of an oval form, bright red, often tinted with rose, or bright pink; flesh pink, solid, filling the fruit to the centre. It is similar to, if not identical with, the Perfected.

Perfected. Lester's Perfected. Pomo d'Oro Lesteriano. A recently introduced and somewhat distinct variety. Plant remarkably healthy and vigorous, often attaining a height or length of six or eight feet, and, in strong soil, of more than ten feet; fruit pinkish-red, or rose-red, of large size, smooth and regular, flattened, well filled to the centre, and, when cooked, yielding a large return in proportion to its bulk; flesh firm, well flavored, with few seeds intermixed; in this last respect, not unlike the Seedless.

When started at the same time, it ripens two weeks after the early varieties, and continues to yield in great abundance until the plants are destroyed by frost. It is considered one of the best sorts for cultivation for the market, and by many is preferred to all others for the garden.

On the authority of a recent writer, the variety has already, to some extent, degenerated. Impure seed, or the influence of some peculiar locality, may have furnished grounds for the statement; but if the variety is genuine, or unmixed, it will, in almost any soil or exposure, commend itself by its hardiness, solidity, and great productiveness.

Red Cherry-tomato. A small, red Tomato, nearly spherical, and about half an inch in diameter. The fruit is produced in great profusion, in large bunches, or clusters, but is of little value, on account of its small size. It is sometimes used as a preserve, and by some esteemed for pickling.

Red Plum-tomato. Fruit bright-red, or scarlet, oval, solid, an inch and a quarter or an inch and a half in depth, and an inch in diameter; flesh pink, or rose-red.

The variety is remarkable for its symmetry and for its uniform size. When ripe, the fruit is not easily distinguished from some varieties of scarlet plums. It is hardy, early, and yields abundantly, but is employed principally for pickling and preserving, — its small size rendering it of little value for stewing or for catchup.

Mixed with the Yellow, the fruit makes a fine garnish and an excellent salad.

Round Red. A small, round, Red variety, an inch in diameter. It is one of the earliest of all the cultivated sorts, uniformly smooth and regular, but of little value, except for pickling or preserving.

Round Yellow. Of the size and form of the foregoing, differing only in color.

Seedless. Very similar to, if not identical with, the Perfected. Fruit almost rose-red, smooth and handsome, solid, with few seeds.

The Cook's Favorite. This recently introduced variety originated in Burlington County, N. J. The plant is strong and vigorous, with fine, broad, light-green foliage. The fruit is of medium size, roundish, or oval, smooth, of a rich, deep color and remarkable solidity, — rarely with a cavity, or hard, unripe parts at the centre. It is a few days earlier than the Perfected. The variety is popular in the

Middle States, where it is said to yield abundantly, and is extensively grown in the vicinity of New York and Philadelphia for marketing. It is also raised to some extent in New England, but has proved somewhat less productive than the Perfected and other larger-fruited sorts.

Originated with Mr. Henry Tilden of Davenport, Ia. The plant is of stocky habit, rather short, with distinct foliage. The fruit is of full medium size, roundish, inclining to oval, very solid, and of a rich, glossy scarlet-color; flesh firm, with few seeds.   *Tilden.* *Tilden's Seedling.*

This new variety has proved early and productive. It is a good keeper, grows uniformly smooth and handsome, is of good quality, bears transportation well, and whether for the garden, or for field-culture for market-purposes, is a truly excellent sort, and is recommended for cultivation.

Mr. Tilden, the originator, obtained five hundred bushels from a single acre.

Like many other garden vegetables, the different varieties of the Tomato readily intermix or hybridize when grown together; and it is with difficulty that any sort is kept in a strictly pure condition. When the seeds or plants are annually purchased, no precaution as to the growing of one kind in the vicinity of another is required; but, when seeds are saved for propagation, each variety should be grown as far as possible apart from all others.

A new variety, raised from seed by Grenier, gardener to M. de Fleurieux, at a place in France called Château de Laye (whence the name), and introduced by M. Vilmorin of Paris.   *Tree-tomato.* *Vil. Hov. Mag.* *New Upright.* *Tomate de Laye.* *French Tree-Tomato.*

It is distinct from all others, rising quite erect to the height of two feet or upwards, with a stem of remarkable size and strength. The branches are short, and not numerous, usually eight or ten inches in length, — thus requiring no heading-in; leaves not abundant, rather curled, much wrinkled, very firm, closely placed on the sturdy branches, and of a remarkably deep, shining-green color; fruit bright red, of large size, smooth, and well filled to the centre, — in many respects resembling the Perfected, though more regular in form.

From the peculiar, tree-like character of the plants, the variety is remarkably well adapted for cultivation in pots; but its late maturity greatly impairs its value as a variety for forcing. It is a slow grower, tardy in forming and perfecting its fruit, and, for ordinary garden-culture, cannot be recommended as being preferable to the Perfected and other earlier and much more prolific varieties. It has been described as strictly self-supporting: but, though the fruit is produced in a remarkably close and almost clasping manner about the sturdy stem and branches, its weight often brings the plants to the ground; and consequently, in exposed situations, it will be necessary to provide stakes, or some similar means of support; though the plants never exhibit the rambling, recumbent character of the Common Tomato.

White Tomato. Plant similar in habit to the Large Red; fruit large, generally ribbed, often irregular, but sometimes smooth. Its distinguishing characteristic is its color, which, if the fruit be screened by foliage, or if grown in the shade, is nearly clear white: if much exposed to the sun, it assumes a yellowish tinge, — much paler, however, than the Large Yellow. Flesh yellowish, more watery than that of the Large Red, and of a somewhat peculiar flavor, much esteemed by some, and unpalatable to others.

The variety is hardy, remarkably productive, as early as the Large Red, bears transportation as well, and is equally as large and solid: but its color, before and after being cooked, is unattractive; and it is rarely seen in the markets, and seldom cultivated for family use.

A yellow variety of the Red Cherry-tomato, — differing only in color. **Yellow Cherry-tomato.**
Quite showy, but of little value for culinary purposes.

A sub-variety of the Red Pear-shaped, with a clear, semi-transparent, yellow skin and yellow flesh. Like the preceding, it is little used, except for preserving and pickling. **Yellow Pear-shaped Tomato. Yellow Fig-Tomato.**

A variety of the Red Plum, of the same size and form, and equally symmetrical, — **Yellow Plum-tomato.**
distinguished only by the color of its skin, which is a fine, clear, transparent yellow. It is used principally for preserving, its small size rendering it of little value in any other form.

When the two varieties are intermixed, the colors present a fine contrast; and a basket of the fruit is quite a beautiful object.

This variety, or more properly species, differs essentially in the character of its foliage, and manner of fructification, from the Garden Tomato. **Grape or Cluster Tomato. Solanum Sp.**
The leaves are much smoother, thinner in texture, and have little of the musky odor peculiar to the Common Tomato-plant. The fruit is nearly globular, quite small, about half an inch in diameter, of a bright-scarlet color, and produced in leafless, simple, or compound clusters, six or eight inches in length, containing from twenty to sixty berries, or tomatoes; the whole having an appearance not unlike a large cluster of currants.

The plants usually grow about three feet in height or length, and, in cultivation, should be treated in all respects like those of other varieties. The flowers are yellow, and comparatively small. Early.

Though quite ornamental, it is of little value in domestic economy, on account of its diminutive size.

Early York. Fruit of medium size, bright red, round, smooth, and generally solid to the centre.

It resembles the Extra Early, and is one of the best sorts for the garden, though not so profitable a market-tomato as many of the larger and later varieties.

Full descriptions of the various medicinal plants usually grown in gardens, with modes of culture and use, will be found in "THE FIELD AND GARDEN VEGETABLES OF AMERICA." Also detailed directions for the raising of edible Mushrooms, including the Agaricus campestris, Boletus, Clavaria, Morel, and the Truffle, with a full description of each species.

CHAPTER XI.

LEGUMINOUS PLANTS.

American Garden-bean. — Asparagus-bean. — Lima Bean. — Scarlet-runner. Sieva Bean. — English Bean. — Pea.

AMERICAN GARDEN-BEAN.

French Bean. — Kidney Bean. — Haricot, of the French. — Phaseolus vulgaris.

THE American Garden-bean is a tender, annual plant from the East Indies, with a dwarfish or climbing stem, and trifoliate leaves. The flowers are variable in color, and produced in loose clusters; the seed-pods are long, flattened, or cylindrical, bivalved, and differ in a remarkable degree in their size, form, and color. The germinative powers of the seeds are retained three or four years.

As catalogued by seedsmen, the varieties are divided into two classes, — the Dwarfs, and the Pole or Running sorts.

Dwarfs. — The plants of this class vary from a foot to two feet in height. They require no stakes or poles for their support, and are grown in hills or drills, as may suit the taste or convenience of the cultivator.

All of the varieties are somewhat tender, and should not be planted before settled, mild weather. They succeed best in warm, light soil; but will flourish in almost any soil or situation, unless it be shaded or very wet.

When planted in drills, they are made from fourteen to twenty inches apart, and from an inch to two inches in depth. The seeds are planted from three to six inches apart; the distance in the drills, as well as the space between the drills, being regulated by the habit of the variety cultivated.

If planted in hills, they should be three feet apart in one direction, and two feet in the opposite. If the variety under cultivation is large and vigorous, four or five plants may be allowed to a hill; if of an opposite character, allow twice this number.

To raise Seed. — Leave a row, or a few hills, entirely unplucked. Seed is of little value when saved at the end of the season from a few scattered pods accidentally left to ripen on plants that have been plucked from time to time for the table.

Varieties : —

Black-eyed China. Plant fifteen inches high; the flowers are white; the pods are five inches long, green and straight while young, and contain five or six seeds, — these are white, spotted and marked about the eye with black, of an oblong form, and measure half an inch in length, and three-eighths of an inch in thickness.

A quart contains fifteen hundred beans, and will plant a drill, or row, of two hundred feet, or a hundred and fifty hills.

The variety is early. Sown at the commencement of the season, the plants blossomed in six weeks, produced pods for the table in seven weeks, pods for shelling in ten weeks, and ripened in eighty-seven days. It yields well, ripens off at once, and, on account of the thick, parchment-like character of the pods, suffers much less from wet and unfavorable seasons than many other sorts.

As a string-bean, it is of fair quality, good when shelled

in the green state, and farinaceous and mild flavored when ripe.

Blue Pod. A half-dwarf variety, growing from two to three feet high. The pods are five inches long, pale green while young, cream-white when fully ripe, and contain five or six seeds.

Its season is intermediate. The plants blossomed in seven weeks, afforded pods for stringing in eight weeks, green beans in ten or eleven weeks, and ripened in ninety-seven days from the time of sowing. It is a week earlier than the White Marrow, and ten days in advance of the Pea-bean. Plantings may be made as late as the last week in June, which will yield pods for the table in seven weeks, and ripen the middle of September, or in about twelve weeks.

The ripe seed is white, oblong, flattened, rounded on the back, often squarely or angularly shortened at the ends, half an inch long, and a fourth of an inch thick. Twenty-seven hundred will measure a quart.

It is a field rather than a garden variety, though the green pods are tender and well flavored. If planted in drills two feet apart, five pecks of seed will be required for an acre; or four pecks for the same quantity of ground, if the rows are two feet and a half apart. If planted in hills, six or eight seeds should be put in each; and, if the hills are three feet apart, twelve quarts of seed will plant an acre.

The Blue Pod is the earliest of the field varieties; more prolific, more generally cultivated, and more abundant in the market, than either the Pea-bean or the White Marrow. It is, however, much less esteemed, and, even in its greatest perfection, is generally sold at a lower price.

On account of its precocity, it is well suited for planting in fields of corn, when the crop may have been partially destroyed by birds or insects, and the season has too far advanced to admit of a replanting of corn. In field culture, Blue-pod beans are planted till the 25th of June.

Canada Yellow.
Round American Kidney.
Law.

The plants of this variety are from fourteen to sixteen inches high; the pods are five inches long, nearly straight, green while young, yellow at maturity, and contain from four to six seeds.

Season intermediate. If sown early, the plants will blossom in six or seven weeks, supply the table with pods in eight weeks, green shelled beans in ten weeks, and ripen off in ninety days. When planted after settled warm weather, the variety grows rapidly, and ripens quickly; blossoming in less than six weeks, and ripening in seventy days, from the time of planting. For green shelled-beans, the seeds may be planted till the middle of July.

The ripe seeds are of an ovoid or rounded form, and measure half an inch in length and three-eighths of an inch in thickness. They are of a yellowish-drab color, with a narrow, reddish-brown line about the eye. Seventeen hundred are contained in a quart; and this amount of seeds will plant two hundred and fifty feet of drill, or a hundred and seventy-five hills.

The variety is quite productive, and excellent as a shelled-bean, green or dry. The young pods are not so tender as those of many other sorts, and are but little used.

Chilian. Plant sixteen or eighteen inches high; flowers pale lilac; the pods are five inches and a half long, and contain five seeds.

Planted early in the season, the variety blossomed in seven weeks, yielded pods for the table in eight weeks, and ripened in a hundred days, from the time of planting.

The ripe seeds are of a clear, bright pink, or rose color, kidney-shaped, and of large size; generally measuring three-fourths of an inch long, and three-eighths of an inch thick. Twelve hundred and fifty are contained in a quart, and will be sufficient for planting a row, or drill, of two hundred feet, or for a hundred and twenty-five hills.

The variety is healthy and productive; much esteemed for the tender, pulpy character of the young pods; and worthy of cultivation for the large size and good quality of the beans, which, either in the green or ripe state, are quite farinaceous and mild flavored.

Crescent-eyed. Half-Moon.

Height fourteen or fifteen inches; flowers white; the pods are five inches and a half long, and contain five seeds.

Season intermediate. If planted early, the variety will blossom in seven weeks, yield pods for stringing in eight weeks, supply the table with green beans in eleven weeks, and ripen in ninety days. When planted and grown under the influence of summer weather, pods may be plucked for the table in fifty days, and the crop will ripen in about twelve weeks.

The beans, when ripe, are white, with a large, rose-red patch about the eye; the colored portion of the surface being striped and marked with brownish-red: they are somewhat kidney-shaped, and measure three-fourths of an inch in length, and three-eighths of an inch in thickness. A quart contains nearly thirteen hundred seeds, and will plant a hundred and fifty hills, or a row of two hundred feet.

The variety yields well, and the green pods are tender and well flavored. It is, however, generally cultivated for its seeds, which are of large size and excellent quality, whether used in a green or ripe state.

Dun-colored.

Plant sixteen inches in height; the pods are five inches and a half long, half an inch broad, yellow and slender when fully ripe, and contain five or six beans.

The ripe seeds are dun-colored, or dark drab, kidney-shaped, five-eighths of an inch long, and a fourth of an inch thick. A quart contains seventeen hundred beans, and will plant a row of two hundred and twenty-five feet, or a hundred and seventy-five hills.

It is one of the earliest of the Dwarf varieties. The plants blossomed in six weeks, produced young pods in seven weeks, and ripened in eighty-five days, from the time of sowing. Planted after settled warm weather, pods were gathered for use in six weeks; and for these the seeds may be sown until the first of August.

As a shelled-bean, green or dry, it is of little value, and hardly worthy of cultivation. As an early string-bean, it is one of the best. The pods are not only succulent and tender, but suitable for use very early in the season. It is also quite prolific, and, if planted at intervals of two weeks till the last of July, will supply the table to the last of September.

The variety has long been cultivated in England and other parts of Europe, and is much esteemed for its hardiness and productiveness.

Dwarf Cranberry. Strictly a Dwarf variety, growing about sixteen inches high. The flowers are pale purple; the pods are five inches long, sickle-shaped, and contain five or six seeds.

The ripe seeds are smaller than those of the Running variety, but of the same form and color. Sixteen hundred are contained in a quart, and will plant nearly two hundred feet of drill, or a hundred and seventy-five hills.

The genuine Dwarf Cranberry is not one of the earliest varieties, but rather an intermediate sort. Sown as soon as the weather was suitable, the plants were in flower in seven or eight weeks, and young pods were gathered for use in nine weeks. In favorable seasons, the crop will be ready for harvesting in ninety days. If planted in June, the variety will ripen in ten weeks.

It is hardy and productive, and the young pods are not only succulent and tender, but are suitable for use at a more advanced stage of growth than those of most varieties. The beans, in their green state, are farinaceous and well flavored, but, after ripening, are little used, the color being objectionable.

A variety with a brownish-red, oval, flattened seed, half an inch in length, is extensively known and cultivated as the Dwarf Cranberry. It is ten or twelve days earlier, the plants are smaller and less productive, the young pods less tender and succulent, and the seeds (green or ripe) less farinaceous, than those of the true variety. With the exception of its earlier maturity, it is comparatively not worthy of cultivation.

Dwarf Horticultural.

Stem sixteen inches high; pods five inches long, green while young, but changing to yellow, marbled and streaked with brilliant rose-red, when sufficiently advanced for shelling in their green state: if well formed, they contain five (rarely six) seeds.

It is a medium, or half-early sort. Planted at the commencement of favorable weather, it blossomed in seven weeks, produced pods for the table in eight weeks, and ripened in ninety-five or a hundred days. Planted and grown in summer weather, the variety produced green pods in seven weeks, and ripened in ninety days.

The ripe seeds resemble those of the Running variety in form and color. Fourteen hundred are contained in a quart; and this quantity of seed will be sufficient for planting a row of a hundred and seventy-five feet, or a hundred and forty hills.

The Dwarf Horticultural Bean is quite productive, and the young pods are tender and of good quality. It is, however, not so generally cultivated for its young pods as for its seeds, which are much esteemed. For shelling in the green state, it is one of the best of the Dwarfs, and deserves cultivation.

Dwarf Sabre.
DWARF CASE-KNIFE.
A half-dwarf, French variety, two and a half to three feet high. The pods are seven or eight inches long, and an inch in width, often irregular and distorted, brownish-white when ripe, and contain seven to eight seeds.

The ripe bean is white, kidney-shaped, flattened, three-fourths of an inch in length, and three-eighths of an inch in width. About twelve hundred are contained in a quart. As the variety is a vigorous grower, and occupies much space, this quantity of seed will plant a row of two hundred feet, or two hundred and twenty-five hills.

Season intermediate. The plants blossomed in seven weeks, produced young pods in eight weeks, pods for shelling in their green state in twelve weeks, and ripened in ninety-seven days, from the time of sowing. If cultivated for its green pods, the seeds may be planted to the middle of July.

The Dwarf Sabre is one of the most productive of all varieties, yielding its long, broad pods in great profusion. From the spreading, recumbent character of the plants, the pods often rest or lie upon the surface of the ground; and, being unusually thin and delicate, the crop often suffers to a considerable extent from the effects of rain and dampness in unfavorable seasons.

The young pods are remarkable for their tender and succulent character; and the beans, both in a green and dried state, are of good quality. It is hardy, productive, and recommended for cultivation.

Early China.
CHINA.
RED-EYED CHINA.
Plant fifteen inches high, with wrinkled foliage and white flowers; the pods are five inches long, yellowish-green as they approach maturity, yellow when fully ripe, and contain five (rarely six) beans.

The ripe seeds are white, colored and spotted about the eye with purplish-red, oblong, six-tenths of an inch long, and three-eighths of an inch thick. Sixteen hundred and fifty measure a quart, and will plant two hundred feet of drill, or two hundred hills.

Plants from seeds sown early in the season blossomed in six weeks, afforded young pods for use in seven weeks, green beans in ten weeks, and ripened in eighty-five days. Planted and grown in summer, the crop ripened in eleven weeks; and plants from seeds sown as late as the first of August afforded an abundant supply of tender pods from the middle to the close of September.

The Early China is very generally disseminated, and is one of the most popular of the Dwarf varieties. It is hardy and productive; but the young pods, though succulent and tender, are inferior to those of some other varieties. The seeds, green or ripe, are thin-skinned, mealy, and mild flavored.

Early Rachel. — A low-growing, branching variety, twelve to fifteen inches high; flowers white; the pods are five inches and a half long, and contain five seeds.

Planted early in the season, the variety blossomed in seven weeks; and in eight weeks the young pods were fit for use. Pods for shelling were plucked in ten weeks, and the crop ripened in eighty days. For the green pods, the seeds may be planted till the middle or 20th of July.

The ripe seed is yellowish-brown, white at one of the ends, kidney-shaped, often abruptly shortened, five-eighths of an inch long, and a fourth of an inch thick. Nearly two thousand are contained in a quart.

The Early Rachel is hardy, and moderately productive, and, as an early string-bean, may be desirable; but as a shell-bean, green or dry, it is of little value. In common with many other early sorts cultivated as string-beans, the pods, though crisp and tender at first, soon become too tough and parchment-like for use. In general, the pods of the later sorts remain crisp and tender a much longer period than those of the earlier descriptions.

Early Valentine.
VALENTINE. Plant about sixteen inches high, with small, yellowish-green leaves and white flowers; the pods are four and a half or five inches long, sickle-shaped, almost cylindrical, green while young, yellow when ripe, and contain five seeds.

The variety is productive, and quite early, though not one of the earliest. Sown at the commencement of the season, the plants blossomed in six weeks, produced pods for use in seven weeks, and ripened in thirteen weeks, or ninety days, from the time of planting. Planted after the beginning of summer weather, pods were gathered for the table in fifty days, and the beans ripened in eleven weeks.

The seeds, when ripe, are of a pale-pink color, marbled or variegated with rose-red, oblong, nearly straight, sometimes distorted and irregular as if pressed out of their natural shape, five-eighths of an inch long, and three-eighths of an inch in thickness. A quart, which contains eighteen or nineteen hundred seeds, is sufficient for planting a hundred and seventy-five hills, or for a drill, or row, of two hundred or two hundred and twenty-five feet.

The Early Valentine has little merit as a shelled-bean, green or ripe; but, of nearly seventy of the most popular of the native as well as foreign sorts experimentally grown, no one excelled it in the tender and succulent character of the pods in the green state. Though these are of moderate size, they are remarkable for their thick, fleshy sides, and for the length of time required for the development of the seeds within. Few, if any, of the Dwarfs harden their pods so slowly, or continue longer in condition for use; and few are more productive.

It has long been grown in England and other parts of

Europe, and is common to gardens in almost every section of the United States.

A variety, imported from France twenty years since, and known as the "Excelsior," strongly resembles, if it is not identical with, the Early Valentine. The plants are similar in habit; the pods have the same form, and solid, fleshy character; and the seeds, in their ripe state, are of the same size and color.

Height sixteen inches; flowers purple; the pods are five inches and a half long, five-eighths of an inch broad, and contain five seeds.

<small>Golden Cranberry. Canadian. Round American Kidney.</small>

Season intermediate. Early plantings blossomed in seven weeks, yielded pods for the table in eight weeks, and ripened in ninety days.

The ripe seeds are pale greenish-yellow, with an olive-green line encircling the eye; roundish-ovoid, three-eighths of an inch long, and nearly the same in thickness. A quart contains nearly eighteen hundred seeds, and will plant a row, or drill, of two hundred feet, or two hundred and twenty-five hills.

As a string-bean, or for shelling in the green state, it is inferior to many other varieties, and is little cultivated for use in these forms; but, as a variety for baking, it is much esteemed, and recommended for cultivation.

Hardy and productive.

The plants of this familiar variety are from fourteen to sixteen inches high; the flowers are pale purple; the pods are five inches long, six-tenths of an inch broad, green at first, gradually becoming paler, cream-yellow when ripe, and contain five (rarely six) beans.

<small>Long Yellow Six-weeks. Six-Weeks. Yellow Six-Weeks.</small>

It is one of the earliest of the Dwarf varieties. Spring plantings were in blossom in six weeks, produced pods for the table in seven weeks, and ripened in eighty-seven days. Sown in summer, the plants afforded pods for the table in six weeks, and ripened in sixty-three days. Planted as late in the season as the last of July or first of August, the variety gave an abundant supply of tender pods from the middle to the last of September.

The ripe seeds are pale yellowish-drab, with an olive-green line about the eye, the drab rapidly changing by age to dull yellowish-brown. They are kidney-shaped, three-fourths of an inch long, and three-tenths of an inch thick. Fourteen hundred beans are contained in a quart, and will plant a row of two hundred feet, or a hundred and fifty hills.

It is quite productive, and an excellent early string-bean, but less valuable as a green shelled-bean, or for cooking when ripe. On account of the tender and delicate character of the pods, the ripe seeds are often injured by damp or continued rainy weather. A popular, early garden-bean, much cultivated both in this country and in Europe.

Mohawk. Stem eighteen inches high, sturdy and
EARLY MOHAWK. branching; flowers pale lilac; the pods are five inches and a half long, five-eighths of an inch wide, and generally contain five beans.

The ripe seeds are variegated with drab, dull purple, and different shades of brown: they are kidney-shaped, and measure nearly three-fourths of an inch in length, and three-eighths of an inch in width. A quart contains fourteen hundred and fifty seeds, and will plant a hundred and seventy-five feet of drill, or a hundred and seventy-five hills.

It is a week later than the earliest varieties. Plants from seeds sown early in spring were in blossom in seven weeks, produced pods for the table in eight weeks, and ripened in a hundred days, from the time of sowing. In ordinary seasons, the variety will ripen perfectly if planted the last week in June; and will yield an abundance of pods for the table, if the planting be made as late in the season as the last of July.

The Early Mohawk is quite productive, and one of the hardiest of the Dwarf varieties. It is well adapted for early planting, and is extensively grown by market-gardeners as an early string-bean. The young pods are tender, and of good quality; and, if gathered as they become of suitable size, the plants will contine to yield them in great abundance. The shelled-beans, green or dry, are considered inferior to many other varieties.

Negro Long-pod.

Plant strong and vigorous, two feet high. The pods are from six to seven inches long, rather narrow, but of even breadth, uniformly green till near maturity, and contain from six to eight slender, small, nearly straight, but somewhat kidney-shaped, glossy-black seeds, about half an inch in length.

Planted May 20, the variety blossomed July 8, and the crop ripened Aug. 10.

The Negro Long-pod is one of the most productive of all the Dwarfs, yielding its long, slender, and succulent pods in profuse abundance. The seeds, either green or ripe, are seldom used.

The variety is of foreign origin, and is common to gardens both in France and England. A sub-variety, known as the Dwarf Negro, less stocky in habit, and with much smaller pods, is also a favorite in the markets of London. The Long-podded, however, is considered much superior to the old Dwarf; but both are highly prized for the narrow, handsome form of the young pods, and for their uniformly fine green color.

Newington Wonder.

The plants of this variety often produce slender, barren runners, eighteen inches or two feet in length; but they are generally of short duration.

The pods are small and straight, usually four inches long, and nearly half an inch broad. They are pale green at first, afterwards change to yellowish-white, tinted or washed with bright pink, and contain six or seven beans.

The ripe seeds are pale brownish-drab, nearly half an inch long, and a fourth of an inch deep. Thirty-six hundred are contained in a quart, which will plant a row four hundred feet in length, or four hundred hills.

The variety is not early, and, when cultivated for its seeds, should have the benefit of the whole season; though, with favorable autumnal weather, the crop will ripen if planted the middle of June.

In its manner of growth and general character, the Newington Wonder resembles the Tampico, or Turtle-soup. As a string-bean, it is one of the best. The pods, though not large, are crisp, succulent, and tender, and are produced in great abundance throughout most of the season. The seeds, both in their green and ripe state, are small, and of little value for the table.

Nonpareil. The plants of this variety are strong and vigorous, and somewhat resemble the Mohawk, or White Kidney, growing eighteen inches high; the flowers are white; the pods are five and a half or six inches long, green at first, cream-yellow at maturity, and contain five or six seeds.

Planted the 20th of May, the variety was in flower July 9, and ripened Aug. 12, or in eighty-four days from the time of planting.

The ripe seeds are strongly kidney-shaped, nearly three-fourths of an inch long, white, with a broad and somewhat irregular patch of red about the eye, and numerous spots of the same color upon the back and sides: fourteen hundred are contained in a quart; and this amount of seed will plant a hundred and seventy-five feet of drill, or a hundred and fifty hills.

The variety is not only hardy and remarkably productive, but the young pods are tender and excellent, and the seeds, green or ripe, are surpassed by few, if any, of the Dwarf sorts, in mildness and delicacy of flavor.

Plant vigorous, much branched, and, like the Blue Pod and White Marrow, inclined to send up running shoots; foliage small, deep green; flowers white; the pods are four inches long, half an inch wide, nearly straight, and contain five beans. *Pea-bean.*

Planted early in spring, it blossomed in fifty days, afforded green pods in fifty-eight days, and ripened in fifteen weeks. In favorable autumns, it will ripen if planted as late as the 20th of June; but it is not so early as the Blue Pod or White Marrow, and, when practicable, should have the advantage of the entire season.

The ripe seeds of the pure variety are quite small, roundish-ovoid, five-sixteenths of an inch long, a fourth of an inch in width and thickness, and of a pure, yet not glossy, white color. Forty-four hundred seeds are contained in a quart.

As a garden variety, it is of little value, though the young pods are crisp and tender. It is cultivated almost exclusively as a field-bean. If planted in rows or drills two feet apart, three pecks of seeds will be required for an acre; or eighteen quarts will seed this quantity of land if the rows are two feet and a half apart. When planted in hills, eight seeds are allowed to a hill; and, if the hills are made three feet apart, eight quarts will plant an acre. The yield varies from fourteen to twenty bushels, according to soil, season, and cultivation.

The Pea-bean, the White Marrow, and the Blue Pod, are the principal, if not the only, kinds of much commercial importance; the names of other varieties being rarely, if ever, mentioned in the regular reports of the current prices of the markets. If equally well ripened, and, in their respective varieties, equally pure, the Pea-bean and the White Marrow command nearly the same prices; the former, however, being more abundant in the market than the latter. By many, and perhaps by a majority, the Pea-bean is esteemed the best of all baking varieties.

Pottawotto-mie. The plants of this variety are remarkable for their strong, vigorous habit, and large, luxuriant foliage. The pods are six inches long, green at first, then mottled and streaked with lively rose-red on a cream-white ground, and contain five (rarely six) seeds.

Plants from seeds sown early in the season were in flower in seven weeks, afforded pods for shelling in eleven weeks, and ripened in a hundred days, from the time of planting.

The ripe seeds are of a light creamy-pink color, streaked and spotted with red or reddish-brown, kidney-shaped, fully three-fourths of an inch long, and three-eighths of an inch broad. One thousand will measure a quart, and will plant a row two hundred feet in length, or a hundred and twenty-five hills.

The young pods are inferior to most varieties in crispness, and tenderness of texture, and are but little used. The seeds are remarkably large, separate easily from the pods, and, green or ripe, are very farinaceous and well flavored, nearly or quite equalling the Dwarf and Running Horticultural.

Red-speckled. Plant nearly a foot and a half high; the pods are five inches and a half long, pale green, with occasional marks and spots of purple, and contain five (rarely six) seeds.

Season intermediate. Plants from seeds sown after settled warm weather blossomed in six weeks, and green pods were plucked for use in fifty days. Pods for shelling in the green state were gathered in ten weeks, and the crop ripened in ninety days. For its young pods, or for green beans, plantings may be made to the last week in June; but the crop will not mature, unless the weather continues favorable, till the first of October.

The ripe seeds are variegated with deep red and pale drab, the red predominating; kidney-shaped, three-fourths of an inch long, and three-tenths of an inch deep. A quart contains fourteen hundred and fifty seeds, and will plant a row of two hundred and twenty-five feet, or a hundred and fifty hills.

The variety is hardy and productive. It is extensively cultivated as a garden-bean in England and France, and has been common to the gardens of this country for nearly two centuries. The young pods are of medium quality; but the seeds, green or dry, are mild and delicate. On account of the parchment-like character of the pods, the seeds seldom suffer from the effects of wet weather.

Plant sixteen to eighteen inches high, and readily distinguished from most varieties by its small, smooth, deep-green, and elongated leaves; flowers purple; the pods are five inches long, nearly cylindrical, greenish-white, streaked with purple when sufficiently advanced for shelling, yellow when ripe, and usually contain five beans.   Refugee. Thousand to One.

The Refugee is not an early sort. The plants blossomed in seven weeks, produced young pods in eight weeks, and ripened in eighty-seven days, from the time of sowing. Plantings for the ripened product may be made till the middle of June; and for the green pods, to the middle of July.

The ripe seeds are light drab, with numerous spots and broad patches of bright purple, nearly straight, cylindrical at the middle, tapering to the ends, five-eighths of an inch long, and three-tenths of an inch thick. Eighteen hundred and fifty are contained in a quart, and will plant a row two hundred and fifty feet in length, or two hundred hills.

The variety is hardy, yields abundantly, and the young pods are thick, fleshy, and tender in texture. As a string-bean, or for pickling, it is considered one of the best of all varieties, and is recommended for general cultivation. The seeds are rarely used either in a green or ripened state.

Rob Roy. Plant half-dwarf, — early in the season producing slender, transient, barren runners two or three feet in length; the pods are five inches long, often produced in pairs, yellow as they approach maturity, yellowish-white when ripe, and contain five or six seeds.

It is one of the earliest of the Dwarfs. Spring plantings blossomed in six weeks, produced pods for the table in seven weeks, and ripened in eighty-two days. Planted in June, pods were plucked for use in six weeks, and the crop was ready for harvesting in sixty-eight days.

The ripe seeds are clear bright yellow, of an oblong form, five-eighths of an inch long, and three-tenths of an inch deep. Fifteen hundred seeds are contained in a quart, and will be sufficient to plant a row of two hundred feet, or a hundred and fifty hills.

The Rob Roy generally matures in great perfection, being seldom stained or otherwise injured by rain or the dampness of ordinary seasons. It is also one of the earliest of the Dwarf varieties, but desirable as a string-bean rather than for its qualities as a green shelled-bean, or for cooking when ripe. If cultivated for its pods only, plantings may be made until the first of August.

Round Yellow Six-weeks.
Round Yellow.
Dwarf Yellow.
Fourteen to sixteen inches high; the pods are five inches long, half an inch broad, pale yellowish-green as they approach maturity, and, when fully ripe, remarkably slender, and more curved than in their green state. They contain five or six beans.

The variety is early; blossoming in six weeks, producing

young pods in seven weeks, and ripening in ninety days, from the time of planting. When planted in June, pods may be plucked for use in seven weeks, and the crop will be ready for harvesting in eighty days. For its green pods, plantings may be made to the last of July.

The ripe seeds are orange-yellow, oblong or ovoid, half an inch long, and three-tenths of an inch thick. A quart contains two thousand seeds, and will plant a row two hundred and twenty-five feet in length, or two hundred and twenty-five hills.

As an early string-bean, the variety is worthy of cultivation, but is little used, and is really of little value, as a shelled-bean, green or ripe. It has been common to the gardens of this country for more than a century; and, during this period, no apparent change has taken place in the character of the plant, or in the size, form, or color of the seed.

Swiss Crimson.
Scarlet Swiss. *Vil.*

Plant vigorous, often producing running shoots; the pods are six inches long, yellow, streaked with brilliant rose-red as they approach maturity, and contain five (rarely six) seeds.

It is a late variety. If planted as early as the weather will permit, the plants will blossom in seven weeks, young pods will be fit for use in nine weeks, and the crop will be ready for harvesting in a hundred and five days. Planted and grown in summer weather, it produced young pods in sixty days, and ripened in thirteen weeks. Plantings for the green beans may be made to the first of July.

The ripe seeds are clear bright pink, striped and spotted with deep purplish-red: they are kidney-shaped, three-fourths of an inch long, and three-eighths of an inch broad. Thirteen hundred seeds are contained in a quart, and will plant a row two hundred feet in length, or a hundred and fifty hills.

It is hardy and productive, and, as a shelled-bean, of excellent quality, either in its green or ripened state. As a variety for stringing, it has little merit.

Turtle-soup.   Plant vigorous, producing numerous slen-
Tampico.   der, barren runners two feet or more in length. The pods are five inches long, sickle-shaped, and contain five or six seeds.

The variety is quite late, and requires most of the season for its full perfection. Plants from early sowings blossomed in eight weeks, the young pods were sufficiently grown for use in ten weeks, and the crop ripened in a hundred and eight days. As the young pods are tender and of excellent quality, and are also produced in great abundance, a planting for these may be made as late as the last week in June, which will supply the table from the last of August till the plants are destroyed by frost.

The ripe seeds are small, glossy-black, somewhat oblong, and much flattened. Thirty-six hundred are contained in a quart, and will plant four hundred feet of drill, or three hundred and fifty hills.

It is very productive, and deserving of cultivation for its young and tender pods, but is of little or no value for shelling while green. The ripened seeds are used, as the name implies, in the preparation of a soup, which, as respects color and flavor, bears some resemblance to that made from the green turtle.

Victoria.   This is one of the earliest of the Dwarf varieties. Plants from early sowings were in blossom in six weeks, yielded pods for the table in seven weeks, produced pods of suitable size for shelling in ten weeks, and ripened in eighty-four days. When planted after the season had somewhat advanced, — the young plants thus receiving the benefit of summer temperature, — pods were gathered for the table in six weeks, and the crop ripened in sixty-three days.

Stalk fourteen to sixteen inches high, with few branches; flowers purple; the pods are four and a half or five inches long, streaked and spotted with purple, tough and parchment-like when ripe, and contain five or six seeds.

The ripe seeds are flesh-colored, striped and spotted with purple, oblong, five-eighths of an inch long, and three-tenths of an inch thick. Fourteen hundred are contained in a quart.

The variety is remarkably early, and, on this account, is worthy of cultivation. The young pods, as well as the seeds, green or dry, are inferior to many other sorts.

White's Early.
Fejee.

A very hardy and vigorous variety, eighteen to twenty inches high. Flowers white, tinged with purple; the pods are five inches and a half long, curved or sickle-shaped, green at first, yellowish-white, striped with purple, when fully ripe, and contain five seeds.

Early plantings will blossom in six weeks, young pods may be plucked for use in seven weeks, and the crop will ripen in eighty-two days. If planted as late in the season as the first week in July, the variety will generally ripen perfectly; and, when cultivated for its green pods, plantings may be made at any time during the month.

The ripe seeds are either drab or light slate, — both colors being common, — marked and spotted with light drab. In some specimens, drab is the prevailing color. They are kidney-shaped, irregularly compressed or flattened, nearly three-fourths of an inch long, and three-eighths of an inch deep. A quart contains sixteen hundred seeds, and is sufficient for planting a row two hundred and fifty feet in length, or two hundred hills.

This variety, as an early string-bean, is decidedly one of the best, and is also one of the hardiest and most prolific. The pods should be plucked when quite young; and, if often gathered, the plants will continue a long time in bearing.

As a shelled-bean, either in its green or ripened state, it is only of medium quality.

The long peduncles, or stems, that support its spikes of flowers, its stocky habit, and fine, deep-green, luxurious foliage, distinguish the variety from all others.

White Flageolet. From sixteen to eighteen inches high; the pods are five inches and a half long, sickle-shaped, and contain six (rarely seven) seeds.

It is a half-early variety; blossoming in six weeks, yielding pods for the table in seven weeks, pods for shelling in eleven weeks, and ripening in ninety days, from the time of planting. Later plantings will ripen in a shorter period, or in eighty days; and, if cultivated as a string-bean, seed sown as late in the season as the last week of July will supply the table from the middle of September with an abundance of well-flavored and tender pods.

The ripe seeds are white, kidney-shaped, three-fourths of an inch long, and three-tenths of an inch broad. Twenty-two hundred are contained in a quart, and will plant a drill, or row, of two hundred and seventy-five feet, or nearly three hundred hills.

The White Flageolet is very productive, and is recommended for cultivation; the young pods are crisp and tender; and the seeds, green or ripe, are farinaceous, and remarkable for delicacy of flavor.

White Kidney.
Kidney.
Large White Kidney.
Royal Dwarf.

The plants of this variety are from sixteen to eighteen inches high, and readily distinguishable, from their large and broad leaves, and strong, branching habit of growth; the flowers are white; the pods are somewhat irregular in form, six inches long, green at first, yellow when ripe, and contain five (rarely six) beans.

The White Kidney-bean is not early. Planted the middle of May, it blossomed in seven weeks, produced young pods in nine weeks, pods for shelling in eleven weeks, and ripened in a hundred and ten days.

The ripe seeds are white, more or less veined, pale yellow about the eye, kidney-shaped, nearly straight, fully three-fourths of an inch long, and about three-eighths of an inch thick. From twelve to thirteen hundred are contained in a quart; and this quantity of seeds will plant a hundred and seventy-five feet of drill, or a hundred and forty hills.

At a string-bean, the variety has little merit; but as a shelled-bean, green or ripe, it is decidedly one of the best of the Dwarfs, and well deserving of cultivation. The seeds are of large size, pure white, separate readily from the pods, and are tender and delicate.

White Marrow.
WHITE MARROWFAT.
DWARF
WHITE CRANBERRY.
WHITE EGG.

Plants vigorous, much branched, and inclined to produce running shoots; flowers white; the pods are five inches long, nearly three-fourths of an inch broad, pale green at first, afterwards pure waxen-white, cream-yellow when ripe, and contain five seeds.

Planted at the commencement of favorable weather, the variety blossomed in seven weeks, yielded pods for the table in eight weeks, and ripened in a hundred and five days. When grown for the ripened product, the planting should not be delayed beyond the 20th of June. Planted at this season, or the last week in June, the crop will blossom the first week in August; and, about the middle of the month, pods may be gathered for the table. By the second week in September, the pods will be of sufficient size for shelling; and, if the season be ordinarily favorable, the crop will ripen the last of the month. It must not, however, be regarded as an early variety, and, when practicable, should be planted before the 10th of June.

The ripe seeds are clear white, ovoid, or egg-shaped, nine-sixteenths of an inch long, and three-eighths of an inch thick. In size, form, or color, they are scarcely distinguishable from those of the White Running Cranberry. If well grown, twelve hundred seeds will measure a quart.

As a string-bean, the White Marrow is of average quality; but, for shelling in the green state, it is surpassed by few, if any, of the Dwarf varieties, as the large seeds not only separate readily from the pod, but are remarkably white and well flavored. As a garden-bean, it deserves more general cultivation. When ripe, it is very farinaceous, of a delicate fleshy-white when properly cooked, and by many preferred to the Pea-bean.

In almost every section of the United States, as well as in the Canadas, it is largely cultivated for market, and is next in importance to the last named for commercial purposes.

In field culture, it is planted in drills, two feet apart, the seeds being dropped in groups, three or four together, a foot apart in the drills. Some plant in hills two and a half or three feet apart by eighteen inches in the opposite direction, seeding at the rate of forty-four quarts to the acre; and others plant in drills eighteen inches apart, dropping the seeds singly, six or eight inches from each other, in the drills.

The yield varies from twenty to thirty bushels to the acre, though crops are recorded of nearly forty bushels.

Yellow-eyed China. Plant sixteen to eighteen inches high; the pods are six inches long, nearly straight, and contain five or six seeds.

It is an early variety. Sown in May, or at the beginning of settled weather, the plants blossomed in six weeks, afforded string-beans in seven weeks, pods for shelling in ten or eleven weeks, and ripened in ninety days, from the time of planting. From sowings made later in the season, pods were plucked for the table in six weeks, and ripened beans in seventy-five days. Plantings for supplying the table with string-beans may be made until the last week in July.

The ripe beans are white, spotted and marked about the eye with rusty yellow, oblong, inclining to kidney-shape, more flattened than those of the Red or Black-eyed, five-eighths of an inch long, and three-eighths of an inch in breadth. Fifteen hundred and fifty are contained in a quart, and will plant two hundred feet of drill, or a hundred and fifty hills. The plants are large and spreading, and most productive when not grown too closely together.

The Yellow-eyed China is one of the most healthy, vigorous, and prolific of the Dwarf varieties; of good quality as a string-bean, and, in its ripened state, excellent for baking, or in whatever manner it may be cooked. It also ripens its seeds in great perfection; the crop being rarely affected by wet weather, or injured by blight or mildew.

POLE OR RUNNING BEANS.

As a class, these are less hardy than the Dwarfs, and are not usually planted so early in the season. The common practice is to plant in hills three feet or three and a half apart; though the lower-growing sorts are sometimes planted in drills fourteen or fifteen inches apart, and bushed in the manner of the taller descriptions of peas.

If planted in hills, they should be slightly raised, and the stake, or pole, set before the planting of the seeds. The maturity of some of the later sorts will be somewhat facilitated by cutting or nipping off the leading runners when they have attained a height of four or five feet.

California. Plant of healthy, vigorous habit, attaining a height of six feet and upwards. The flowers are white; the pods are long, broad, and flat, green at first, cream-yellow at maturity, and contain from six to eight seeds.

Planted May 20, the variety blossomed July 12, green

pods were plucked for use July 24, and the crop ripened the middle of August.

The ripe seeds are of a clear ochre-yellow color, broadly kidney-shaped, five-eighths of an inch long, and three-eighths of an inch in width. If well grown, one thousand will measure a quart; and this amount of seed will be sufficient for a hundred hills.

The California Bean is hardy and productive, yielding its long and broad pods in great abundance till destroyed by frost. Though much used as a string-bean, it is principally valued for the excellent quality of the seeds in their green state.

From reliable authority, the variety is grown to a considerable extent on the Pacific coast of South America, in some parts of California, and also in the Sandwich Islands.

The true name appears to be wanting. Though it is popularly known in this section of the country as the "California," the name seems to have been given in accordance with a custom, much too prevalent, of applying the term to whatever fruits, flowers, or vegetables may have been originally received from the State of California.

Case-knife. This variety, common to almost every garden, is readily distinguished by its strong and tall habit of growth, and its broad, deep-green, blistered leaves. The flowers are white; the pods are remarkably large, and often measure nine or ten inches in length, nearly an inch in width, and, if well formed, contain eight or nine seeds.

Early plantings blossomed in seven or eight weeks, yielded pods for stringing in ten weeks, green beans in twelve or thirteen weeks, and ripened in a hundred and five days. Later plantings, with the exclusive advantage of summer weather, produced green pods in seven weeks, pods for shelling in eight or nine weeks, and ripened in ninety-six days. Plantings for the green beans may be made till near the middle of July, and for the young pods to the 25th of the month.

The ripe seeds are clear white, kidney-shaped, irregularly flattened or compressed, three-fourths of an inch long, and three-eighths of an inch deep. A quart contains fifteen hundred seeds, and will plant a hundred and seventy-five hills.

It is one of the most prolific of the running varieties. As a shelled-bean, green or ripe, it is of excellent quality. The large pods, if plucked early, are succulent and tender, but coarser in texture than those of many other sorts.

Plant six feet and upwards in height, of healthy, Concord. vigorous habit; flowers white; the pods are four inches in length, and three-fourths of an inch in breadth; they are green at first, afterwards greenish-yellow, brownish-white at maturity, and contain five seeds, which have the form of the Horticultural, from which variety the Concord appears to have been derived: these seeds are white with a patch of yellowish-drab about the eye, the colored portion of the surface being spotted and marked with bright rose-red.

It is one of the earliest of the running sorts. Planted May 20, the variety was in flower July 8, and began to ripen Aug. 10.

The young pods are tough and stringy, and less valuable for the table than many other sorts; but as a shelled-bean, green or ripe, it is one of the best of the running varieties. The plants are healthy growers, attach themselves readily to the poles, and yield abundantly; the seeds, which separate easily from the pods, have the flavor and general character of the Horticultural. Recently introduced, and recommended for cultivation.

Horticultural.
MARBLED PRAGUE.
 vu.
LONDON HORTICULTURAL.
WREN'S EGG.

Stem six feet or more in height; flowers purple; the pods are from five to six inches long, nearly three-fourths of an inch broad, pale green while young, greenish-white, streaked and blotched with brilliant rose-red, when more advanced, much contorted, hard, parchment-like, and very tenacious of their contents when ripe, and enclose five or six seeds.

Planted at the commencement of the season, the variety blossomed in seven weeks, produced pods for stringing in nine weeks, green beans in twelve weeks, and ripened in a hundred days. Plantings made during the last week in June will mature their crop if the season be favorable. For the green beans, plantings may be made until the last of June, and for the young pods until the first of July.

The ripe beans are flesh-white, streaked and spotted with bright pink or red. They are egg-shaped, half an inch in length, and four-tenths of an inch in width and depth. From the time of ripening, the soft, flesh-like tint gradually loses its freshness, and finally becomes cinnamon-brown, the variegations growing relatively duller and darker. A quart contains eleven hundred seeds, and will plant a hundred and twenty-five hills.

The Horticultural Bean was introduced into this country from England about the year 1825. It has now become very generally disseminated, and is one of the most popular of the running sorts. As a string-bean, it is of good quality; shelled in its green state, remarkably farinaceous and well flavored; and, when ripe, one of the best for baking or stewing. It is hardy and productive, but is liable to deteriorate when raised many years in succession from seed saved in the vegetable garden from the scattered pods accidentally left to ripen on the poles. To raise good seed, leave each year a few hills unplucked, allowing the entire product to ripen.

Indian Chief.
WAX-BEAN.
BUTTER-BEAN.
ALGERIAN.
D'ALGER OF THE FRENCH.

Stem six or seven feet high, with large broad foliage and purple flowers; the pods are five inches long, nearly as thick as broad, sickle-shaped, green at first, but soon change to a fine, waxen, semi-transparent cream-white, — the line marking the divisions being orange-yellow. At this stage of growth, the color indicates approaching maturity; but the pods will be found crisp and succulent, and are in their greatest perfection for the table. When ripe, they are nearly white, much shrivelled, and contain six or seven seeds.

When cultivated for the ripened product, the seed should be planted as early in the season as the weather will permit. The plants will then blossom in eight or nine weeks, afford young pods in eleven weeks, pods for shelling in thirteen or fourteen weeks, and ripen in a hundred and twenty-four days. Plantings for green pods may be made until the first of July.

At the time of harvesting, the seeds are deep indigo-blue, oblong, often shortened abruptly at the ends, half an inch long, nearly the same in depth, and three-tenths of an inch thick. Fourteen hundred seeds measure a quart, and will plant a hundred and seventy-five hills.

The Indian-chief Bean is remarkable for its fine, tender, succulent, and richly colored pods; and for these it is well worthy of cultivation. They are not only produced in profuse abundance, but continue fit for use longer than those of most varieties. In moist seasons, they remain crisp and tender till the seeds have grown sufficiently to be used in the green state. The ripe seeds are of little value.

The real merits of the variety appear to be little known; yet, of all the running sorts cultivated for the green pods, it must be classed as one of the best.

Mottled Cranberry.
STRINGLESS.

A strong-growing, but not tall variety. The flowers are white; the pods are four inches and a half long, three-fourths of an inch wide, yellow at maturity, and contain four or five seeds.

If planted early, the variety will blossom in seven weeks, yield pods for the table in eight or nine weeks, green beans in eleven weeks, and ripen in a hundred days. When planted after settled warm weather, it will ripen in ninety days.

The ripe seeds are white, the eye surrounded with a broad patch of purple, which is also extended over one of the ends: they are of a rounded-oval form, half an inch long, and three-eighths of an inch in width and thickness. A quart contains fourteen hundred and fifty seeds, and will plant a hundred and fifty hills. As the plants are of dwarfish character, the seeds are sometimes sown in drills; a quart being required for two hundred feet.

The Mottled Cranberry is moderately productive, and is cultivated to some extent for its young pods: the seeds, while green, are of good quality.

Red Cranberry. This is one of the oldest and most familiar of garden-beans, and has probably been longer and more generally cultivated in this country than any other variety.

The plants are five or six feet high, of medium strength and vigor. The pods are quite irregular in form, — often reversely curved, or sickle-shaped; four inches and a half long; clear white when suitable for shelling; yellowish-white, shrivelled, and contorted, when ripe; and contain five or six seeds.

Its season is intermediate. Planted the 10th of May, the variety blossomed in seven weeks, yielded young pods in nine weeks, green beans in eleven weeks, and ripened in ninety-five days. In favorable seasons, the crop will ripen if the seeds are planted the last of June; but, for the young pods or for green beans, plantings may be made till near the middle of July.

The seeds are clear, deep purple, round-ovoid, half an inch long, and three-eighths of an inch in depth and thickness. Fourteen hundred and fifty are contained in a quart, and will plant a hundred and fifty hills.

It is a hardy and productive variety, principally grown as a string-bean. The pods are succulent and tender; and these qualities are retained to a very advanced stage of growth, or until quite of suitable size for shelling. The dark color of the bean, which is, to some extent, imparted to the pods in the process of cooking, is by some considered an objection, and the White Cranberry, though perhaps less prolific, is preferred. As a shelled-bean, it is of good quality in its green state, but in its ripened state little used.

Plant seven feet and upwards in height, **Rhode-Island Butter.** with large, broad, deep-green, wrinkled foliage; the pods are six inches long, nearly three-fourths of an inch broad, cream-white, much shrivelled when ripe, and contain seven seeds.

If planted early in the season, green pods may be plucked for the table in nine or ten weeks, pods for shelling in twelve weeks, and the crop will ripen in a hundred and twenty-three days. Planted early in June, the pods will generally all ripen; but, if the planting is delayed to the last of the month, the crop will but partially mature, unless the season prove more than usually favorable. The vines will, however, yield a plentiful supply of pods, and also of green beans.

The seeds, at maturity, are cream-yellow, with well-defined spots and stripes of deep yellowish-buff. They are broad kidney-shaped, five-eighths of an inch long, and nearly half an inch broad. Fourteen hundred are contained in a quart, and will plant a hundred and fifty hills.

The variety yields abundantly; and the large pods are tender, succulent, and excellent for table use. The beans, in their green state, are of good quality, though little used when ripe.

Sabre, or Cimeter. Stem seven or eight feet high; the pods are large, broad, and thin, curved at the ends in the form of a sabre, or cimeter, green when young, cream-white when ripe, and contain eight beans.

The variety blossomed in eight weeks, afforded young pods for the table in ten weeks, green beans in eleven weeks, and ripened in a hundred days, from the time of planting. Sown in June, the crop matured in ninety days. Plantings for the green seeds may be made till the last of June, and for the young pods to the middle of July.

The ripe seeds are clear white, kidney-form, three-fourths of an inch long, and three-eighths of an inch broad. Sixteen hundred are contained in a quart, and will plant a hundred and sixty hills.

The Sabre Bean is remarkably productive; the young pods are crisp and tender, excellent for table use, and good for pickling; the seeds, green or dry, are farinaceous, and of delicate flavor and appearance.

In height and foliage, size and form of the pods, color and size of the ripe seeds, it resembles the Case-knife. The principal difference between the varieties is in the earlier maturity of the Sabre.

White Cranberry. Stem five or six feet high; the pods are five inches and a half long, striped and marbled with red when near maturity, yellowish-buff when ripe, and contain five or six beans.

It is not an early variety. From plantings made at the usual season, young pods were gathered in nine weeks, pods for shelling green in twelve weeks, and ripened beans in a hundred and five days. For stringing, or for shelling in a green state, the variety may be planted the first of July; but, in ordinary seasons, few of the pods will reach maturity.

The ripe seeds are white, egg-shaped, sometimes nearly spherical, half an inch long, and three-eighths of an inch in breadth and thickness. In size, form, and color, they strongly resemble the Dwarf White Marrow, and are not easily distinguished from the seeds of that variety. Twelve hundred and fifty are contained in a quart, and will plant a hundred and twenty-five hills.

The White Cranberry is hardy, yields well, and the young pods are tender and well flavored. For shelling green, it is decidedly one of the best of all varieties; and for baking, or otherwise cooking, is, when ripe, fully equal to the Pea-bean or White Marrow.

Wild-goose. — Plant seven or eight feet high; the pods are sickle-shaped, and contain six seeds closely set together.

The variety requires the entire season for its full perfection. When planted early, it will blossom in nine weeks, produce young pods in eleven weeks, green beans in thirteen weeks, and ripen in a hundred and twenty days. If planted and grown under the influence of summer weather, the plants will blossom in seven weeks, yield young pods in nine weeks, green beans in twelve weeks, and ripen in a hundred days. Plantings for the green seeds may be made to the middle of June, and for the young pods to the first of July.

The ripe beans are pale cream-white, spotted with deep purplish-black, round-ovoid, four-tenths of an inch long, and three-eighths of an inch in width and thickness. A quart contains nearly seventeen hundred seeds, and will plant two hundred hills.

The variety has been long cultivated both in Europe and this country. It is hardy and productive. The young pods are of fair quality, and the seeds, green or ripe, are excellent for table use, in whatever form prepared.

Yellow Cranberry. — Five to six feet high; the pods are five inches long, three-fourths of an inch broad, often sickle-shaped, shrivelled, and irregular in form, like those of the Red variety, at maturity, and contain five or six seeds.

It is a few days later than the White Cranberry, and nearly two weeks later than the Red. Planted at the commencement of the season, it blossomed in eight weeks, yielded pods for the table in ten weeks, pods for shelling in twelve or thirteen weeks, and ripened in a hundred and ten days. Early summer plantings blossomed in seven weeks, produced pods for the table in less than nine weeks, and ripened in a hundred days. When grown for the ripened crop, it should have the advantage of the entire season; but, when cultivated for its young pods, plantings may be made till the first of July.

The seeds are yellow, round-ovoid, half an inch long, and three-eighths of an inch in breadth and thickness. Thirteen hundred and fifty are contained in a quart, and will plant a hundred and twenty-five hills.

The variety is hardy and prolific, of good quality as a string-bean, or for shelling in the green state. When ripe, the seeds are nearly equal to the White Marrow for baking, though the color is less agreeable.

ASPARAGUS-BEAN.

Long-podded Dolichos. — Dolichos sesquipedalis.

The Asparagus-bean, in its manner of growth, inflorescence, and in the size and character of its pods, is quite distinct from the class of beans before described. It is a native of tropical America, and requires a long, warm season for its full perfection.

The stem is from six to seven feet high; the leaves are long, narrow, smooth, and shining; the flowers are large, greenish-yellow, and produced, two or three together, at the extremity of quite a long peduncle; the pods are nearly cylindrical, pale green, pendent, and grow with remarkable rapidity, — when fully developed, they are eighteen or twenty inches long, and contain eight or nine seeds.

These should be sown as early in spring as the appearance of settled warm weather; and the plants will then blossom in ten or eleven weeks, afford pods for use in fourteen weeks, and ripen off their crop in gradual succession until destroyed by frost.

The ripe seeds are cinnamon-brown, with a narrow, dark line about the hilum; kidney-shaped, half an inch long, and a fourth of an inch broad. Nearly four thousand are contained in a quart, and will plant four hundred and fifty hills.

The seeds are quite small, and are rarely eaten either in a green or ripe state. The variety is cultivated exclusively for its long, peculiar pods, which are crisp, tender, of good flavor, and much esteemed for pickling. It is, however, much less productive than many of the running kinds of garden-beans, and must be considered more curious than really useful.

A species or variety known as the Chinese Long Pod produces pods of much greater length, often measuring nearly three feet.

LIMA BEAN.

Phaseolus lunatus.

Stem ten feet or more in height; leaves long and narrow, smooth and shining; flowers small, greenish-yellow, in spikes; the pods are four inches and a half long, an inch and a quarter broad, much flattened, green and wrinkled while young, yellowish when ripe, and contain three or four beans.

The Lima is one of the latest, as well as one of the most tender, of all garden-beans, and seldom, if ever, entirely perfects its crop in the Northern States. Little will be gained by very early planting, as the seeds are not only liable to decay before vegetating, but the plants suffer greatly from cold, damp weather. In the Northern and Eastern States, the seeds should not be planted in the open ground before the beginning of May; nor should the planting be delayed beyond the 10th or middle of the month. In ordinary seasons, the Lima Bean will blossom in eight or nine weeks, and pods may be plucked for use the last of August, or beginning of September.

The ripe seeds are dull white or greenish-white, with veins radiating from the eye; broad kidney-shaped, much flattened, seven-eighths of an inch long, and two-thirds of an inch in width. A quart contains seven hundred seeds, and will plant eighty hills.

The pods are tough and parchment-like in all stages of their growth, and are never eaten. The seeds, green or ripe, are universally esteemed for their peculiar flavor and excellence, and by most persons are considered the finest of all the garden varieties. If gathered when suitable for use in their green state, and dried in the pods in a cool and shaded situation, they may be preserved during the winter. When required for use, they are shelled, soaked a short time in clear water, and cooked as green beans; thus treated, they will be nearly as tender and well flavored as when freshly plucked from the plants.

The seeds are sometimes started on a hot-bed, in thumb-pots, or on inverted turf, or sods, cut in convenient pieces, and about the last of May, if the weather is warm and pleasant, transplanted to hills in the open ground.

When cultivated in the vicinity of the Sieva, the varieties readily intermix, or hybridize; and, unless a fresh supply of seed is procured every year or two, the Lima rapidly degenerates. If raised for a succession of years, in Northern latitudes, from seeds of Northern growth, the variety gradually becomes earlier; but the plants decline in stockiness and vigor, and the pods and seeds yearly decrease in size, until the Lima is little, if at all, superior to some of the improved forms of the Sieva.

Plants from seeds of Southern growth are generally healthy and vigorous, and produce beans of remarkable size and excellence; but the pods develop slowly, and few reach full maturity.

In tropical climates, the Lima Bean is perennial.

Green Lima. A sub-variety of the Common Lima, differing principally in the pea-green color of the seeds.

As generally found in the market, the seeds of the Common and Green Lima are more or less intermixed. By some, the Green is considered more tender, and thought to remain longer on the plants without becoming hard, than the White. The habits of the plants are the same, and there is no difference in the season of maturity. A careful selection of seeds for planting, and skilful culture, would undoubtedly give a degree of permanency to this difference in color, which appears to be the principal, if not the only, point of variation.

Mottled Lima. This, like the Green, is a sub-variety of the Common Lima. The ripe seeds are dull white, or greenish-white, mottled and clouded with purple.

In the habit of the plant, in the foliage, pods, form, or size of the seeds, or season of maturity, there are no marks of distinction when compared with the Common Lima.

SCARLET-RUNNER.
Phaseolus multiflorus.

From South America. Though nearly allied to the Common Kidney-bean, it is considered by botanists a distinct species, differing in its inflorescence, in the form of its pods, and particularly in the fact that the cotyledons, or lobes, of the planted seed, do not rise to the surface of the ground in the process of germination. It is, besides, a perennial plant. The roots are tuberous, and, though small, not unlike those of the Dahlia.

If taken up before frost in the autumn, they may be preserved in a conservatory, or warm parlor or sitting-room, during winter, and reset in the open ground on the approach of warm weather, when new shoots will soon make their appearance, and the plants will blossom a second time early and abundantly.

Plant twelve feet or more in height or length, with deep-green foliage and brilliant scarlet flowers; the latter being produced in spikes, on long footstalks. The pods are six inches long, nearly an inch broad, somewhat hairy while young, sickle-shaped and wrinkled when more advanced, light reddish-brown when ripe, and contain four or five seeds.

It requires the whole season for its perfection, and should be planted as early as the weather will admit. The plants will then blossom in seven or eight weeks, produce young pods in nine weeks, green seeds in twelve weeks, and ripen in a hundred and fifteen days.

The ripe seeds are lilac-purple, variegated with black, or deep purplish-brown, — the edge, or border, little, if any, marked; hilum long and white; form broad-kidney-shaped; size large, — if well grown, measuring seven-eighths of an inch long, six-tenths of an inch broad, and three-eighths of an inch thick. Five hundred and fifty are contained in a quart, and will plant eighty hills.

In this country, it is usually cultivated as an ornamental, climbing annual; the spikes of rich, scarlet flowers, and its deep-green foliage, rendering the plant one of the most showy and attractive objects of the garden.

Though inferior to some of the finer sorts of garden-beans,

its value as an esculent has not been generally appreciated. The young pods are tender and well flavored; and the seeds, green or ripe, are much esteemed in many localities. "In Britain, the green pods only are used; on the Continent, the ripened seeds are as much an object of culture; in Holland, the Runners are grown in every cottage-garden for both purposes; while, in France and Switzerland, they are grown chiefly for the ripened seeds. In England, they occupy a place in most cottage-gardens, and are made both ornamental and useful. They cover arbors; are trained over pales and up the walls of cottages, which they enliven by the brightness of their blossoms; while every day produces a supply of wholesome and nutritious food for the owner. The French, now enthusiastically fond of this legume, at one time held it in utter detestation."

Painted Lady-runner. A sub-variety of the Scarlet-runner, with variegated flowers, the upper petals being scarlet, the lower white. The ripe seeds are paler, and the spots and markings duller. Cultivation and uses the same.

White-runner. A variety of the Scarlet-runner. The plants are less vigorous, the pods are longer and less wrinkled, and the flowers and seeds pure white.

The green pods are used in the same manner as those of the Scarlet-runner, and are similar in texture and flavor; but the shelled-beans, either green or ripe, are generally considered superior to those of the Scarlet variety. They are sometimes seen in vegetable markets under the name of the "Lima," and are probably often cultivated, as well as purchased and consumed, as the Lima. The White-runner beans, however, are easily distinguished by their greater thickness, more rounded form, and especially by their uniform whiteness.

SIEVA.

Carolina. — Saba. — West-Indian. — Small Lima. — Carolina Sewee. — Phaseolus lunatus var.

The Sieva is a variety of the Lima, and attains a height of ten or twelve feet. The leaves and flowers resemble those of the Common Lima. The pods, however, are much smaller, and remarkable for their uniform size, generally measuring three inches in length, and seven-eighths of an inch in width : they are green and wrinkled while young, pale yellowish-brown when ripe, and contain three, and sometimes four seeds.

Though several days earlier than the Lima, the Sieva Bean requires the whole season for its complete maturity : and even when planted early, and receiving the advantage of a warm summer and a favorable autumn, it is seldom fully perfected in the Northern States ; for, though much of the crop may ripen, a large portion is prematurely destroyed by frost.

The variety blossomed in eight weeks from the time of planting, afforded pods for shelling in twelve weeks, and ripened from near the middle of September till the close of the season.

The seeds are white or dull yellowish-white, broad-kidney-shaped, much flattened, five-eighths of an inch long, and nearly half an inch broad. A quart contains sixteen hundred, and will plant a hundred and fifty hills.

The Sieva is one of the most productive of all varieties. The young pods, however, are tough and hard, and are never eaten. The beans, in their green or ripe state, are similar to the Lima, and are nearly as delicate and richly flavored. It is from two to three weeks earlier than the last named, and would yield a certain abundance in seasons when the Lima would uniformly fail. As a shelled-bean, green or dry, it must be classed as one of the best, and is recommended for cultivation.

A sub-variety of the Common Sieva: the principal if not the only mark of distinction is in the variegated character of the seeds, which are dull-white, spotted and streaked with purple. **Mottled Sieva.**

It is sometimes described as being earlier than the Common variety; but, from various experiments in the cultivation of both varieties, there appears to be little if any difference in their seasons of maturity. The color and form of the flower are the same as the Sieva; the pods are of the same size and shape; and the leaves have the same elongated form, and smooth, glossy appearance.

Mr. John M. Ives states that the variety originated in Danvers, Essex County, Mass.

ENGLISH BEAN.

Horse-bean. — Garden-bean of the English. — Vicia faba.

The English Bean differs essentially from the Common American Garden or Kidney Bean usually cultivated in this country. Aside from the great difference in their general appearance, and manner of growth, the soil, climate, and mode of cultivation, required by the two classes, are very dissimilar: the American Garden-bean thrives best in a light, warm soil, and under a high temperature; and the English Bean, in stiff, moist soil, and in cool, humid seasons.

It is an annual plant, with an upright, smooth, four-sided, hollow stem, dividing into branches near the ground, and growing from two to four feet and upwards in height. The flowers are large, nearly stemless, purple or white, veined and spotted with purplish-black; the pods are large and downy; the seeds are rounded, or reniform, flattened, and vary to a considerable extent in size and color in the different varieties, — they will vegetate until more than five years old.

Soil and Planting. — As before remarked, the English Bean requires a moist, strong soil, and a cool situation; the principal obstacles in the way of its successful cultivation in this country being the heat and drought of the summer. The seeds should be planted early, in drills two feet asunder for the smaller-growing varieties, and three feet for the larger sorts, — dropping them six inches from each other, and covering two inches deep. A quart of seed will plant a hundred and fifty feet of row or drill.

English Bean.

Cultivation. — " When the plants have attained a height of five or six inches, they are earthed up slightly for support; and, when more advanced, they are sometimes staked along the rows, and cords extended from stake to stake to keep the plants erect. When the young pods appear, the tops of the plants should be pinched off, to throw that nourishment, which would be expended in uselessly increasing the height of the plant, into its general system, and consequently increase the bulk of crop, as well as hasten its maturity. This often-recommended operation, though disregarded by many, is of very signal importance." — *McInt.*

Taking the Crop. — The pods should be gathered for use when the seeds are young, or when they are of the size of a morrowfat pea. As a general rule, all vegetables are most tender and delicate when young; and to few esculents does this truth apply with greater force than to the class of plants to which the English Bean belongs.

Use. — The seeds are used in their green state, cooked and served in the same manner as shelled kidney-beans. The young pods are sometimes, though rarely, used as string-beans.

Varieties. — In England, where this vegetable is grown in great perfection, and where it is much esteemed and generally used as a table esculent, the number of varieties cultivated nearly equals the number of kinds of the Common Garden-bean grown in this country. Under the climate of the United States, the crop has generally proved a failure. The plants are not only much infested with vermin, and more or less injured by mildew, but the yield is so small, and the quality so inferior, that its cultivation is generally abandoned.

Nineteen varieties are described in "THE FIELD AND GARDEN VEGETABLES OF AMERICA."

The *White Windsor* produces fine large pods, and is a favorite kind. Nine of the seeds, if well grown, will weigh an ounce. The *Green Windsor* is also a popular sort; eleven of the seeds weighing an ounce. Other esteemed varieties are the *European Long-pod*, *Early Mazagan*, *Dutch Long-pod*, and the *Dwarf Fan*, or *Cluster*.

THE PEA.

Pisum sativum.

The Pea is a hardy, annual plant; and its cultivation and use as an esculent are almost universal.

To give in detail the various methods of preparing the soil, sowing, culture, gathering, and use, would occupy a volume.

The following directions are condensed from an elaborate treatise on the culture of this vegetable, by Charles McIntosh, in his excellent work entitled "The Book of the Garden:"—

Soil and its Preparation. — The Pea comes earliest to maturity in light, rich soil. For early crops, mild manure, such as leaf-mould, should be used; for general crops, a good dressing may be applied; and for the dwarf kinds, such as Tom Thumb, Bishop's New Long Pod, and the like, the soil can hardly be too rich.

Seed and Sowing. — A quart of ripe peas is equal to two pounds' weight, and contains, of the largest sized varieties, thirteen hundred, and of the smaller descriptions two thousand seeds. A pint of the small-seeded sorts, such as the Daniel O'Rourke, Early Frame, and Early Charlton, will sow a row sixty feet in length; and the same quantity of larger growing sorts will sow a row of nearly a hundred feet, on account of being sown so much thinner. A fair average depth for covering the seed is two and a half or three inches; though some practise planting four or five inches deep, which is said to be a preventive against the premature decay of the vines near the roots.

As to distance between the rows, when peas are sown in the usual manner (that is, row after row throughout the whole field), they should be as far asunder as the length of the stem of the variety cultivated: thus a pea that attains a height or length of two feet should have two feet from row to row, and so on to those taller or lower growing.

They are sometimes sown two rows together, a foot apart, and ten, twenty, or even fifty feet between the double rows; by which every portion of the crop is well exposed to the sun and air, and the produce gathered with great facility. There is no loss of ground by this method; for other crops can be planted within a foot or two of the rows, and this amount of space is necessary for the purpose of gathering.

A common practice in ordinary garden culture is to sow in double rows twelve or fourteen inches apart, slightly raising the soil for the purpose. When so planted, all of the sorts not over two feet in height may be successfully grown without sticking. When varieties of much taller growth are sown, a greater yield will be secured by bushing the plants, which is more economically as well as more strongly done if the planting is made in double rows. The staking, or bushing, should be furnished when the plants are three or four inches high, or immediately after the second hoeing: they should be of equal height, and all straggling side twigs should be removed for appearance' sake.

Early Crops. — The earliest crops produced in the open garden without artificial aid are obtained by judicious selection of the most approved early varieties; choosing a warm, favorable soil and situation, and sowing the seed either in November, just as the ground is closing, or in February or March, at the first opening of the soil, — the latter season, however, being preferable, as the seed then vegetates with much greater certainty, and the crop is nearly or quite as early. Great benefit will be derived from reflected heat, when planted at the foot of a wall, building, or tight fence, running east and west.

Subsequent Cultivation. — When the crop has attained the height of five inches, a little earth should be drawn around the stems, forming a sort of ridge, with a slight channel in the middle; the intention being to give a slight support to the plants until they take hold of the stakes.

Gathering. — The crop should be gathered as it becomes fit for use. If even a few of the pods begin to ripen, young pods will not only cease to form, but those partly advanced will cease to enlarge.

Use. — "In a sanitary point of view, peas cannot be eaten too young, nor too soon after they are gathered; and hence people who depend on the public markets for their supply seldom have this very popular vegetable in perfection, and too often only when it is almost unfit for use. This is a formidable objection to the use of peas brought from long distances. It is, of course, for the interest of the producer to keep back his peas till they are fully grown, because they measure better, and we believe, by many, are purchased quicker, as they get greater bulk for their money. This may be so far excusable on the part of such; but it is inexcusable that a gentleman having a garden of his own should be served with peas otherwise than in the very highest state of perfection, which they are not, if allowed to become too old, or even too large."

Varieties. — These are very numerous, and, like those of the Broccoli and Lettuce, not only greatly confused, but often based on trifling and unimportant distinctions.

"New sorts are yearly introduced; and it would be injudicious not to give them a fair trial; for as we progress in pea-culture, as in every other branch of horticulture, we may reasonably expect that really improved and meritorious sorts will arise, and be substituted for others that may be inferior."

Advancer. Height three feet; pods single or in pairs, long and well filled, yielding seven or eight large peas. The ripe seeds are green, but vary in depth of color; wrinkled; and somewhat resemble those of the Champion of England.

Sown May 1, the plants blossomed June 14, and pods were gathered for use June 28.

The variety is of recent introduction, and is the dwarfest and earliest of the wrinkled marrow peas. English writers describe it as being but a few days later than the Dan O'Rourke. It is very prolific, podding well up the stem, and nearly as tender and sugary as the Champion of England.

It is one of the best sorts for the garden; and its earliness and great productiveness make it worthy the attention of market-gardeners.

Plant from four to five feet high, according to the soil in which it is grown, producing from twelve to fifteen pods, each of which contains eight or ten peas, closely compressed, and of the size of the Early Frames. The ripe seed is white. *Auvergne. Cot. Gard.*

Plants from seed sown May 1 were in blossom June 26; and the pods were sufficiently grown for plucking July 12.

Although the Auvergne Pea very far surpasses most of the White varieties, it has never become much disseminated, and is very little known or cultivated. It is, however, a most characteristic variety, and always easily distinguishable by its long, curved pods. It is one of the most productive of all the garden peas.

Plant three feet in height; pods narrow, exceedingly well filled, containing seven or eight peas of medium size, which, when ripe, are small, smooth, and of a bluish-green color. *Batt's Wonder. Trans.*

Planted May 1, the variety was in flower July 1, and the pods were fit for use the middle of the month.

The variety withstands drought well, and the pods hang long before the peas become too hard for use. It is an excellent pea for a second crop.

Beck's Prize-taker. *Trans.*

Plant four and a half to five feet in height; pods roundish, containing seven to eight middle-sized peas of a fine green color when young, and mixed olive and white when ripe.

Sown May 1, the plants blossomed June 25, and the pods were suitable for plucking the 12th of July.

It is one of the best varieties for the main crop. Similar to, if not identical with, Bellamy's Early Green Marrow.

Bedman's Imperial. *Cot. Gard.*

Plant from three to four feet high: the pods are usually in pairs, and contain from six to seven peas, which are of an ovate form, and about a third of an inch in their greatest diameter. The ripe seed is pale blue.

Planted May 1, the variety blossomed the last of June, and furnished peas for use the 18th of July.

For many years, this variety stood foremost among the Imperials, but is now giving place to other and greatly superior sorts.

Bellamy's Early Green Marrow. *Cot. Gard.*

Plant four and a half or five feet high, producing from twelve to eighteen pods, which contain, on an average, from six to seven large bluish-green peas. The ripe seed has a mixed appearance; some being dull yellowish-white, and others light olive-green, in about equal proportions.

Plants from seed sown the first week in May were in blossom the last week in June, and pods were plucked for use the middle of July.

The variety is highly recommended, both as a good bearer and a pea of excellent quality, whether for private use or for marketing: for the latter purpose it is peculiarly adapted, as the pod is of a fine, deep color, handsomely and regularly shaped, and always plumply filled.

Pods two inches long; pea a fourth of an inch in diameter, cream-colored, with blotches of white, particularly about the eye. The plant grows little more than a foot high, and is fairly productive. Early sowings will give a supply for the table in ten weeks. **Bishop's Early Dwarf.** *Law.*

This once popular Early Dwarf sort is now rapidly giving place to Bishop's New Long-podded, — a more prolific and much superior variety.

Stem two feet high; pods nearly straight, containing six or seven white peas. It is an early variety, an abundant bearer, of excellent quality, and in all respects much superior to the Common Bishop's Early Dwarf. **Bishop's New Long-podded.**

Planted the 1st of May, it blossomed June 14, and yielded peas for the table the 10th of July.

Plant five feet high; pods three inches and a quarter in length, containing about six large, round, cream-white or brownish-white, black-eyed seeds, three-eighths of an inch in diameter. **Black-eyed Marrow.**

Its season is nearly the same with the Dwarf and Missouri Marrow. Sown the 1st of May, the plants blossomed the 28th or 30th of June, and yielded peas for the table July 15.

This is a very prolific as well as excellent variety. It is little cultivated in gardens at the North, though sometimes grown as a field-pea in the Canadas. In the Middle States, and at the South, it is a popular market-sort; and its cultivation is much more extensive.

The dark color of the eye of the ripened seed distinguishes the variety from all others.

Plant three feet high; pods cimeter-shaped, and generally well filled; seeds of good quality, larger than those of the Prussian Blue, from which the variety doubtless originated. **Blue Cimeter.** *Thomp.* **Sabre.**

Planted the 1st of May, it blossomed the 28th of June, and the pods were suitable for plucking the middle of July.

It bears abundantly, but not in succession, and, for this reason, is much prized by market-gardeners. The most of the pods being fit to pluck at the same time, the crop is harvested at once, and the land immediately occupied with other vegetables.

Blue Imperial.
Dwarf Blue Imperial.
Plant strong and vigorous, four feet in height; pods single and in pairs, containing six or seven large peas.

The ripe seed is somewhat indented and irregularly compressed, three-eighths of an inch in diameter, and of a greenish-blue color.

Sown the 1st of May, the plants were in blossom the 26th of June, and pods were plucked for use the 12th of July.

It is very hardy; yields abundantly; thrives well in almost any description of soil or situation; and, though not so sweet and tender as some of the more recent sorts, is of good quality. It vegetates with much greater certainty, and its crops are more reliable, than the higher-flavored varieties; and these qualities will still secure its cultivation by those who prefer a certain and plentiful supply, of fair quality, to a precarious and limited yield of extraordinary sweetness and excellence. It has long been grown in this country, and is considered a standard variety.

Blue Prussian.
Cot. Gard.
Stem three feet high. The pods are generally produced in pairs, and vary from twelve to sixteen on each plant. They contain about seven peas. The ripe seed is blue.

Sown the 1st of May, the plants blossomed June 28, and yielded peas for use the middle of July.

It produces abundantly, and is a valuable sort for late

summer use. "It is unquestionably the parent of the Blue Imperial and all like varieties."

Plant from a foot and a half to three feet high. The pods are single and in pairs in about equal proportion, and contain from six to seven peas each. The ripe seed is pale blue.   *Blue Spanish Dwarf. Cot. Gard.*

Plants from sowings made the first of May blossomed the last of June, and yielded peas for use the middle of July.

It is a good variety for small gardens, as it is a low grower and a fair bearer; but it is now much surpassed by Bishop's Long-podded and Burbridge's Eclipse, both of which are considered more prolific and better flavored.

From six to seven feet high. The pods are generally single, but frequently in pairs, three inches and three-quarters long, of a bright-green color, and contain from five to seven exceedingly large peas.   *British Queen. Cot. Gard.*

Sown May 1, the plants blossomed the 30th of June, pods were plucked for use the 15th of July, and the crop ripened off the 1st of August.

This is one of the best late peas in cultivation, and belongs to the class known as Wrinkled, or Knight's Marrows; but is much superior in every respect to all the old varieties usually called Knight's Marrows, being much more prolific and richly flavored. As an intermediate variety, it deserves a place in every garden.

Plant from a foot and a half to two feet high; pods three inches and a quarter long, containing from five to seven peas.   *Burbridge's Eclipse. Cot. Gard.*

Seed was planted May 1, the plants blossomed June 26, and pods were plucked for use July 14.

This may be classed among the valuable contributions which have been made to the list of peas during the last few years. Unlike many of the dwarf varieties, it is a most productive sort; and thus its dwarf character is not its chief recommendation. For private gardens, or for cultivation for market, few peas surpass this and Bishop's Long-podded.

Carter's Victoria. *Trans.* Plant six to seven feet high; pods slightly curved, containing seven or eight large peas, which are sweet, and of excellent quality. The ripe seeds are white, and much shrivelled or wrinkled.

Plants from seeds sown May 1 blossomed July 1, and the pods were fit for plucking the 18th of the month.

The variety continues long in bearing, and the peas exceed in size those of Knight's Tall White Marrow. It is one of the best late tall peas.

Charlton. *Cot. Gard. Law. Thomp.* EARLY CHARLTON. The original character of this variety may be described as follows: —
Plant five feet high, and of vigorous growth; leaves large, with short petioles; tendrils small; pods broad, containing six or seven peas of excellent quality. They are rather larger than those of the Early Frame, with which this is often confounded. The Early Charlton is, however, a fortnight later than the Early Frame; so that, when sown at the same time, it forms a succession.

The various names by which it has been known are Reading Hotspur, Master's or Flander's Hotspur, Golden Hotspur, Brompton Hotspur, Essex Hotspur, Early Nicol's Hotspur, Charlton Hotspur, and finally Early Charlton, the last name becoming general about 1750.

An English writer remarks, "that the variety now exists only in name. That which is sold for the Early Charlton is often a degenerated stock of Early Frames, or any stock of Frames which cannot be warranted or depended upon, but which are, nevertheless, of such a character as to admit of their being grown as garden varieties. The Early Charlton, if grown at all by seed-growers as a distinct variety, is certainly cultivated to a very limited extent."

Of the popular American improved early sorts, the Hill's Early, Hovey's Extra Early, Landreth's Extra Early, are hardy as well as very prolific, and are not only well adapted for private gardens, but may be recommended as the most profitable kinds for cultivating for early marketing. In an experimental trial of these kinds with the Early Dan O'Rourke, and some of the most approved of the earliest foreign varieties, they proved to be nearly or quite as early, fully as prolific, continued longer in bearing, and were much more stocky and vigorous in habit.

Plant five or six feet high, producing from eight to ten pods. These are three inches and a quarter to three inches and three-quarters long, and contain from six to seven large peas, which are close together without being compressed. Champion of Paris, or Paradise Marrow. *Cot. Gard.*

The ripe seed is white, medium-sized, somewhat flattened and pitted. Sown May 1, the plants blossomed June 28, and pods were ready for plucking July 16.

This is a very excellent pea, an abundant cropper, and considerably earlier than the Auvergne and Shillings Grotto, to both of which it is also greatly superior.

Plant six feet high; pods large, and well filled. Champion of Scotland.

Sown May 1, the variety blossomed July 1, and pods were gathered for use the 20th of the month.

In its general character, the Champion of Scotland somewhat resembles the Competitor, often remaining fresh and green till the middle of September. From the time of the first plucking, the plants continued to grow, blossom, and pod for nearly five weeks.

It is of excellent quality, and, as a late sort, one of the best for cultivation.

Stalk remarkably strong and vigorous, at- Competitor.

taining a height of six feet and upwards; pods long and broad, generally yielding from six to eight large peas.

The seeds, when ripe, are cream-yellow, above medium size, and much shrivelled and indented.

Sown May 1, the plants blossomed the last of June, and pods were plucked for use the 20th of July.

The Competitor Pea is of recent origin, and is described as the latest of all the sorts now in cultivation. Aside from its large size and excellence, it is one of the most valuable of all varieties for the length of time the plants continue in bearing. In an experimental growth of this pea, the pods were first plucked, as stated above, the 20th of July; and from this time the plants continued to yield abundantly until the last of August, or for a period of nearly six weeks.

Dantzic. *Law.* Plant six to seven feet high; pods in pairs, two and a half inches long, and half an inch broad. When ripe, the seed is the smallest of all the light peas, quite round or spherical, of a bright-yellow color, beautifully transparent, with whitish eyes.

Sown the 1st of May, the plants blossomed the 8th of July, afforded peas for the table the 25th of the same month, and ripened from the 10th to the middle of August.

It is not a productive variety, and is seldom cultivated in England or in this country, but is grown extensively on the shores of the Baltic, and exported for splitting, or boiling whole.

Dickson's Favorite. *Trans.* Plant five feet high; pods ten to twelve on a stalk, long, round when full grown, curved, and hooked at the extremity, like the Auvergne: they are remarkably well filled, and contain from eight to ten peas of medium size, round, and very white.

Planted the 1st of May, the variety blossomed June 25, and pods were gathered for use the 12th of July.

This pea is highly deserving of cultivation as a second early variety.

The plant is of slender habit of growth, produces a single stem two feet high, and bears, on an average, from seven to nine pods: these are smaller than those of the Dan O'Rourke, generally single, but occasionally in pairs, almost straight, and contain seven peas each. The seed, when ripe, is white. **Dillistone's Early.** *Cot. Gard.*

As described by English cultivators, the plants were a mass of bloom three days before the last named had commenced blossoming, and the crop was ready for gathering seven days before the Dan O'Rourke.

In an experimental growth of this pea, it proved little, if at all, earlier than the Dan O'Rourke, and really seemed to have few distinctive characteristics when compared with that variety.

Plant very stocky, forming a dwarfish, spreading bush, twelve to fifteen inches high. **Drew's New Dwarf.** The pods are single or in pairs, and contain from six to eight large peas of excellent quality. The ripe seeds are cream-yellow, ovate, compressed, wrinkled, and indented.

Season intermediate. Sown May 1, the plants were in flower June 26, and pods were gathered for use the 14th of July.

To secure its greatest perfection, the seeds should be sown quite early, and a space of ten or twelve inches allowed between the plants in the rows. When grown late in the season, it is not only much less productive, but the plants, to a considerable extent, lose the strong, dwarfish, bushy habit for which the variety is so justly prized. Properly treated, the plants are remarkably prolific, — sometimes yielding forty or fifty pods each.

Plant from three to four feet in height; pods three inches to three inches and a half long, containing about six closely set peas: these are cream-colored and white, slightly wrinkled, and measure nearly three-eighths of an inch in diameter. **Dwarf Marrow.** DWARF MARROWFAT.

Planted the 1st of May, the variety blossomed the last of June, and afforded peas for the table the 15th of July.

The Dwarf Marrow is hardy and productive. Though not so sweet or well flavored as some of the more recent sorts, its yield is abundant and long-continued; and for these qualities it is extensively cultivated. The variety, however, is rarely found in an unmixed state; much of the seed sown under this name producing plants of stronger habit of growth than those of the true Dwarf Marrow, and more resembling the Tall White variety.

Early Dan O'Rourke.
Cot. Gard.

Plant from three and a half to four feet high, — in general habit not unlike the Early Frame, of which it is probably an improved variety; pods usually single, two inches and three-fourths long, containing five or six peas.

When fully ripe, the pea is round, cream-colored, and measures nearly a fourth of an inch in diameter.

Plants from seed sown May 1 were in bloom June 7, and pods were gathered for use from the 25th of the month.

The Dan O'Rourke is remarkable for its precocity, and, with the exception of one or two American varieties, is the earliest of all the sorts now in cultivation. It is hardy, prolific, seldom fails to produce a good crop, appears to be well adapted to our soil and climate, is excellent for small private gardens, and one of the best for extensive culture for market.

Its character as an early pea can be sustained only by careful culture, and judicious selection of seeds for propagation. If grown in cold soil, from late-ripened seeds, the variety will rapidly degenerate; and, if from the past any thing can be judged of the future, the Dan O'Rourke, under the ordinary forms of propagation and culture, will shortly follow its numerous and once equally popular predecessors to quiet retirement as a synonyme of the Early Frame, or Charlton.

Early Frame.
Thomp.

Plant three to four feet in height; pods two and a half inches long by half an inch in breadth. The peas, when fully ripe, are round and plump, cream-colored, and measure nearly a fourth of an inch in diameter.

Sown the 1st of May, the variety blossomed June 20, and the pods were ready for plucking the 6th of July.

This well-known pea, for a long period, was the most popular of all the early varieties. At present, it is less extensively cultivated, having been superseded by much earlier and equally hardy and prolific sorts.

Early Hotspur.

Similar to, if not identical with, the Early Frame.

Early Warwick.

Once at the head of early peas; now considered by the most experienced cultivators to be identical with the Early Frame.

Early Washington.
CEDO NULLI.

A sub-variety of the Early Frame, differing slightly, if at all, either in the size or form of the pod, color and size of the seed, or in productiveness.

Once popular, and almost universally cultivated; now rarely found on seedsmen's catalogues.

Eugénie.
ALLIANCE.

Plant three feet in height; pods single or in pairs, three inches long, containing five or six peas. When ripe, the peas are of medium size, cream-colored, and much shrivelled and indented.

Plants from sowings made May 1 were in blossom June 14, green peas were plucked July 10, and the pods ripened from the 18th to the 25th of the same month.

English catalogues describe the variety as being "the earliest white, wrinkled marrow-pea in cultivation, podding from the bottom of the stalk to the top, with fine large pods."

In a trial growth, it proved hardy and very prolific; and the peas, while young, were nearly as sweet as those of the Champion of England. The pods were not remarkable for diameter, but, on the contrary, were apparently slender. The peas, however, were large; and, the pods being thin in texture, the peas, when shelled, seemed to be equal in diameter to the pods themselves. As a new variety, it certainly promises well, and appears to be worthy of general cultivation. It will come to the table immediately after the earliest sorts, and yield a supply till the Marrows are ready for plucking.

Fairbeard's Champion of England. *Cot. Gard.* CHAMPION OF ENGLAND. Plant of strong and luxuriant habit of growth, with a stem from five to six feet in height. The pods are generally single, but sometimes in pairs, about three inches and a half long, and contain six or seven quite large peas, which are closely packed together and compressed. The ripe seed is wrinkled, and of a pale olive-green.

Sown the 1st of May, the plants were in flower June 25, and pods were gathered for use the 12th of July.

This is, without doubt, one of the most valuable acquisitions which have been obtained for many years, being remarkably tender and sugary, and, in all respects, of first-rate excellence. The rapid progress of its popularity, and its universal cultivation, are, however, the best indications of its superiority.

Fairbeard's Nonpareil. *Cot. Gard.* Stem three and a half to four feet high. The pods are full and plump, and contain from six to eight peas, which are close together, much compressed, and of that sweet flavor which is peculiar to the Knight's Marrows. The ripe seed is yellowish-white, and wrinkled.

It is earlier than Fairbeard's Champion of England,

nearly as early as the Frames, and a most valuable acquisition.

Stem four feet high. The pods are three inches long, and contain from six to seven peas, which are of good size, but not so sweet as those of the Champion of England. The ripe seed is somewhat oval, and of a pale olive-green color.   *Fairbeard's Surprise. Cot. Gard.*

The variety is a day or two earlier than the last named.

Plant three feet in height; the pods are numerous, varying from twelve to eighteen, generally produced in pairs, and contain from six to eight very large ovate peas. The ripe seed is blue.   *Flack's Imperial. Cot. Gard.*

Plants from seed sown May 1 blossomed June 28, and pods were plucked for the table July 15.

It is one of the most prolific peas in cultivation; grows to a convenient height; and, whether considered for private gardens or for market supplies, is one of the most valuable varieties which has been introduced for years.

Plant from six to seven feet high; the pods number from ten to fourteen on each plant, and contain eight very large peas, which are of a deep, dull green color. The ripe seed is white and olive mixed.   *General Wyndham. Cot. Gard.*

This is a valuable acquisition, and was evidently procured from the Ne Plus Ultra; but it is a more robust grower, and produces much larger pods.

The plant continues growing, blooming, and podding till late in the season; and, when this is in the full vigor of growth, the Ne Plus Ultra is ripening off. The peas, when cooked, are of a fine, bright green, and unlike those of any other variety.

Hair's Dwarf Mammoth. Plant from three to three feet and a half high; pods single or in pairs, containing six large peas, which are sugary, tender, and excellent. The ripe seeds are shrivelled, and vary in color; some being cream-white, and others bluish-green.

Sown May 1, the plants blossomed July 1, and pods were ready for use the 15th of the same month.

Very prolific, and deserving of cultivation.

Harrison's Glory. *Trans.* Plant three feet high; pods rather short, containing five or six medium-sized peas, of good quality. When ripe, the seeds are light olive, mixed with white, and also slightly indented.

Planted May 1, the variety was in flower June 23, and the pods were fit for gathering the 10th of July.

It is a good variety; but, like Harrison's Perfection, the pods are frequently not well filled.

Harrison's Perfection. *Trans.* Plant three feet in height; pods small, straight, containing five peas; of good size and quality.

Sown the 1st of May, the variety was in flower June 23, and the pods were ready for plucking the 12th of July.

The only defect in this variety is, that the pods are often not well filled. When growing, it is scarcely distinguishable from Harrison's Glory; but, in the mature state, the seeds of the former are smooth and white, while those of the latter are indented, and of an olive color.

King of the Marrows. Plant six feet in height; pods single or in pairs, containing five or six large seeds, which, when ripe, are yellowish-green, and much shrivelled and indented, like those of the Champion of England.

Planted May 1, the variety blossomed the last of June, and pods for the table were plucked the 15th of July.

Though late, it is one of the best of the more recently

introduced sorts, and well deserving of general cultivation. When the pods are gathered as fast as they become fit for use, the plants will continue to put forth new blossoms, and form new pods, for an extraordinary length of time; in favorable seasons, often supplying the table for five or six weeks.

It is tender and sugary, and little, if at all, inferior to the Champion of England.

In common with most of the colored peas, the ripe seeds, when grown in this country, are much paler than those of foreign production; and, when long cultivated in the climate of the United States, the blue or green is frequently changed to pale blue or yellowish-green, and often ultimately becomes nearly cream-white.

A dwarfish sub-variety of Knight's Marrows, with wrinkled, blue seeds. **Knight's Dwarf Blue Marrow.**

Plant three feet high; pods three inches long. The ripe peas are of a light bluish-green color. It differs from the foregoing principally in the height of the plant, but also, to some extent, in the form of the pods. **Knight's Dwarf Green Marrow.**

Plant three feet high; pods three inches long, and well filled; pea, on an average, about three-eighths of an inch in diameter, flattened, and very much wrinkled; color white, and sometimes of a greenish tinge. It is a few days earlier than the Dwarf Green. **Knight's Dwarf White Marrow.** *Law.*

A sub-variety of Knight's Tall Marrows, with blue, wrinkled, and indented seeds. It resembles the Tall White and Tall Green Marrows. **Knight's Tall Blue Marrow.**

Knight's Tall Green Marrow. *Law. Thomp.* Plant very strong and vigorous, attaining a height of six or seven feet; pods large, broad, and well filled. The seeds, when ripe, are green, and much wrinkled or indented.

Planted the first of May, the variety blossomed the last of June, and supplied the table the middle of July.

The peas are exceedingly tender and sugary; the skin also is very thin. "From their remarkably wrinkled appearance, together with the peculiar sweetness which they all possess, Knight's Marrows may be said to form a distinct class of garden peas, possessing qualities which, together with their general productiveness, render them a valuable acquisition both to cultivators and consumers."

Knight's Tall White Marrow. Height and general character of the plant similar to Knight's Tall Green Marrow. Pods in pairs. The ripe seed is white. Very productive and excellent.

Lord Raglan. Plant three feet high; the pods are large and broad, and contain six or seven large peas. When ripe, the seeds are shrivelled, and of a blue or greenish-blue color; the American-grown, however, being usually much paler than those received from England.

Sown May 1, the plants were in flower July 1, and pods were plucked for use the 15th of the month.

The variety is prolific, appears to be adapted to our soil and climate, grows to a convenient height, is of excellent quality, — nearly or quite equalling the Champion of England, — and is recommended for cultivation.

By some of the most reliable of English cultivators, it is described as differing slightly, if at all, from Hair's Dwarf Mammoth.

Matchless Marrow. *Cot. Gard.* This is a good marrow-pea, but now surpassed by the improved varieties of the Early

Green Marrow. It possesses no qualities superior to that variety, and is not so early.

Plant from four and a half to five feet high, producing from twelve to sixteen pods, each containing six or seven large peas, which are roundish, and somewhat compressed, half an inch long, and nearly the same broad.   *Milford Marrow. Cot. Gard.*

Its season is near that of Bellamy's Early Green Marrow. Planted May 1, it blossomed June 28, and the pods were fit for plucking the middle of July.

Plant three feet and a half or four feet high; pods three inches long, containing about six peas, rather closely set together. When ripe, the pea is similar to the Dwarf Marrow in form, but is larger, paler, more wrinkled, and much more regular in size.   *Missouri Marrow. MISSOURI MARROW-FAT.*

Plants from seed sown May 1 were in blossom the 30th of June, and pods were gathered for use the 14th of July. It is a few days later than Fairbeard's Champion of England, and nearly of the season of the Dwarf Marrowfat, of which it is probably but an improved or sub-variety.

It is of American origin, very productive, of good quality, and well deserving of cultivation.

Plant three feet and a half high; pods three inches long, containing five or six peas. When ripe, these are of medium size, pale blue or olive, sometimes yellowish, shaded with blue, and, like the Eugénie, much wrinkled and indented.   *Napoléon. CLIMAX.*

Sown the beginning of May, the variety blossomed the 15th of June, pods were plucked for use the 10th of July, and the crop ripened the 25th of the same month.

English catalogues represent the Napoléon as being " the earliest blue pea in cultivation, podding from the bottom of the haum to the top with fine large pods." In a trial growth, it proved early and productive; not only forming a great number of pods, but well filling the pods after being formed. In quality it is tender, very sweet, and well flavored, resembling the Champion of England. Its season is nearly the same with that of the Eugénie, and the variety is well deserving of cultivation.

Ne Plus Ultra.
Cot. Gard.

This variety belongs to the wrinkled class of peas; is as early as Bellamy's Green Marrow; and possesses, both in pod and pea, the same fine, deep, olive-green color.

The plant is from six to seven feet high: it begins to produce pods at two or two and a half feet from the ground; and the number, in all, is from twelve to eighteen. The pods are generally in pairs, three inches and a half long, of a deep, bright-green color, and contain seven very large peas, each of which is half an inch long, and nearly the same broad.

Sown the first of May, the variety blossomed the last of June, and afforded peas for use the 15th of July.

It is one of the best tall Marrows in cultivation. The ripe seed is mixed white and olive.

Noble's Early Green Marrow.
Cot. Gard.

A sub-variety of Bellamy's Early Green Marrow. It is a much more abundant bearer, producing from eighteen to twenty pods on a plant, which are singularly regular in their size and form.

Prince Albert.
EARLY MAY. EARLY KENT.

Plant from two and a half to three feet in height; pods generally in pairs, two inches and a half in length, and half an inch broad. The ripe seeds are round, cream-colored, and measure a fourth of an inch in diameter.

Sown May 1, the plants blossomed June 15, and pods were plucked for use July 6.

The Prince Albert was, at one period, the most popular of all the early varieties, and was cultivated in almost every part of the United States. As now found in the garden, the variety is not distinguishable from some forms of the Early Frame; and it is everywhere giving place to the Early Dan O'Rourke and other more recent sorts, which have proved of quite as good quality, and much more productive.

A very dwarfish variety, from six to nine inches high. Stem thick and succulent; foliage dark bluish-green. Each plant produces from four to six pods, which are of a curious, elliptic form, and contain three or four large peas. Ripe seed white, of medium size, egg-shaped, unevenly compressed. Queen of the Dwarfs. *Cot. Gard.*

The plants are tender; the pods rarely fill well; and the variety cannot be recommended for cultivation.

Plant three and a half to four feet high. The pods contain from six to seven large peas, which are nearly round, and measure seven-tenths of an inch in diameter in the green state. The ripe seed is white. Ringwood Marrow. *Cot. Gard.*

The variety is early. Planted May 1, it blossomed the 25th of June, and the pods were ready to pluck the 10th of July.

It is a valuable sort, producing a large, well-filled pod, and is a most abundant bearer. It has, however, a peculiarity, which by many is considered an objection, — the pod is white, instead of green, and presents, when only full grown, the appearance of over-maturity. This objection is chiefly made by those who grow it for markets, and who find it difficult to convince their customers, that, notwithstanding the pod is white, it is still in its highest perfection. So far from being soon out of season, it retains its tender and marrowy character longer than many other varieties.

Royal Dwarf, or White Prussian.
Cot. Gard.

Plant of medium growth, with an erect stem, which is three feet high. The pods are nearly three inches long, generally well filled, and contain from five to six peas, which are ovate, not compressed, four-tenths of an inch long, and a third of an inch in thickness. The ripe seed is white.

Plants from seed sown the 1st of May blossomed June 25, and supplied the table the middle of July. The crop will ripen the 25th of the same month.

This is an old and prolific variety, well adapted for field culture, and long a favorite in gardens, but now, to a great extent, superseded.

Sebastopol.

Plant of rather slender habit, three feet and a half in height; pods two inches and three-quarters in length, containing from five to seven peas, which, when ripe, are nearly round and smooth, cream-colored, and scarcely distinguishable, in their size, form, or color, from the Early Frame and kindred kinds.

Planted May 1, the variety blossomed June 16, afforded pods of sufficient size for shelling July 7, and ripened the 20th of the same month.

It is early, productive, of superior quality, and an excellent sort for growing for market, or in small gardens for family use. In an experimental cultivation of the variety, it proved one of the most prolific of all the early sorts.

Shillings Grotto.
Cot. Gard.

Plant with a simple stem, four feet and a half to five feet high; the pods are generally single, three inches and a half long, and contain, on an average, seven large peas. The ripe seed is white.

A great objection to this variety is the tardiness with which it fills, the pods being fully grown, and apparently filled, when the peas are quite small, and only half grown. Though considered a standard sort, it is not superior to the Champion of England, and will probably soon give place to it, or some other of the more recent varieties.

Plant a foot high, branching on each side in the manner of a fan; and hence often called the "Dwarf Fan." The pods are sometimes single, but generally in pairs, two inches and a half long, and contain from five to six rather large peas. The ripe seed is cream-white.

<small>Spanish Dwarf.
Cot. Gard.
EARLY SPANISH DWARF. DWARF FAN. STRAWBERRY.</small>

Sown May 1, the plants were in blossom June 26, and pods were plucked for use July 14.

The Spanish Dwarf is an old variety, and still maintains its position as an Early Dwarf for small gardens, though it can hardly be considered equal to Burbridge's Eclipse or Bishop's Long-podded.

There is a variety of this which is called the Improved Spanish Dwarf, and grows fully nine inches taller than the old variety; but it possesses no particular merit to recommend it.

Plant six to seven feet in height, seldom branched; the pods are from three to three inches and a half long, three-fourths of an inch broad, and contain six or seven peas. When ripe, the pea is nearly of the color of the Dwarf Marrow, but is more perfectly spherical, less wrinkled, and, when compared in bulk, has a smoother, harder, and more glossy appearance.

<small>Tall White Marrow.
TALL MARROWFAT.</small>

Planted May 1, the variety blossomed the 1st of July, and supplied the table from the 15th to the 30th of the same month. It is a few days later than the Dwarf.

In this country, it has been longer cultivated than any other sort; and, in some of the forms of its very numerous sub-varieties, is now to be found in almost every garden. It is hardy, abundant, and long-continued in its yield, and of excellent quality. In England, the variety is cultivated in single rows, three feet apart. In this country, where the growth of the pea is much less luxuriant, it may be grown in double rows, three feet and a half apart, and twelve inches between the single rows.

Taylor's Early. Similar in habit, production, and early maturity, to the Early Dan O'Rourke.

Thurston's Reliance.
Cot. Gard.
Six to seven feet high; the pods are broad and flat, like the pods of the Blue Cimeter, and contain seven or eight very large peas; ripe seed white, large, and unevenly compressed.

This is a quite distinct and useful pea; an abundant bearer; and the pods are of a fine deep-green color, which is a recommendation for it when grown for market. It comes in at the same time as the Auvergne and Shillings Grotto, but is of a more tender constitution.

Tom Thumb.
Bush Pea.
Plant of remarkably low growth, seldom much exceeding nine inches in height, stout and branching; pods single, rarely in pairs, two inches and a half in length, half an inch broad, containing five or six peas, which are cream-yellow, and measure a fourth of an inch in diameter.

Planted the 1st of May, the variety blossomed the 12th of June, and the pods were of suitable size for plucking July 4.

In the color of its foliage, its height and general habit, the variety is very distinct, and readily distinguishable from all other kinds. It is early, of good quality, and, the height of the plant considered, yields abundantly. It may be cultivated in rows ten inches apart.

Mr. Landreth, of Philadelphia, remarks as follows: "For sowing at this season (November, in the Middle States), we recommend trial of a new variety, which we have designated

'Tom Thumb,' in allusion to its extreme dwarfness. It seldom rises over twelve inches, is an abundant bearer, and is, withal, quite early. It seems to be admirably adapted to autumn sowings in the South, where, on apprehended frost, protection may be given : it is also equally well suited to early spring planting for the same reason. It is curious, as well as useful, and, if planted on ground well enriched, will yield as much to a given quantity of land as any pea known to us."

It is a desirable variety in the kitchen garden, as, from its exceeding dwarfish habit, it may be so sown as to form a neat edging for the walk, or border.

Plant three feet and a half to four feet high, somewhat branched; pods ten or twelve on a stalk or branch, large, flat, straight, containing six or eight large peas, which are very sugary and excellent. The ripe seeds are large, of a light olive-green color, some being nearly white. *Veitch's Perfection. Trans.*

Planted the 1st of May, the variety will be in flower June 28, and the pods will be fit for use the middle or 20th of July. It is one of the best peas for main or late crops.

Plant from six to seven feet high; pods nearly four inches in length, generally in pairs, straight, roundish, well filled, containing from six to eight peas of extraordinary size and of good quality. The ripe peas are olive-green. *Victoria Marrow. Thomp.*

The Victoria Marrow is not early. Planted May 1, it blossomed the last of June, and was fit for the table from the middle of July.

This variety bears some resemblance to Knight's Tall Marrow; but, like nearly all others, it is less sugary. Those who have a fancy for large peas will find this, perhaps, the largest.

Warner's Early Emperor. *Thomp.*
EARLY EMPEROR.

This variety grows somewhat taller, and is a few days earlier, than the Prince Albert: the pods and peas are also somewhat larger. It is an abundant bearer, and, on the whole, must be considered a good sub-variety of the Early Frame.

Woodford's Marrow. *Cot. Gard.*
NONPAREIL.

Plant of robust habit, three feet and a half high. The pods are three inches and a half long, and contain, on an average, seven peas, which are of a dark olive-green color, rather thick in the skin, and closely packed, — so much so as to be quite flattened on the sides adjoining.

Sown May 1, the variety blossomed June 28, and peas were gathered for the table July 17.

This is a very characteristic pea, and may at once be detected from all others, either by the ripe seed or growing plants, from the peculiar dark-green color, which, when true, it always exhibits. It is well adapted for a market-pea, its dark-green color favoring the popular prejudices.

EATABLE-PODDED OR SUGAR PEAS.

String-peas. — Skinless Peas. — Pisum macrocarpum. — Dec.

In this class are included such of the varieties as want the tough, inner film, or parchment lining, common to the other sorts. The pods are generally of large size, tender and succulent, and are used in the green state like string-beans; though the seeds may be used as other peas, either in the green state or when ripe. "When not ripe, the pods of some of the sorts have the appearance of being swollen, or distended with air; but, on ripening, they become much shrivelled, and collapse closely on the seeds." The varieties are not numerous, when compared with the extensive catalogue of the kinds of the Common Pea offered for sale by seedsmen, and described by horticultural writers. The principal are the following: —

Stalk two feet high, dividing into branches; pods single or in pairs, six-seeded, three inches long, crooked or jointed-like with the seeds, as in all of the Sugar Peas, very prominent, especially on becoming ripe and dry; pea fully a fourth of an inch in diameter, white, and slightly wrinkled.

Common Dwarf Sugar. *Law. Vil.*

The variety is quite late. Sown the beginning of May, the plants blossomed the last week in June, and pods were gathered for use July 17.

It is prolific, of good quality as a shelled-pea, and the young pods are tender and well flavored.

Plant twenty inches high, branching. The pods are two inches and three-quarters in length, somewhat sickle-shaped, and contain five or six peas, which, when ripe, are roundish, often irregularly flattened or indented, wrinkled, and of a yellowish-white color.

Early Dwarf Dutch Sugar.

The variety is the lowest-growing and earliest of all the Eatable-podded kinds. If sown at the time of the Common Dwarf Sugar, it will be fit for use twelve or fourteen days in advance of that variety. It requires a good soil; and the pods are succulent and tender, but are not considered superior to those of the Common Dwarf Sugar.

Stalk four to five feet high; flower reddish; pods thick and fleshy, distended on the surface by the seeds, which are widely distributed, curved, and much contorted, six inches long, and sometimes nearly an inch and a half in diameter, — exceeding in size that of any other variety. They contain but five or six seeds, which, when ripe, are irregular in form, and of a greenish-yellow color, spotted or speckled with brown.

Giant Eatable-podded. *Vil.*

It is a week later than the Large Crooked Sugar.

Large Crooked Sugar. *Thomp.*
Six-Inch-Pod Sugar.

Plant nearly six feet in height; the pods are from four to five inches in length, and an inch in width, — broad, flat, and crooked. When young, they are tender, and easily snap or break in pieces, like the young pods of kidney-beans; and are then fit for use. The sides of the pods exhibit prominent marks where pushed out by the seeds, even at an early stage of growth. The ripe peas are somewhat indented or irregularly compressed, and of a yellowish-white-color.

It is one of the best of the Eatable-podded sorts, and is hardy and productive. It is, however, quite late.

Sown May 1, it blossomed the last of June, and produced pods for use in the green state the 20th of July.

Purple-podded or Australian. *Law.*
Blue-Podded.
Botany-Bay Pea.

Plant five feet high, generally without branches; pods usually in pairs, with thick, fleshy skins, and commonly of a dark-purple color: but this characteristic is not permanent, as they are sometimes found with green pods; in which case, they are, however, easily distinguished from those of other peas by their thick and fleshy nature. When ripe, the peas are of medium size, often much indented and irregularly compressed, and of a light, dunnish, or brown color. Season intermediate.

It is very productive, and seems possessed of properties which entitle it to cultivation.

Red-flowered Sugar. *Vil.*
Chocolate.

Stem four or five feet in height; leaves tinged with red where they connect with the stalk of the plant; flowers pale red. The pods are three inches long, more or less contorted, and contain from six to eight peas. The ripe seeds are large, pale brown, marbled with reddish-brown.

Season nearly the same as that of the Common Dwarf Sugar. It is productive, remarkably hardy, and may be sown very early in spring, as it is little affected by cool and wet weather; but the green peas are not much esteemed, as they possess a strong and rather unpleasant flavor. The green pods are tender and good; and for these the variety may be worthy of cultivation.

Tamarind Sugar. LATE DWARF SUGAR.

Plant similar to the Common Dwarf Sugar; flowers white; pods six to eight seeded, very large and broad, — often measuring four inches in length and an inch in breadth, — succulent, and generally contorted and irregular in form. A few days later than the Common Dwarf Sugar.

Hardy, prolific, and deserves more general cultivation.

White-podded Sugar. *Vil.*

Stem four to five feet high; flowers purple; the pods are nearly three inches long, five-eighths of an inch wide, of a yellowish-white color, and contain five or six peas. The ripe seeds are irregularly flattened and indented, of a greenish-yellow color, marbled or spotted with brown or black.

The variety is quite late. Sown May 1, the pods were not fit for use till July 24.

The pods are crisp and succulent, though inferior in flavor to most of the Eatable-podded varieties.

Yellow-podded Sugar. *Vil.*

Stem three to four feet high; flowers white, tinted with yellow; pods four inches long, greenish-yellow, thick and fleshy, containing six or seven peas widely separated. The ripe seeds are oblong, rather regular in form, and of a creamy-white color.

It is one of the earliest of the Eatable-podded sorts, coming to the table, if planted May 1, about the middle of July. It is of good quality, but not hardy or productive; and seems to have little to recommend it, aside from the singular color of its pods.

For descriptions, and modes of culture, of the less common leguminous plants, including the Chick-pea, Chickling Vetch, Japan Pea, Lentil, Lupin, Vetch or Tare, and the Winged Pea, and also for more complete descriptions of many of the varieties of the Common Pea, the reader is referred to "THE FIELD AND GARDEN VEGETABLES OF AMERICA."

CHAPTER XII.

MISCELLANEOUS VEGETABLES.

Alkekengi, or Ground Cherry. — Martynia. — Okra, or Gumbo. — Rhubarb, or Pie-plant. — Tobacco.

ALKEKENGI.

Strawberry-tomato. — Winter Cherry. — Ground Cherry. — Barbadoes Gooseberry. — Physalis edulis.

THIS is a hardy, annual plant, with an angular, branching, but not erect stem, attaining a height or length of more than three feet. The flowers are solitary, yellow, spotted or marked with purple, and about half an inch in diameter; the fruit is roundish or obtuse-heart-shaped, half an inch in diameter, yellow, semi-transparent at maturity, and enclosed in a peculiar thin, membranous, inflated, angular calyx, or covering, which is of a pale-green color while the fruit is forming, but at maturity changes to a dusky white or reddish-drab. The pedicel, or fruit-stem, is weak and slender, and most of the berries fall spontaneously to the ground at the time of ripening.

The seeds are small, yellow, lens-shaped, and retain their germinative properties three years.

The plants are exceedingly prolific, and will thrive in almost any description of soil. Sow at the same time, and thin or transplant to the same distance, as practised in the cultivation of the Tomato. On land where it has been grown, it springs up in great abundance, and often becomes troublesome in the garden.

Use. — The fruit has a juicy pulp, and, when first tasted, a pleasant, strawberry-like flavor, with a certain degree of sweetness and acidity intermixed. The after-taste is, however, much less agreeable, and is similar to that of the common Tomato.

By many the fruit is much esteemed, and is served in its natural state at the table as a dessert. With the addition of lemon-juice, it is sometimes preserved in the manner of the plum, as well as stewed and served like cranberries.

If kept from the action of frost, the fruit retains its natural freshness till March or April.

Purple Alkekengi.
PURPLE GROUND CHERRY. PURPLE STRAWBERRY-TOMATO. PURPLE WINTER CHERRY. PHYSALIS SP.

This species grows naturally and abundantly in some of the Western States. The fruit is roundish, somewhat depressed, about an inch in diameter, of a deep-purple color, and enclosed in the membranous covering peculiar to the genus.

Compared with the preceding species, the fruit is more acid, less perfumed, and not so palatable in its crude state, but by many considered superior for preserving. The plant is less pubescent, but has much the same habit, and is cultivated in the same manner.

MARTYNIA.

Unicorn Plant. — *Gray.* — *Martynia proboscidea.*

A hardy, annual plant, with a strong, branching stem, two feet and a half or three feet high. The leaves are heart-shaped, viscous, and of a peculiar musk-like odor when bruised or roughly handled; the flowers are large, bell-shaped, somewhat two-lipped, dull white, tinged or spotted with yellow and purple, and produced in long, leafless racemes, or clusters; the seed-pods are green, very downy or hairy, fleshy, oval, an inch and a half in their greatest diameter, and taper to a long, slender, incurved horn, or beak. The fleshy, succulent character of the pods is of short duration: they soon become fibrous, the elongat-

The Martynia.

ed beak splits at the point, the two parts diverge, the outer green covering falls off, and the pod becomes black, shrivelled, hard, and woody. The seeds are large, black, wrinkled, irregular in form, and retain their germinative properties three years.

Sowing and Cultivation. — The Martynia is of easy cultivation. As the plants are large and spreading, they should be two feet and a half or three feet apart in each direction. The seeds may be sown in April or May, in the open ground where the plants are to remain; or a few seeds may be sown in a hot-bed, and the seedlings afterwards transplanted.

Gathering and Use. — The young pods are the parts of the plant used. These are produced in great abundance, and should be gathered when half grown, or while tender and succulent: after the hardening of the flesh, they are worthless. They are used for pickling, and by many are considered superior to the Cucumber, or any other vegetable employed for the purpose.

OKRA, OR GUMBO.

Ocra. — *Hibiscus esculentus.*

Okra is a half-hardy annual, with a simple stem, from two to six feet in height, according to the variety; the leaves are large, palmate, deep green; the flowers are large, five-petaled, yellowish on the border, purple at the centre; the seed-pods are angular, or grooved, more or less sharply pointed, an inch or an inch and a half in diameter at the base, and from four to eight inches in length; the seeds are large, round-kidney-shaped, of a greenish-drab color, black or dark brown at the eye, and retain their power of germination five years.

Soil, Sowing, and Cultivation. — Okra may be raised in any common garden-soil, and is propagated by seeds sown in April or May. The plants may be grown in rows two feet apart, and a foot from each other in the rows. The pods will be fit for use in August and September.

It requires a long, warm season, and is most productive when started in a hot-bed, and grown in a warm, sheltered situation.*

Use. — The green pods are used while quite young, sliced in soups and similar dishes, to which they impart a thick, viscous, or gummy consistency. Thus served, they are esteemed not only healthful, but very nutritious.

The ripe seeds, roasted and ground, furnish a palatable substitute for coffee.

Varieties: —

Buist's Dwarf Okra. *Count. Gent.* A variety recently introduced by Mr. Robert Buist of Philadelphia. Height two feet, being about half that of the old variety. Its superiority consists in its greater productiveness, and the little space required for its development, while the fruit is of larger size and superior quality. It is said to produce pods at every joint.

Stem two feet and a half high, sometimes branched at the top, but generally undivided; leaves large, and, as in all varieties, five-lobed; flowers yellow, purple at the centre; pods erect, obtusely pointed, nearly as large in diameter as those of the Giant, but generally about five inches in length.

Dwarf Okra.

It is the earliest of the Okras, and the best variety for cultivation in the Northern and Eastern States.

Between this and the Tall, or Giant, there are numerous sub-varieties, the result both of cultivation and climate. The Tall sorts become dwarfish and earlier if long cultivated at the North; but the Dwarfs, on the contrary, increase in height, and grow later, if long grown in tropical climates.

Dwarf Okra.

The seeds of all the sorts are similar in size, form, and color.

Stem five to six feet in height; pods erect, sharply tapering to a point, eight to ten inches in length, and an inch and a half in diameter near the stem, or at the broadest part.

Tall or Giant Okra.
White-Podded.

With the exception of its larger size, it is similar to the Dwarf, and, if long cultivated under the influence of short and cool seasons, would probably prove identical.

It yields abundantly, but is best adapted to the climate of the Middle and Southern States.

RHUBARB.

Pie-plant. — Rheum sp. et var.

This is a hardy, perennial plant, cultivated almost exclusively for its leaf-stalks. The flower-stalk is put forth in June, and is from five to seven feet in height, according to the variety; the flowers are red, or reddish-white, in erect, loose, terminal spikes; the seeds are brown, triangular, membranous at the corners, and retain their germinative properties three years.

Soil and Cultivation. — Rhubarb succeeds best in deep, somewhat retentive, soil: the richer its condition, and the deeper it is stirred, the better, as it is scarcely possible to cultivate too deeply, or to manure too highly.

It may be propagated by seeds, or by a division of the roots; the latter being the usual method. When grown from seeds, the plants not only differ greatly in size and quality, but are much longer in attaining a growth suitable for cutting.

"Whether grown from seed, or increased by a division of the roots, a deep, rich soil, trenched to the depth of two or even three feet, is required to insure the full development of the leaf-stalks; for upon their size, rapidity of growth, and consequent tenderness of fibre, much of their merit depends. The seed should be sown in April, in drills a foot asunder, — thinning the plants, when a few inches high, to nine inches apart. In the autumn or spring following, they will be fit for transplanting in rows three feet asunder, and the plants set three feet apart. If propagated by dividing the roots, it may be done either in autumn or spring, the same distance being given to the sets that is allowed for seedling plants. As, however, some of the varieties grow to a much larger size than others, a corresponding distance should be accorded them, extending to five feet between the rows, and three feet from plant to plant." — *McInt.*

After-culture. — This consists in keeping the soil well enriched, open, and clear of weeds, and in breaking over the flower-stalks, that they may not weaken the roots, and consequently reduce the size and impair the quality of the leaf-stalks.

Gathering the Crop. — "This is usually done in spring, commencing as soon as the stalks have attained a serviceable size. No leaves, however, should be plucked the first year, and only a few of the largest and first formed during the second; and this plucking should not be made too early in the season, because, in that case, the plants would be weakened. From the third year, as long as the roots or plantations last, it may be gathered with freedom. A plantation in good soil, and not overmuch deprived of its foliage, will last from ten to fifteen years.

Rhubarb is sometimes blanched. This may be effected, without removing the plants, by means of sea-kale pots, or by empty casks open at the top, put over the crowns in March.

Use. — As before remarked, it is cultivated for its leaf-stalks, which are used early in the season, as a substitute for fruit, in pies, tarts, and similar culinary preparations. When fully grown, the expressed juice forms a tolerably palatable wine, though, with reference to health, of doubtful properties. "In 1810, Mr. Joseph Myatts of Deptford, England, long known for his successful culture of this plant, sent his two sons to the borough-market with five bunches of Rhubarb stalks, of which they could sell but three." It is now disposed of by the ton, and many acres in the vicinity of nearly all large towns and cities are devoted exclusively to its cultivation.

Varieties. — These are quite numerous, as they are readily produced from the seed; but the number really deserving of cultivation is limited. Old kinds are constantly giving place to new, either on account of superior earliness, size, productiveness, or quality. The following are the prominent sorts cultivated: —

Cahoon. Stalk short and thick, — if well grown, measuring from twelve to sixteen inches in length, and three inches or more in diameter; skin thick, uniformly green.

Its remarkable size is its principal recommendation. The texture is coarse, the flavor is harsh and strong, and it is rarely employed for culinary purposes.

In some localities, it is cultivated to a limited extent for the manufacture of wine, the juice being expressed from the stalks, and sugar added in the ratio of three pounds and a half to a gallon. This wine, though quite palatable, has little of the fine aroma of that made from the grape, and, if not actually deleterious, is much less safe and healthful. Any of the other varieties may be used for the same purpose, the principal superiority of the Cahoon consisting in its larger stalks, and consequently its greater product of juice.

Downing's Colossal. A large variety, nearly of the size of Myatt's Victoria. It is described as being less acid than the last named, and of a fine, rich, aromatic flavor.

Early Prince Imperial. Stalks of medium size; recommended by D. T. Curtis, Esq., Chairman of the Vegetable Committee of the Massachusetts Horticultural Society, as in all respects the best flavored of any variety ever tested, and commended for general cultivation, as particularly adapted to the wants of the family, if not to the wishes of the gardener, to whom size and productiveness are more than flavor. When cooked, it is of the color of currant-jelly, and remarkably fine flavored.

In 1862, it received the first prize of the Massachusetts Horticultural Society, as the best for family use.

Elford. *Thomp.* An early sort, well adapted for forcing. The stalks are rather slender, covered with a thin skin of a bright-scarlet color; and their substance throughout is of a fine red, which they retain when cooked, if not peeled,—a process which, owing to the thinness of the skin, is not considered necessary. Even when grown in the dark, the stalks still preserve the crimson tinge.

Hawke's Champagne. A new variety, said to equal Mitchell's Royal Albert in earliness, and also to be of a deeper and finer color, and much more productive. It forces remarkably well, is hardy in open culture, and commands the highest market-prices, both from its great size, and fine, rich color.

Mitchell's Royal Albert. *Thomp.* Stalks large, red, and of excellent flavor. Early and prolific.

Myatt's Linnæus. LINNÆUS. A medium-sized, recently introduced sort. "Besides being the earliest of all, and remarkably productive as well as high flavored, and possessing little acidity, it has a skin so thin, that removing it is hardly necessary; and its pulp, when stewed, has the uniform consistence of baked Rhode-Island Greenings, and it continues equally crisp and tender throughout the summer and early autumn." One of the best sorts for a small garden or for family use.

Myatt's Victoria. VICTORIA. Leaf-stalks very large, varying from two inches and a half to three inches in their broadest diameter, and frequently measuring upwards of two feet and a half in length: the weight of a well-developed stalk, divested of the leaf, is about two pounds. They are stained with red at the base, and are often reddish, or finely spotted with red, to the nerves of the leaf.

It has a thick skin, is more acid than many other varieties, and is not particularly high flavored: but no kind is more productive; and this, in connection with its extraordinary size, makes it not only the most salable, but one of the most profitable kinds for growing for the market. It is a fortnight later than the Linnæus.

Tobolsk Rhubarb. Leaf-stalks below medium size, stained with red at the base. It is perceptibly less acid than most varieties, and remarkable for fineness of texture, and delicacy of flavor.

TOBACCO.

Nicotiana, sp.

All the species and varieties of Tobacco in common cultivation are annuals; and most, if not all, are natives of this continent. "Like other annual plants, it may be grown in almost every country and climate, because every country has a summer; and that is the season of life for all annual plants. In hot, dry, and short summers, like the northern summers of Europe or America, Tobacco-plants will not attain a large size, but the Tobacco produced will be of delicate quality and good flavor. In long, moist, and not very warm summers, the plants will attain a large size, — perhaps as much so as in Virginia; but the Tobacco produced will not have that superior flavor, which can only be given by abundance of clear sunshine, and free, dry air."

The species and varieties are as follow: —

Connecticut Seed-leaf.
PEACH-LEAF.
VIRGINIA TOBACCO.
NICOTIANA TABACUM.
Leaves oblong, regularly tapering, stemless and clasping, eighteen inches to two feet long, and from nine to twelve inches in diameter. When fully developed, the stem of the plant is erect and strong, five feet high, and separates near the top into numerous, somewhat open, spreading branches; the flowers are large, tubular, rose-colored, and

quite showy and ornamental; the capsules are ovoid, or somewhat conical, and, if well grown, nearly half an inch in their greatest diameter; the seeds, which are produced in great abundance, are quite small, of a brownish color, and retain their germinative properties four years.

Connecticut Seed-leaf Tobacco.

This species is extensively cultivated throughout the Middle and Southern States, and also in the milder portions of New England. In the State of Connecticut, and on the banks of the Connecticut River in Massachusetts, it is a staple product; and in some towns the value of the crop exceeds that of Indian Corn, and even that of all the cereals combined.

Guatemala Tobacco. A variety with white flowers. In other respects, similar to the foregoing.

Numerous other sorts occur, many of which are local, and differ principally, if not solely, in the size or form of the leaves. One of the most prominent of these is the Broad-leaved, which is considered not only earlier and more productive, but the best for manufacturing; also the Oronoco, with somewhat smaller leaves, and the Japan, intermediate in size and vigor.

Propagation. — It is propagated by seeds sown annually. Select a warm, rich locality in the garden, spade it thoroughly over, pulverize the surface well, and the last of April, or beginning of May, sow the seeds thinly, broadcast; cover with a little fresh mould, and press it well upon them either by the hoe, or back of the spade. As they are exceedingly minute, much care is requisite in sowing, especially that they should not be too deeply covered. When the plants appear, keep them clear of weeds, and thin them out sufficiently to allow a free growth. A bed of seedlings nine or ten feet square will be sufficient for an acre of land. If preferred, the plants may be raised in drills eight inches apart, slightly covering the seeds, and pressing the earth firmly over them as above directed. When the seedlings are four or five inches high, they are ready for transplanting.

Soil and Cultivation. — Tobacco requires a warm, rich soil, not too dry or wet; and, though it will succeed well on recently-turned sward or clover-turf, it gives a greater yield on land that has been cultivated the year previous, as it is less liable to be infested by worms, which sometimes destroy the plants in the early stages of their growth. The land should be twice ploughed in the spring; first as soon as the frost will permit, and again just previous to setting. Pulverize the surface thoroughly by repeated harrowing and rolling, and it will be ready to receive the young plants. The time for transplanting is from the 1st to the 20th of June, taking advantage of a damp day, or setting them immediately after a rain. If the ground is not moist at the time of transplanting, it will be necessary to water the plants as they are set.

"The ground should be marked in straight rows three feet apart, and slight hills made on these marks two feet and a half apart; then set the plants, taking care to press the earth firmly around the roots. As soon as they are well established, and have commenced growing, run a cultivator or horse-hoe between the rows, and follow with the hand-hoe, resetting where the plants are missing. The crop should be hoed at least three times, at proper intervals, taking care to stir the soil all over.

"When the plants begin to flower, the flower-stem should be broken or cut off; removing also the suckers, if any appear; leaving from twelve to sixteen leaves to be matured."

Harvesting and Curing. — In ordinary seasons, the crop will be ready for harvesting the beginning of September; and should all be secured by the 20th of the month, or before the occurrence of frost. The stalks must be cut at the surface of the ground, and exposed long enough to the sun to wilt them sufficiently to prevent breaking in handling. They should then be suspended in a dry, airy shed, or building, on poles, in such a manner as to keep each plant entirely separate from the others, to prevent mouldiness, and to facilitate the drying by permitting a free circulation of air. Thirty or forty plants may be allowed to each twelve feet of pole. The poles may be laid across the beams, about sixteen inches apart.

"When erected for the purpose, the sheds are built of sufficient height to hang three or four tiers, the beams being four feet apart, up and down. In this way, a building forty feet by twenty-two will cure an acre and a half of Tobacco. The drying-shed should be provided with several doors on either side for the free admission of air."

When the stalk is well dried (which is about the last of November or the beginning of December), select a damp day; remove the plants from the poles; strip off the leaves from the stalk, and form them into small bunches, or hanks, by tying the leaves of two or three plants together, winding a leaf about them near the ends of the stems; then pack down while still damp, lapping the tips of the hanks, or bunches, on each other, about a third of their length, forming a stack with the buts, or ends, of the leaf-stems outward; cover the top of the stack, but leave the ends or outside of the mass exposed to the air. In cold weather, or by midwinter, it will be ready for market; for which it is generally packed in damp weather, in boxes containing from two to four hundred pounds.

A fair average yield per acre is from fourteen to eighteen hundred pounds.

To save Seed. — " Allow a few of the best plants to stand without removing the flowering-shoots. In July and August, they will have a fine appearance; and, if the season be favorable, each plant will produce as much seed as will sow a quarter of an acre by the drill system, or stock half a dozen acres by transplanting." A single capsule, or seed-pod, contains a thousand seeds.

Green Tobacco.
Turkish Tobacco.
Nicotiana Rustica.

Leaves oval, from seven to ten inches long, and six or seven inches broad, produced on long petioles. Compared with the preceding species, they are much smaller, deeper colored, more glossy, thicker, and more succulent. When fully grown, the plant is of a pyramidal form, and about three feet in height; the flowers are numerous, greenish-yellow, tubular, and nearly entire on the borders; the seed-vessels are ovoid, more depressed at the top than those of the Connecticut Seed-leaf, and much more prolific; seeds small, brownish.

The Green Tobacco is early, and remarkably hardy, but not generally considered worthy of cultivation in localities where the Connecticut Seed-leaf can be successfully grown. It is well adapted to the northern parts of New England and the Canadas, where it will yield an abundance of foliage, and perfect its seeds. "It is very generally cultivated, almost to the exclusion of the other species, in the north of Germany, Russia, and Sweden, where almost every cottager grows his own tobacco for smoking. It also seems to be the principal sort grown in Ireland."

Green Tobacco.

There are several varieties, all of which have the hardiness and productiveness common to the species, but are not considered remarkably well flavored.

The plants should be started in spring, and transplanted as directed for the Connecticut Seed-leaf; but, on account of its smaller size and habit, two feet, or even twenty inches, between the plants, will be all the space required.

INDEX.

ALKEKENGI	327
Purple	328
ALLIACEOUS PLANTS	65
ALLIUM ampeloprasum	66
,, cepa	68
,, porrum	66
,, sativum	65
AMERICAN GARDEN-BEAN	253
APIUM graveolens	177
,, petroselinum	219
ARRACH	159
ASPARAGINOUS PLANTS	77
ASPARAGUS	77
Battersea	81
Deptford	81
Dutch	81
Giant Purple-top	81
Gravesend	81
Grayson's Giant	81
Green-top	81
Mortlake	81
Reading	81
Red-top	81
ASPARAGUS OFFICINALIS	77
ATRIPLEX HORTENSIS	159
BALM	211
BARBADOES GOOSEBERRY	327
BASIL	212
Bush	213
Common	212
Green Bush	213
Large Sweet	212
Lettuce-leaved	213
Purple	212
Purple Bush	213
BEAN, American Garden	253
Dwarf varieties	253
Black-eyed China	254
Blue Pod	255
Canada Yellow	256

BEAN, Canadian	263
Chilian	256
China	260
Crescent-eyed	257
Dun-colored	257
Dwarf Case-knife	260
Dwarf Cranberry	258
Dwarf Horticultural	259
Dwarf Sabre	260
Dwarf White Cranberry	275
Dwarf Yellow	270
Early China	260
Early Mohawk	264
Early Rachel	261
Early Valentine	262
Excelsior	263
Fejee	273
Golden Cranberry	263
Half-moon	257
Kidney	274
Long White Kidney	274
Large Yellow Six-weeks	263
Mohawk	264
Negro Long Pod	265
Newington Wonder	265
Nonpareil	266
Pea	267
Pottawottomie	268
Red-eyed China	260
Red-speckled	268
Refugee	269
Rob-Roy	270
Round American Kidney	256–263
Round Yellow	270
Round Yellow Six-weeks	270
Royal Dwarf	274
Scarlet Swiss	271
Six-weeks	263
Swiss Crimson	271
Tampico	272
Thousand to One	269

BEAN, Turtle-soup 272
    Valentine 262
    Victoria 272
    White Cranberry 275
    White's Early 273
    White Egg 275
    White Flageolet 274
    White Kidney 274
    White Marrow 275
    White Marrowfat 275
    Yellow-eyed China 276
    Yellow Six-weeks 263
BEAN, Running or Pole 277
    Algerian 281
    Asparagus 286
    Butter 281
    California 277
    Carolina 292
    Carolina Sewee 292
    Case-knife 278
    Chinese Long Pod 287
    Cimeter 284
    Concord 279
    D'Alger 281
    Green Lima 289
    Horticultural 280
    Indian Chief 281
    Lima 287
    London Horticultural 280
    Long-podded Dolichos 286
    Marbled Prague 280
    Mottled Cranberry 281
    Mottled Lima 289
    Mottled Sieva 293
    Painted Lady-runner 291
    Red Cranberry 282
    Rhode-Island Butter 283
    Saba 292
    Sabre 284
    Scarlet-runner 289
    Sieva 292
    Small Lima 292
    Stringless 281
    Wax 281
    West-Indian 292
    White Cranberry 284
    White-runner 291
    Wild-goose 285
    Wren's Egg 280
    Yellow Cranberry 285
BEAN, English 293
    Cluster 295
    Dutch Long Pod 295

BEAN, Early Dwarf 295
    Early Mazagan 295
    Evergreen Long Pod 295
    Green Windsor 295
    Horse-bean 293
    White Broad Windsor 295
    Windsor 295
BEAN, French 253
    Kidney 253
BEET 1
    Bark-skinned 4
    Bassano 5
    Common Long Blood 9
    Cow-horn Mangel-wurzel . . . 5
    Dwarf Blood 8
    Early Blood Turnip-rooted . . 6
    Early Bassano 5
    Early Mangel-wurzel 6
    Early Turnip 6
    Extra Early 5
    Fine Dwarf Red 8
    German Red Mangel-wurzel . 7
    German Yellow Mangel-wurzel 8
    Half Long Blood 8
    Improved Long Blood 8
    Long Blood 9
    Long Red Mangel-wurzel . . 10
    Long Smooth Blood 8
    Long Yellow Mangel-wurzel . 11
    Olive-shaped Mangel-wurzel, Red 11
    Olive-shaped Mangel-wurzel, Yellow 11
    Orange Globe Mangel-wurzel . 14
    Pine-apple Short-top 12
    Red Castelnaudary 12
    Red Globe Mangel-wurzel . . 12
    Red Mangel-wurzel 10
    Red Oval Mangel-wurzel . . . 11
    Serpent-like 5
    Sutton's Large Globe Mangel-Wurzel 13
    White Globe Mangel-wurzel . 13
    White Silesian 13
    White Sugar 13
    White Turnip-rooted 14
    Wyatt's Dark Crimson 14
    Yellow Castelnaudary 12
    Yellow Globe Mangel-wurzel . 14
    Yellow Oval Mangel-wurzel . 11
    Yellow Turnip-rooted 15
BEET LEAF 153

INDEX.

BETA CICLA 153
BORECOLE, or KALE 127
   Dalmeny Sprouts 128
   Dwarf Green Curled 128
   Green Marrow-stem 128
   Neapolitan 128
   Purple 128
BEAN, Red Marrow-stem 128
   Thousand-headed 128
   Variegated 128
BRASSICA campestris Ruta-baga . 45
   " caulo-rapa 147
   " oleracea 128, 132, 143
   " oleracea bullata ... 148
   " oleracea capitata 133
   " oleracea sabellica ... 127
   " rapa 55
BRASSICACEOUS PLANTS 127
BROCCOLI 128
   Brimstone 131
   Early Purple 129
   Early Sprouting 129
   Grange's Early Cauliflower . 130
   Green Cape 130
   Frogmore Protecting 129
   Late Dwarf Purple 130
   Late Willcove 131
   Portsmouth 130
   Purple Cape 130
   Reading Giant 131
   Snow's Superb White Winter . 131
   Sulphur 131
   Walcheren 131
   Willcove 131
BRUSSELS SPROUTS 132
   Dwarf 133
   Giant 133
   Tall 133

CABBAGE 133
   American Drumhead 137
   American Green Glazed ... 137
   Champion of America 134
   Battersea 135
   Early Battersea 135
   Early Drumhead 135
   Early Dutch Drumhead ... 135
   Early Low Dutch 135
   Early Sugar-loaf 136
   Early Wakefield 136
   Early York 136
   Green Glazed 137
   Large Flat Dutch 139

CABBAGE, Large French Ox-heart, 138
   Large Late Drumhead 137
   Large Ox-heart 138
   Large York 137
   Little Pixie 138
   Marblehead Mammoth Drum-
     head 138
   Mason 139
   Pointed-head 141
   Pomeranian 139
   Premium Flat Dutch 139
   Small Ox-heart 140
   Stone-mason 140
   Tom Thumb 138
   Vannack 141
   Waite's New Dwarf 141
   Winnigstadt 141
CABBAGE, Red Varieties 142
   Early Blood-red 142
   Early Dwarf Red 142
   Large Red Dutch 142
   Small Red 142
   Superfine Black 143
   Utrecht Red 143
CAPSICUM annuum 233
   " frutescens 235
   " cerasiforme 236
CARAWAY 213
CAROLINA POTATO 52
CARROT 16
   Altrincham 17
   Altringham 17
   Blood Red 21
   Dutch Horn 18
   Early Forcing Horn 18
   Early Frame 18
   Early Half-long Scarlet ... 18
   Early Horn 18
   Early Short Scarlet 18
   Green-top White 21
   Half-long Red 18
   James's Scarlet 20
   Long Lemon 20
   Long Orange 19
   Long Red 20
   Long Red Belgian 20
   Long Surrey 20
   Long Yellow 20
   New Intermediate 21
   Purple 21
   White Belgian 21
   Yellow Belgian 20
CARUM CARUI 213

CAULIFLOWER	143	CHICCORY, Magdeburg Large-rooted	186
Early Leyden	146	Spotted	185
Early London	144	Turnip-rooted	186
Early Paris	145	Variegated	185
Erfurt Early	145	CICHORIUM endivia	189
Erfurt Extra Early	145	" intybus	184
Fitch's Early London	144	COCHLEARIA ARMORACIA	192
Frogmore Early Forcing	145	CONVOLVULUS BATATAS	52
Large Asiatic	145	CORIANDER	214
Legge's Walcheren Broccoli	146	CORIANDRUM SATIVUM	214
Le Normand	145	CORN, Garden Varieties	161
London Particular	144	Adams's Early White	161
Mitchell's Hardy Early	146	Black Sweet	161
New Erfurt	146	Burr's Improved	162
Dwarf Mammoth	146	Burr's Sweet	162
Stadtholder	146	Darling's Early	163
Waite's Alma	146	Darling's Early Sweet	163
Walcheren	146	Early Dwarf Sugar	163
Wellington	147	Early Jefferson	163
CELERIAC	183	Extra Early Dwarf	163
Curled-leaved	184	Golden Sweet	164
CELERY	177	Golden Sugar	164
Boston Market	180	Mammoth Eight-rowed Sugar	164
Cole's Superb Red	180	Mexican	161
Cole's Superb White	180	Narraganset	164
Early Dwarf Solid White	180	Old-Colony	165
Fine White Solid	182	Parching, white kernel	166
Giant White	182	Parching, yellow	166
Laing's Improved Mammoth Red	181	Pop	166
Lion's Paw	182	Red-cob Sweet	167
Manchester Red	181	Rhode-Island Asylum	167
Manchester Red Giant	181	Rice, Red Kernel	167
New Large Purple	181	" White Kernel	168
New Large Red	181	" Yellow Kernel	168
Prussian	182	Slate Sweet	161
Red Solid	181	Stowell's Evergreen	168
Seymour's Superb White Solid	181	Stowell's Evergreen Sweet	168
Seymour's White Champion	182	Turkey Wheat	169
Shepherd's Giant Red	182	Tuscarora	169
Shepherd's Red	182	Twelve-rowed Sweet	170
Tours Purple	181	CORN, Field Varieties	170
Turkey	182	Baden	175
Turkish Giant Solid	182	Brown	173
Wall's White	182	Canada Yellow	170
White Lion's Paw	182	Dutton	171
White Solid	182	Early Canada	170
CHICCORY	184	Early Dutton	171
Brunswick Large-rooted	186	Golden Flint	176
Coffee	186	Hill	172
Improved	185	Illinois White	173
Large-rooted	186	Illinois Yellow	173

INDEX.

CORN, Improved King Philip . . . 173
   King Philip 173
   Long White Flint 175
   New-England Eight-rowed . . 174
   Old-Colony Premium 172
   Smutty White . . . . , 172
   Southern White 175
   Southern Yellow 175
   Webster 172
   Western White 173
   Western Yellow 173
   White Flint 176
   White Gourd-seed 175
   White Horse-tooth 175
   Whitman 172
   Whitman Improved 172
   Yellow Flint 176
   Yellow Horse-tooth 175
CRAMBE MARITIMA 151
CRESS, or PEPPERGRASS 187
   Broad-leaved 188
   Common 188
   Curled 188
   Garnishing 188
   Golden 188
   Normandy Curled 189
   Plain-leaved 188
CUCUMBER 83
   Carter's Champion 87
   Coleshill 87
   Conqueror of the West 87
   Cuthill's Black Spine 87
   Doctor 87
   Early Cluster 85
   Early Frame 85
   Early Green Cluster 85
   Early Long Green Prickly . . 90
   Early Russian 86
   Early Short Green Prickly . . 91
   Early White-spined 91
   Eggleston's Conqueror 87
   Extra Long Green Turkey . . 90
   Flanigan's Prize 87
   Giant of Arnstadt 88
   Henderson's Number One
      Black-spined 88
   Hunter's Prolific 88
   Improved Sion House 88
   Irishman 88
   London Long Green 86
   Long Green Prickly 90
   Long Green Turkey 90
   Long Prickly 90

CUCUMBER, Lord Kenyon's Fa-
    vorite 88
   Manchester Prize 88
   Napoleon III. 89
   Nepal 89
   New-York Market 91
   Norman's Stitchworth-park
      Hero . . . . 7 . . 89
   Old Sion House 89
   Prize-fighter 89
   Rifleman 89
   Ringleader 89
   Roman Emperor 89
   Short Green 85
   Short Green Prickly 91
   Short Prickly 91
   Southgate 89
   Star of the West 89
   Stockwood 89
   Sugden's Aldershott 89
   Victory of Bath 90
   White Spanish 91
   White-spined 91
CUCUMIS anguria 104
   " melo 93
   " sativus 83
CUCURBITA citrullus 98
   " pepo 105
CUCURBITACEOUS PLANTS 83

DAUCUS CAROTA 16
DOLICHOS SESQUIPEDALIS . . . 286

EATABLE-PODDED PEAS 322
EGG-PLANT 229
   American Large Purple . . . 230
   Chinese Long White 231
   Guadaloupe Striped 231
   Large Round Purple 232
   Long Purple 231
   New-York Improved 231
   Round Purple 232
   Scarlet-fruited 232
   White 232
ENDIVE 189
ENDIVES, Batavian 191
   Broad-leaved 191
   Curled 191
   Large 191
   Lettuce-leaved 191
   Small 191
   White 191

INDEX

ENDIVES, Curled 191
    Dutch Green Curled 191
    Early Fine Curled Rouen . . . 191
    Green Curled Summer 191
    Italian Green Curled 181
    Large Green Curled 191
    Long Italian Green 191
    Staghorn 191
    Triple Curled Moss 191
    White Curled 191
ENGLISH BEAN 293
    "   TURNIP 55
ESCULENT ROOTS 1

FRENCH BEAN 253
    "   SPINACH 159
    "   TURNIP 45

GARDEN-BEAN, American 253
    "   "   English 293
GARLIC 65
    Common 65
    Early Rose 66
    Great-headed 66
GHERKIN 104
GREEN MINT 227
GROUND CHERRY 327
    Purple 328
GUMBO 330

HARICOT 253
HIBISCUS ESCULENTUS 330
HORSE-BEAN 293
HORSE-RADISH 192

IPOMŒA BATATAS 52

JAMAICA CUCUMBER 104

KALE (see "BORECOLE") 127
KIDNEY-BEAN 253
KOHL RABI 147
    Green 147

LACTUCA SATIVA 193
LAVENDER 215
    Blue-flowering 217
    Broad-leaved 216
    Common 217
    Narrow-leaved Blue-flowering, 217
    Spike 216
LAVENDULA SPICA 215
LEAF-BEET, or SWISS CHARD . . 153

LEAF-BEET, Curled 154
    Large-ribbed Curled 154
    Large-ribbed Scarlet Brazilian 154
    Large-ribbed Silver 154
    Large-ribbed Yellow Brazilian 154
    Red-stalked 154
    Sea-kale 154
    Silver-leaf 154
    Swiss Chard 154
    Yellow-stalked 154
LEEK 66
    Broad Flag 68
    Common Flag 67
    Large Flag 68
    Large Rouen 67
    London Flag 68
    Long Flag 67
    Musselburgh 68
    Scotch Flag 68
    Yellow Poitou 68
LEEK-LEAVED SALSIFY 51
LEGUMINOUS PLANTS 253
LEPIDIUM SATIVUM 187
LETTUCE 193
LETTUCES, Cabbage 195
    American Brown Dutch . . . 205
    Black-seeded Gotte 196
    Boston Curled 197
    Brown 201
    Brown Batavian 196
    Brown Dutch Black-seeded . . 195
    Brown Silesian 196
    Button 202
    Capuchin 202
    Curled 197
    Drumhead 200, 204
    Early Cape 196
    Early White Spring 196
    Endive-leaved 197
    English Endive-like Curled-leaved 197
    Green Ball 202
    Green Curled 197
    Green Winter 198
    Hammersmith Hardy 198
    Hardy Green Hammersmith . 198
    Hardy Hammersmith 202
    Hardy Winter 198
    Ice 198–200
    Ice Cos 200
    Imperial Head 199

INDEX. 349

LETTUCES, India 199
   Large Brown 200
   Large Drumhead 204
   Large India 199
   Large Red 200
   Large White 202
   Large Winter 200
   Madeira 200
   Malta 200
   Mammoth 200
   Marseilles 196
   Mogul 200
   Naples 201
   Neapolitan 201
   Palatine 201
   Red-bordered 203
   Royal 202
   Royal Cape 196
   Spanish 204
   Stone Tennis-ball 202
   Sugar 203
   Summer 202
   Summer Cape 196
   Tennis-ball 202
   Turkey 199–203
   Versailles 203
   Victoria 203
   White 200
   White Batavian 204
   White Dutch 205
   White Gotte, Black-seeded . . 204
   White Gotte, White-seeded . . 204
   White Silesian 204
   White Stone 205
   White Tennis-ball 204
   Yellow-seeded Brown Dutch . 205
LETTUCES, Cos 206
   Ady's Fine Large 207
   Alphange, Black-seeded . . . 206
   Alphange, White-seeded . . . 206
   Bath 207
   Bath Green 207
   Brown 207
   Florence, Black-seeded 206
   Florence, White-seeded 206
   Gray Paris 207
   Green Paris 207
   Green Winter 208
   Kensington 207
   London White 208
   Magnum Bonum 206
   Sutton's Superb Green 207
   Sutton's Superb White 208

LETTUCES, Wellington 207
   White Paris 208
LIMA BEAN 287
   Green 289
LONG-PODDED DOLICHOS 286
LOVE-APPLE 239

MARJORAM 217
   Common 217
   Knotted 218
   Pot 218
   Sweet 218
   Winter Sweet 219
MARTYNIA 328
   ,,   proboscidea 328
MELISSA OFFICINALIS 211
MELON 92
MELON, Musk 93
   Beechwood 94
   Christiana 94
   Citron 94
   Common Musk 95
   Early Cantaloupe 95
   Green Citron 94
   Green-fleshed Citron 94
   Large-ribbed Netted Musk . . 95
   Monroe's Green Flesh 96
   Nutmeg 96
   Pine-apple 96
   Skillman's Fine-netted 96
   Ward's Nectar 97
   White Japan 97
MELON, Persian Varieties 97
MELON, Water 98
   Apple-seeded 98
   Black Spanish 99
   Bradford 99
   California Pie 103
   Carolina 99
   Citron 100
   Clarendon 100
   Dark-speckled 100
   Ice-cream 101
   Imperial 101
   Mountain Sprout 101
   Mountain Sweet 101
   Odell's Large White 102
   Orange 103
   Pie 103
   Ravenscroft 103
   Spanish 99
   Souter 104

350 INDEX.

MENTHA VIRIDIS 227
MISCELLANEOUS VEGETABLES . 327
MOUNTAIN SPINACH 159
MUSKMELON 93
MUSTARD 209
   Black 209
   Brown 209
   Red 209
   White 210

NASTURTIUM ARMORACIA 192
NEW-ZEALAND SPINACH 155
NICOTIANA 336
   „ tabacum 336
   „ rustica 340

OCRA 330
OCYMUM basilicum 212
   „ minimum 213
OKRA 330
   Buist's Dwarf 330
   Dwarf 331
   Giant 331
   Tall 331
   White-podded 331
OLERACEOUS PLANTS 211
ONION 68
   Brown Deptford 70
   Danvers 70
   Danvers Red 70
   Danvers Yellow 70
   Deptford 70
   Early Red Wethersfield 71
   Early Silver-skin 71
   Egyptian 75
   Intermediate Red Wethersfield 71
   Large Red 72
   New Deep Blood-red 72
   Potato 72
   Silver-skin 73
   Silver-skin of New England . . 76
   Strasburg 74
   Top 75
   Tree 75
   Underground 72
   Wethersfield Large Red . . . 72
   White Globe 75
   White Portugal 73
   Yellow 76
   Yellow Globe 75
   Yellow Strasburg 74
ORACH 159

ORACH, Dark Green 160
   Green 160
   Lurid 160
   Pale Red 160
   Purple 160
   Red 160
   White 160
ORIGANUM heracleoticum 219
   „ marjorana 218
   „ onites 218
   „ vulgare 217
OYSTER-PLANT 51

PARSLEY 219
   Common 221
   Curled 220
   Dwarf Curled 220
   Hamburg 221
   Large-rooted 221
   Mitchell's Matchless Winter . 221
   Myatt's Extra Fine-curled . . 221
   Myatt's Garnishing 221
   Myatt's Triple-curled 221
   Plain 221
   Rendle's Treble Garnishing . . 221
   Sutton's Dwarf Curled 220
   Turnip-rooted 221
   Usher's Dwarf Curled 220
   Windsor Curled 221
PARSNIP 22
   Common 24
   Dutch 24
   Early Short Horn 24
   Guernsey 25
   Hollow-crowned 25
   Long Smooth 25
   Long Smooth Dutch 24
   The Student 25
   Sutton's Student 25
   Turnip-rooted 26
PASTINACA SATIVA 22
PEA 296
   Advancer 298
   Alliance 309
   Auvergne 299
   Batt's Wonder 299
   Beck's Prize-taker 300
   Bedman's Imperial 300
   Bellamy's Early Green Marrow 300
   Bishop's Early Dwarf 301
   Bishop's New Long-podded . 301
   Black-eyed Marrow 301

PEA, Blue Cimeter 301
   Blue Imperial 302
   Blue Prussian 302
   Blue Spanish Dwarf 303
   British Queen 303
   Brompton Hotspur 304
   Burbridge's Eclipse 303
   Bush 320
   Carter's Victoria 304
   Cedo Nulli 309
   Champion of England 310
   Champion of Paris 305
   Champion of Scotland . . . 305
   Charlton 304
   Charlton Hotspur 304
   Climax 315
   Competitor 305
   Dantzic 306
   Dickson's Favorite 306
   Dillistone's Early 307
   Drew's New Dwarf 307
   Dwarf Blue Imperial 302
   Dwarf Fan 319
   Dwarf Marrow 307
   Dwarf Marrowfat 307
   Early Charlton 304
   Early Dan O'Rourke 308
   Early Emperor 322
   Early Frame 309
   Early Hotspur 309
   Early Kent 316
   Early May 316
   Early Nicol's Hotspur 304
   Early Spanish Dwarf 319
   Early Warwick 309
   Early Washington 309
   Eugénie 309
   Fairbeard's Champion of England 310
   Fairbeard's Nonpareil 310
   Fairbeard's Surprise 311
   Flack's Imperial 311
   Flander's Hotspur 304
   General Wyndham 311
   Golden Hotspur 304
   Hair's Dwarf Mammoth . . . 312
   Harrison's Glory 312
   Harrison's Perfection 312
   Hill's Early 305
   Hovey's Extra Early 305
   King of the Marrows 312
   Knight's Dwarf Blue Marrow . 313
   Knight's Dwarf Green Marrow, 313

PEA, Knight's Dwarf White Marrow 313
   Knight's Tall Blue Marrow . . 313
   Knight's Tall Green Marrow . 314
   Knight's Tall White Marrow . 314
   Landreth's Extra Early 305
   Lord Raglan 314
   Matchless Marrow 314
   Master's Hotspur 304
   Milford Marrow 315
   Missouri Marrow 315
   Missouri Marrowfat 315
   Napoléon 315
   Ne Plus Ultra 316
   Noble's Early Green Marrow . 316
   Nonpareil 322
   Paradise Marrow 305
   Prince Albert 316
   Queen of the Dwarfs 317
   Reading Hotspur 304
   Ringwood Marrow 317
   Royal Dwarf 318
   Sabre 301
   Sebastopol 318
   Shillings Grotto 318
   Single-blossomed Frame . . . 319
   Spanish Dwarf 319
   Strawberry 319
   Tall Marrowfat 319
   Tall White Marrow 319
   Taylor's Early 320
   Thurston's Reliance 320
   Tom Thumb 320
   Veitch's Perfection 321
   Victoria Marrow 321
   Warner Early Emperor 322
   White Prussian 318
   Woodford's Marrow 322
PEAS, Eatable-podded or String . 322
   Australian 324
   Blue-podded 324
   Botany Bay 324
   Chocolate 324
   Common Dwarf 323
   Early Dwarf Dutch 323
   Giant 323
   Large Crooked 324
   Late Dwarf 325
   Purple-podded 324
   Red-flowered 324
   Six-inch Pod 324
   Tamarind 325
   White-podded 325

Peas, Yellow-podded	325
Pepper	233
Bell	233
Bird	234
Bull-nose	233
Cayenne	235
Cherry	236
Cherry Yellow-fruited	236
Chili	236
Large Bell	233
Large Red Cherry	237
Long Red	236
Long Yellow	237
Round	237
Squash	237
Sweet Mountain	238
Sweet Spanish	238
Tomato-shaped	237
Peppergrass	187
Persian Melons	97
Phaseolus lunatus	287
,, multiflorus	289
,, vulgaris	253
Physalis Edulis	327
Pie-Plant	332
Pisum sativum	296
,, macrocarpum	322
Potato	27
Buckeye	31
Carter	31
Chenango	37
Cuzco	32
Danvers Red	32
Danvers Seedling	32
Davis's Seedling	32
Dykeman	33
Early Blue	33
Early Dykeman	33
Early Handsworth	33
Early Goodrich	34
Garnet Chili	34
Gillyflower	34
Harrison	35
Jackson White	35
Jenny Lind	36
Lady's Finger	36
Lapstone Kidney	36
Long Red	37
Mercer	37
Meshannock	37
Monitor	37
Nichol's Early	36
Potato, Peach-blow	38
Pink-eyed	38
Rhode-Island Seedling	36
Rohan	38
Ruffort Kidney	36
Sebec	31
State of Maine	38
Western Red	39
White Chenango	37
White Peach-blow	39
Prickly-Fruited Gherkin	104
Pumpkin	105
Canada	106
Cheese	106
Common Yellow Field	106
Connecticut Field	107
Hard-shell	108
Long Yellow Field	107
Nantucket	108
Nigger-head	108
Small Sugar	109
Striped Field	109
Sugar	109
Vermont	106
Radish	39
Radishes, Spring or Summer	41
Early Scarlet Short-top	42
Early Scarlet Turnip-rooted	41
Early White Turnip-rooted	42
Gray Olive-shaped	42
Gray Turnip-rooted	42
Long Purple	42
Long Scarlet	42
Long White	43
Olive-shaped Scarlet	43
Scarlet Turnip-rooted	43
White Turnip-rooted	44
Radishes, Autumn and Winter	44
Black Spanish	44
Large Purple Winter	44
Purple Spanish	44
Rose-colored Chinese	45
Scarlet Chinese Winter	45
Winter White Spanish	45
Raphanus Sativus	39
Red Beet	1
Rheum	332
Rhubarb	332
Cahoon	334
Downing's Colossal	334
Early Prince Imperial	334
Elford	334

INDEX.

RHUBARB, Hawke's Champagne . 335
   Linnæus 335
   Mitchell's Royal Albert 335
   Myatt's Linnæus 335
   Myatt's Victoria 335
   Tobolsk 336
   Victoria 335
ROSMARINUS OFFICINALIS 222
ROSEMARY 222
   Common 223
   Green-leaved 223
   Narrow-leaved 223
RUSSIAN TURNIP 45
RUTA-BAGA TURNIP 45

SAGE 223
   Common 224
   Green-leaved 225
   Green-top 225
   Purple-top 224
   Red-leaved 224
   Red-top 224
SALAD PLANTS 177
SALSIFY 51
SALVIA OFFICINALIS 224
SATUREJA hortensis 225
   ,,   montana 226
SAVORY 225
   Summer 225
   Winter 226
SAVOY 148
SAVOY CABBAGE 148
   Cape 149
   Drumhead 149
   Earliest Ulm 150
   Early Dwarf 149
   Early Green 149
   Early Ulm 150
   Green Curled 150
   Green Globe 150
   Large Green 150
   New Ulm 150
SCARLET-RUNNER BEAN 289
   ,,   Painted-lady 291
   ,,   White-runner 291
SEA-KALE 151
SICILIAN BEET 153
SINAPIS alba 210
   ,,   nigra 209
SKINLESS PEAS 322
SMALLAGE 177
SOLANUM lycopersicum 239
   ,,   melongena 229

SOLANUM TUBEROSUM 27
SPANISH POTATO 52
SPEARMINT 227
   Curled-leaved 227
SPINACEA OLERACEA 156
SPINACEOUS PLANTS 153
SPINACH 156
   Common Prickly 159
   Flanders 157
   Large Prickly-seeded 157
   Large Winter 157
   Lettuce-leaved 158
   Round Dutch 158
   Round-leaved 158
   Sorrel-leaved 158
   Summer 158
   White Sorrel-leaved 159
   Winter 159
   Yellow Sorrel-leaved 159
SQUASH 110
SQUASH, Autumn and Winter Varieties 114
   Acorn 122
   Autumnal Marrow 114
   Boston Marrow 114
   Bush Vegetable Marrow . . . 115
   Canada Crookneck 116
   Cashew 116
   Cocoa 117
   Cocoanut 117
   Commodore Porter 123
   Cuckaw 124
   Cushaw Pumpkin 116
   Custard 117
   Dwarf Vegetable Marrow . . . 115
   Honolulu 118
   Hubbard 119
   Improved Turban 123
   Mammoth 120
   Porter's Valparaiso 123
   Puritan 120
   Sweet Potato 121
   Turban 122
   Turk's Cap 122
   Valparaiso 123
   Vegetable Marrow 123
   Winter Crookneck 124
   Winter Striped Crookneck . . 125
   Yokohama 125
SQUASH, Summer Varieties 111
   Apple 111
   Bush Summer Warted Crookneck 111

Squash, Cymling	112, 113	Thyme, Lemon	228
Early Apple	111	Thymus citriodorus	228
Early Summer Crookneck	111	,, vulgaris	228
Early White Bush Scalloped	112	Tobacco	336
Early Yellow Bush Scalloped	113	Broad-leaved	338
Egg	113	Connecticut Seed-leaf	336
Green Striped Bergen	114	Green	340
Large Summer Warted Crookneck	114	Guatemala	338
		Japan	338
Orange	114	Oronoco	338
White Pattypan	112	Peach-leaf	336
White Summer Scalloped	112	Turkish	340
Yellow Pattypan	113	Virginian	336
Yellow Summer Scalloped	113	Tomato	239
Yellow Summer Warted Crookneck	111	Apple	242
		Apple-shaped	242
Strawberry-Tomato	327	Bermuda	243
Purple	328	Cluster	251
String-Peas	322	Early Apple	245
Succory	184	Early Red	243
Sugar-Peas	322	Early York	252
Swede or Ruta-Baga Turnip	45	Extra Early	243
Ashcroft	47	Fejee	244
Common Purple-top Yellow	47	Fig	244
Green-top White	48	French Tree-tomato	249
Green-top Yellow	47	Giant	245
Laing's Improved Purple-top	48	Grape	251
Long White French	50	Improved Apple	245
Purple-top White	48	Large Red	246
River's	49	Large Yellow	246
Skirving's Improved Purple-top	49	Lester's Perfected	247
Skirving's Purple-top	49	Mammoth	245
Sutton's Champion	50	Mammoth Chihuahua	245
Sweet German	50	Mexican	247
White French	50	New Upright	249
Sweet Potato	52	Perfected	247
American Red	54	Pomo d'Oro Lesteriano	247
Kentucky Early Red	53	Red Cherry	247
Large White	53	Red Pear-shaped	244
Nansemond	54	Red Plum	248
Red-skinned	54	Round Red	248
Red Nansemond	53	Round Yellow	248
Yellow Carolina	54	Seedless	248
Yellow Nansemond	54	Tilden	249
Yellow-skinned	54	Tilden's Seedling	249
Swiss Chard	153	The Cook's Favorite	248
		Tomate de Laye	249
Tetragonia Expansa	155	Tree	249
Thousand-Headed Cabbage	132	White	250
Thyme	227	White's Extra Early	243
Broad-leaved	228	Yellow Cherry	251
Common	227	Yellow Fig	251
Evergreen	227		

INDEX.

TOMATO, Yellow Pear-shaped	251
Yellow Plum	251
TRAGOPOGON PORRIFOLIUS	51
TURNIP	55
Altrincham	56
Altringham	56
Chivas's Orange Jelly	56
Cow-horn	56
Early Dwarf	61
Early Flat Dutch	57
Early Stone	63
Early White Dutch	57
Early Yellow Dutch	57
Finland	57
Golden Ball	57
Green Globe	58
Green Norfolk	58
Green-top Flat	58
Green-top Yellow Aberdeen	58
Long White Clairfontaine	59
Long White Maltese	59
Petrosowoodska	59
Purple-top Flat	59
Purple-top Strap-leaved	59
Purple-top Yellow Aberdeen	60
Red Globe	60
Red Norfolk	61
Red Tankard	61
Red-top Flat	59
Robertson's Golden Stone	61
Six-weeks	61
TURNIP, Snowball	61
Stone Globe	62
Waite's Hybrid Eclipse	62
White Dutch	57
White Garden Stone	63
White Globe	62
White Norfolk	63
White Stone	63
White-top Flat	63
White-top Strap-leaved	63
Yellow Dutch	57
Yellow Globe	57
Yellow Malta	64
Yellow Stone	64
TURNIP CABBAGE	147
TURNIP-ROOTED CELERY	183
UNICORN PLANT	328
VEGETABLE OYSTER	51
VICIA FABA	293
WATERMELON	98
WEST-INDIAN BEAN	292
,, ,, CUCUMBER	104
WHITE BEET	153
WILD ENDIVE	184
WINTER CHERRY	327
Purple	328
ZEA MAYS	161

PRINTED BY GEO. C. RAND & AVERY, NO. 3, CORNHILL, BOSTON.

www.ingramcontent.com/pod-product-compliance
Lightning Source LLC
Chambersburg PA
CBHW031422230426
43668CB00007B/394